FORBIDDEN WORKERS

Also by Peter Kwong

The New Chinatown

Chinatown, New York: Labor and Politics, 1930–1950

FORBIDDEN

WORKERS

ILLEGAL CHINESE IMMIGRANTS
AND AMERICAN LABOR

PETER KWONG

THE NEW PRESS

NEW YORK

PUBLISHED IN THE UNITED STATES BY THE NEW PRESS, NEW YORK
DISTRIBUTED BY W. W. NORTON & COMPANY, INC., NEW YORK

Established in 1990 as a major alternative to the large,
commercial publishing houses, The New Press is the first full-scale
nonprofit American book publisher outside of the university presses.

The Press is operated editorially in the public interest,
rather than for private gain; it is committed to publishing
in innovative ways works of educational, cultural,
and community value that, despite their intellectual merits,
might not normally be commercially viable.

The New Press's editorial offices are located
at the City University of New York.

BOOK DESIGN BY BAD

PRINTED IN THE UNITED STATES OF AMERICA

97 98 99 00   9 8 7 6 5 4 3 2 1

TO DUŠANKA
MY STAUNCH SUPPORTER AND
UNWAVERING FRIEND

CONTENTS

ACKNOWLEDGMENTS
[xi]

INTRODUCTION
[1]

1. The Pig Trade: The Contemporary Version
[19]

2. Going to America
[47]

3. Snakeheads
[69]

4. The Limits of Kinship Networks
[91]

5. Manufacturing Ethnicity
[113]

6. The Exclusion of Chinese Labor
[139]

7. Ineffectual Enforcement of Immigration and Labor Law
[161]

8. Waiting for Organized Labor
[185]

9. The Undocumented Immigrant as Part of American Labor
[207]

CONTENTS

A FINAL NOTE

[235]

ENDNOTES

[241]

BIBLIOGRAPHY

[257]

INDEX

[269]

FORBIDDEN WORKERS

ACKNOWLEDGMENTS

THIS BOOK IS AN EXPOSÉ OF NOT JUST THE MISTREATMENT OF CHINESE illegal immigrants, but also the darker side of American realities that create these types of conditions. I salute the many victims who, although fearful and weary, spoke out under my nudging to tell their stories. I hope this book will provoke reactions from the larger American society and help to end these abuses and build a better America for all Americans, including those who come here to seek democracy, equality, and economic opportunity.

I am indebted to the Alfred P. Sloan Foundation and the Research Foundation of the City University of New York whose financial assistance helped me to complete the book.

My genuine gratitude goes to three friends, Robert Fitch, Ida Susser, and Wing Lam, for giving me moral support so many times when I felt discouraged. I thank them for reading parts of the manuscript and giving helpful suggestions. Many thanks to Wah Lee of the Chinese Staff and Workers Association for keeping me regularly informed of the latest news and developments in the Chinese community. I also wish to acknowledge my wonderful experience working with my old friends Ying Chan and Jon Alpert in the production of a video documentary on Chinese human smuggling, upon which part of this book is based. I am also indebted to my dear friend and long-time editor from my *Village Voice* days, Dan Bischoff, for his fine editing and his respect for the purpose of this project.

This book, situated at the intersection of immigration, labor, and racial issues, would have gone nowhere without the wonderful people at The New Press, who understood and appreciated my less then conventional approach. I salute the women and men working there, particularly my editor and The New Press director, André Schiffrin, for his audacious and amazingly successful undertaking of publishing risky books on diverse and controversial subjects—books that are often shunned by the increasingly centralized and bottom-line–conscious publishing industry.

As usual, I am indebted to my wife Dušanka, not only for having to spend extraordinary amounts of time interrupting her own writing to edit and advise me on this book, but also for having the humor to deal with the various manifestations of emotional malaise stemming from my difficulties in writing.

Peter Kwong
July 1997

INTRODUCTION

IN THE WEE HOURS OF THE MISTY MORNING OF JUNE 6, 1993, THE
Indonesian captain of a Honduran-registered, forty-two-year-old
cargo steamer named (with what would later seem transliterate irony)
the *Golden Venture* hove to in international waters just outside New
York Harbor. The smuggler-in-charge on the ship, Lee Ginsing, tried
to get in touch by shortwave radio with his ground contact in
Queens, who was supposed to send out small fishing boats to meet
the ship and take off its secret cargo: 286 illegal would-be immigrants
from mainland China, who had been living in the dank and smelly
hold of the ship for the nearly four months it had taken to voyage
from Asia.

For hours the radio receiver turned up nothing but static. Lee,
impatient and nervy after the long journey, placed his revolver at the
Indonesian captain's temple and ordered him to steer the ship close
enough to the shore for the passengers to disembark in the shallow
water without assistance. The captain steamed toward the mouth of
New York harbor, guarded here by the sandy flats of the southern tip
of Long Island, and soon refused to navigate any further. Lee took
over the helm forcibly. From the ship's bridge he could barely make
out, through a sparse rain, the few scattered lights of Rockaway
Beach, deserted now but soon to fill with crowds of summer bathers.
In the distance glimmered the lights of the World Trade Center's twin
towers.

Then, when the ship was just a few hundred yards from the
Rockaway Beach U.S. Coast Guard Station, the *Golden Venture* ran
aground. The lurch of the ship's bow digging into a sandbar brought
the illegals out on deck. They gazed longingly at their dreamed-of
shore, knowing that with the sun would come the American authorities, and then maybe jail or deportation. Their months of seasickness
in the rusty hold, subsisting on little more than rice and water,

enduring the taunts of the snakeheads (human smugglers)—not to mention the thousands of U.S. dollars they had already paid for passage—would all go for nought. Many could no longer be restrained. They jumped into the chest-constricting, fifty-three-degree water to swim the last few hundred feet to America.

By daybreak, ten of the *Golden Venture's* illegal passengers had drowned. Alerted to the disaster, the Coast Guard sent out small seacraft and helicopters to begin a rescue effort. Local media were called to witness the extraordinary sight of a high-walled, deep-sea freighter tilting in the sand off one of the most popular recreational beaches in New York City. The entire world soon saw images of soaked Chinese nationals huddling under blankets on the windy beach, staring in confusion at the television cameras.

THE STORY OF THE *GOLDEN VENTURE* BECAME A NATIONAL OBSESSION. For weeks, every television station and newspaper around the country carried its own investigation into what seemed to be an invasion of illegal aliens. As a recognized expert on Chinese American issues and the human smuggling problem, I received endless calls. As early as 1989 I had spoken publicly about the revival of indentured servitude in New York's Chinatown created by the exorbitant smuggling fees charged by the "snakeheads." These enormous fees had long since forced illegal immigrants to accept practically any labor conditions, usually for years on end, to work off their debts. Consequently, working circumstances in the Chinese community have declined dramatically, making the eighty-four-hour workweek, home work, child labor, below-minimum wages, and even wage withholding common—just as they were in the primitive stages of late-nineteenth-century capitalism, when American tycoons imported immigrants to replace their assertive, even rebellious, unionized workforce. Of course, the media were rarely interested in my involved sociohistorical analysis. They wanted quick, simple answers. The public was attracted by the shocking and the exotic: the snakeheads, the smuggling routes, the role of international crime syndicates. The immigrants themselves were of little interest, and their aspirations were thought of, if at all, as both typical and obvious.

Most of the people who had boarded the *Golden Venture* in search of the promised land were peasants from Fujian Province in southern coastal China. They had traveled halfway around the world, spent 112 days at sea, and had promised to pay $30,000 to their smugglers if they successfully reached the United States. Scattered along chilly Rockaway Beach that early June morning, shivering under their thin blankets, this motley group seemed hapless enough—less a threat to American borders than survivors of a misdirected ship of fools that had unwittingly crashed right into the financial and media center of the world. Many American television viewers were even sympathetic. But with media emphasis squarely on the sensational, it was easy to conclude that America was being overwhelmed by an Asian-controlled, internationally based crime syndicate capable of operating human smuggling networks on a vast scale, and that hundreds of thousands of uneducated, inassimilable, illegal aliens were already here.

All of this fed nicely into the growing national anti-immigrant sentiment, which had begun the previous decade in the border states over the massive influx of Mexican immigrants. These states were humming with complaints that illegals take away "our" jobs and spend "our" tax revenues to cover "their" families' health, education, and welfare costs.

Their hostility comes as no surprise against the backdrop of the present uncertain economy, with high unemployment rates in many traditional industries and downsizing and job insecurity afflicting others, while massive immigration continues. Over one million legal immigrants arrived in the United States each year during the first half of the 1990s, not counting those who came in illegally and those who overstayed their non-immigrant visas. Historically, such a high influx rate has only been surpassed at the beginning of this century.

Adding to the anxiety is the fact that new immigrants nowadays come mainly from Asia and Latin America and are culturally and racially dramatically different from the earlier European stock. Their arrival has changed the previously essentially white/black binary character of American society to an uncharted multiracial society. Yet, as they introduce unfamiliar social and political dynamics, undermining customary European practices, they also generate apprehension on the part of the old-timers, manifested in recent heated debates on the issues of core versus multicultural curricula in schools and English-only versus bilingual ballots. And as the country gropes to define the new ideal, the popularity of "cultural" and "identity" studies in the academic community reveals a general disorientation in the society.

Even though America portrays itself as a country of immigrants, the truth is that the American people have always been leery of immigrants; the older immigrants have always seen the newcomers as competition, and as a threat to continuity and homogeneity of American society. Since 1945, opinion polls have consistently indicated that American people wish for a decrease in immigration. And as the immigration rates grew to historical highs in the first half of the 1990s, so did the desire of the American public to stop the trend: a 1993 *New York Times*–CBS News poll found that 61 percent of the American public wanted immigration to be decreased; in 1995, a Roper poll showed that 83 percent favored reductions and 70 percent wanted immigration to be no greater than 300,000 annually[1] (the current legal cap is set at 750,000).

OFFICIAL WHITE HOUSE REACTION AFTER THE *GOLDEN VENTURE* fiasco was swift. "We must not—we will not—surrender our borders to those who wish to exploit our history of compassion and justice," intoned President Clinton, declaring illegal immigration and human smuggling threats to national security. He ordered the National Security Council to coordinate the resources of the FBI, the CIA, and other major federal law enforcement organizations to combat the problem. As it turned out, the *Golden Venture* incident and the World Trade Center bombing were the two most important news events contributing to the escalation of border state anti-immigrant senti-ment into a national phenomenon.

The extent of anti-immigrant hostility was revealed by the over-whelmingly popular passage of Proposition 187 in California in No-vember 1994. Prop 187 denied health care, education, and other public services to undocumented immigrants and their offspring, and required social service providers to report to law enforcement au-thorities any service user suspected of undocumented status. Al-though still hung up in the courts as of this writing, Prop 187 had an inspiriting ripple effect on legislatures across the country. After a time even Congress took its cue from the state referendum, interpreting it as the American public consensus on the subject, and legislated sev-eral of its own punitive measures.

The anti-immigrant fever ran so high that even liberal Democrats began to vie among themselves to introduce tough measures against illegal immigration. First came the Anti-Terrorism and Effective Death Penalty Act of 1996, which suspended several traditional rights under the U.S. Constitution, including the right to a fair trial and an appeal, which had previously been granted generously to all immi-grants, including illegals. Intended to deter illegal immigration ex-peditiously, the Act allows illegal aliens seeking admission to the United States to be summarily excluded and deported, and for their political asylum claims to be administratively determined before a non-judicial officer while they are held in detention. That was fol-lowed by the 1996 immigration bill, which funded stiffer border controls, increased the number of alien smuggling investigators, im-posed harsher sentences on human smugglers, and extended wiretap authority to smuggling and document fraud cases. The Welfare Re-form Bill, also passed in 1996, effectively cut off all forms of benefits to illegal immigrants.

The hostility has now turned against legal immigrants as well: the new 1996 immigration bill requires U.S. citizens who wish to sponsor their relatives in coming to America to meet an income requirement of at least 125 percent of the federal poverty level; the new welfare law excludes legal immigrants from most housing, welfare, social security, Medicaid, and food stamps benefits unless they can prove that they have worked legally and paid into the Social Security system. Elderly permanent residents who are not eligible for social security are barred from receiving welfare assistance as well. A recent *Washington Post* editorial has qualified the ongoing anti-immigration discourse in this country as "startling and truly mean";[2] in the *New York Times* A. M. Rosenthal sees it as "moving America toward exceptionally ugly results, which we are too delicate to face straight on."[3]

The spirit of these measures is not difficult to discern. "Our goals are to do all we can to discourage the unchecked flow of illegal immigrants and to encourage those illegal immigrants already here to go home," said Republican Congressman Elton Gallegly of California. The legislation was drafted by the Republicans with the acquiescence of the Democrats, and President Clinton signed all three bills into law right before the 1996 presidential election.

These punitive measures may have bought the President some votes, but they will not work—if their goal is curtailing illegal immigration—because they don't address the heart of the problem: the ever-healthy demand of American business for vulnerable, unprotected labor. Even with all the public attention generated by the *Golden Venture* fiasco and the new measures signed into law by a president campaigning triumphantly for reelection, Chinese illegal migration will continue. It will continue because the sensational headlines, punitive legislation, and political demagoguery all work together to reinforce the essential appeal of illegal Chinese laborers to the American businesses that employ them: illegal aliens continue to be cheaper, more pliable, and more dependent on their employers than legitimate labor. More than any other single fact, this explains how human smuggling has grown in the last half of the last decade of the twentieth century into an industry boasting $4 billion in annual profits.

And what about the *Golden Venture* and its cargo? No one would ever have heard of the old tramp steamer if snakehead Lee's contact in Queens had answered the radio that night in June 1993. What no one aboard knew at that time, however, was that the contact had been killed by rival snakehead operators for poaching on their business. As for the snake people, those who weren't killed in the surf were brought ashore by the Coast Guard and immediately incarcerated by the Immigration and Naturalization Service. At most a dozen were given immediate asylum and released. One third agreed voluntarily to deportation to Central American countries, and another third were eventually returned to China.

The remaining fifty-three would-be immigrants were kept in a number of federal prisons for three years and eight months. Finally, in February of 1997, the Clinton administration agreed to parole them. The Indonesian captain and crew of the *Golden Venture*, as well as snakehead Lee and his gang of enforcers, were already out—they had been freed after only six months to a year detention. As this book goes to press, the relatives of the newly freed *Golden Venture* inmates have been contacted by snakeheads.[4] They say each family owes them $20–30,000. After all, they made it to the Golden Mountain.

IT IS MY CONTENTION THAT THE PROBLEM OF ILLEGAL IMMIGRATION, including Chinese immigration, can only be understood in the context of the underlying supply-and-demand principle enshrined in traditional U.S. economics. In that sense, the illegal immigration problem is no different from our national drug problem, where all the traffic interdiction and supply eradication efforts in Latin America and Southeast Asia over the past twenty years have had little impact on U.S. sales and consumption. Quite to the contrary, these efforts have had the paradoxical effect of making the traffic in illegal drugs more profitable and the criminal cartels that control it more sophisticated and menacing. Similarly, harsh immigration laws will only make illegal aliens more vulnerable to smugglers and employers, raise the costs of smuggling even higher, and force the smuggling syndicates to grow even more brutal and immune to government powers.

As an Asian American specialist, I have studied the Chinese Ameri-can communities for more than two decades. The findings have been published in several books and in a number of articles. And since 1991, I have conducted hundreds of personal interviews with Chinese undocumented workers in their living quarters, at their workplaces, in coffee shops, in prisons, and on waiting lines of employment agencies, in all parts of New York City, from the relatively circum-scribed precincts of south Manhattan's traditional Chinatown to the ballooning Chinese neighborhoods of Queens and Brooklyn. These contacts have brought to my attention circumstances affecting Chi-nese workers far beyond the New York metropolitan area, from Con-necticut suburbs to newly opened restaurants in North Carolina and even into Southern California and elsewhere around the country.

My access to these illegal immigrants has been anything but au-tomatic, although it was easier for me to communicate with them because of my command of several Chinese dialects. In fact, it takes years of painful cultivation to gain the trust of someone whose daily work is carried out in constant fear of detection by immigration officials and whose private life is shadowed by the threat of torture from fellow Chinese debt enforcers. In-depth interviews with them have been very difficult, especially in regard to sensitive issues con-cerning their smugglers and employers. The problem is compounded by the lack of free time from their long working hours to talk with me. I have to intrude on them late at night when they are usually exhausted or on their days off when they are usually busy with personal chores with their families and relatives.

Aside from these critical personal interviews, my knowledge of the illegals is informed by my regular contacts with federal and local police officers, immigration officials, social workers, immigration lawyers, and Chinatown reporters. I am able to maintain regular ex-changes and share my ideas and findings with immigration scholars, labor organizers, congressional aides and policymakers through participation in various forums—including the Columbia University Seminar on Cultural Pluralism and seminars sponsored by Center for

Immigration, Ethnicity, and Citizenship at The New School of Social Research, seminars on "The Impact of Globalization and International Affairs on American Society" co-sponsored by Council on Foreign Relations and The Stanley Foundation. Some of my research findings have been published as cover stories in *The Village Voice* and *The Nation* and as video documentaries on NBC and PBS programs.

The most significant factor shaping my macro perspective on the Chinese human smuggling is that after the *Golden Venture* made its sudden appearance as an unannounced seaside attraction for Rockaway Beach tourists in 1993, I traveled to China to investigate the origins of emigration by the Fuzhounese, who had displaced the Cantonese as the majority of ethnic Chinese immigrants to the United States in the 1980s. There I had the opportunity to interview snakehead operators, local party officials, and average citizens and farmers, including those who had made great sacrifices to send relatives on the dangerous journey to America. Together they gave a fairly complete picture of the Fuzhounese smuggling network and the system of family-centered chain migration it supports that has brought some two hundred thousand illegal immigrants to the United States in the past fifteen years.

The Fuzhounese are not alone. Other coastal regions in China are also increasingly involved in illegal migration, pushed by the massive social dislocations created by rapid economic development. China's internal migration—from rural to urban, north to south, interior to coastal regions—has indeed spilled over into global emigration, as it has so often threatened to do in the past. What's more, Chinese migration is a part of a larger international mobility, a consequence of a global economy determined to champion free trade and open markets.

And so, while this book provides answers as to who the bulk of illegal Chinese immigrants in the United States are, where they come from, and what drives their migration, it is not to be merely descriptive. It looks at the Fuzhounese illegals and the conditions of virtual indentured servitude under which they are forced to live in our midst as a key to understanding contemporary American society. How is it possible that at the close of the twentieth century, more than a hundred years after the abolition of slavery, such conditions have re-emerged in a country that sees itself as the champion of human rights and democracy? What does this neglect of basic rights bode for the general well-being of our society? What can we do to solve the constellation of problems highlighted by the Chinese illegal immigration, and related to America's immigration policy, organized crime, ethnic labor exploitation, absence of state intervention, an ineffective labor movement, and America's racial and ethnic tensions?

AMERICA'S IMMIGRATION HISTORY IS PUNCTUATED BY AMERICAN industry's need for labor. Immigrants have historically been recruited for two reasons: during times of economic expansion, when all levels of skilled and unskilled laborers were in great demand, and whenever business forces felt a need to increase the labor pool in order to undermine wage levels and the bargaining power of existing domestic labor organizations.

Today's immigration is no different: professionals are recruited abroad to service the technical, financial, and high-tech fields, which continue to expand; and less-skilled immigrants are recruited to serve the needs of the decentralized, restructured American economy, which has all but eliminated union protections for unskilled labor. In addition to moving production overseas, to wherever the labor is cheaper and less organized, American businesses also subcontract work to smaller domestic production sites whose operations remain more flexible because they employ unregulated labor. The cited rationale for this restructuring is cost-cutting, but its much more important objective is a readjustment in the balance of power between labor and capital established since the 1930s. The destruction of the powerful labor movement that was able to make significant gains in collective bargaining, higher wages, health and retirement benefits, unemployment compensation, and other social welfare safety nets is the chief objective of this new business order in the United States.

The best way to achieve this objective is by hiring the least organized and most vulnerable labor available—new immigrants or, preferably, undocumented aliens who have no protection at all. The American labor market is currently composed of the highly paid native-born unionized workers; the native-born historically disadvantaged minorities, who work in lower-wage competitive industries; the unorganized new immigrants; and the completely unprotected illegal aliens. Among this last group, and exploited as they are, Latin American immigrants rarely enter with such crushing debts as the Fuzhounese, who must maintain a killing pace in several below-minimum-wage jobs for years just to repay their smugglers. That leaves the Fuzhounese with the unpleasant distinction of being one of the lowest rungs on the ladder of labor, and reduction to their status the ultimate goad that owners can use on the rest of American labor.

Most Americans see the Fuzhounese as an aberration—an isolated ethnic phenomenon at the fringes of society. But an increasing number of mainstream garment manufacturers, aware of the Fuzhounese's unique predicament, now offer job orders to Chinese subcontractors who hire illegal Chinese workers. The same is true of mainstream restaurant owners and construction companies who service a general American clientele.

The peculiar Fuzhounese condition in the United States is indicative of the changing pattern of immigrant incorporation into America. European immigrants came to service America's first great industrial expansion after the Civil War. They were recruited to work in large industrial complexes in concentrated urban areas, and they worked alongside native-born Americans. The immigrant ghettos they initially settled in were just transitional way stations, necessary only until they adjusted to the new society and learned English. The pressures of economic survival invariably forced them to move on—to wherever work was available. Eventually, they found homes outside the ghetto, learned English, and integrated into American society.

Today, the unskilled immigrant workers are recruited to work in decentralized industries and are employed by subcontractors, many of whom have shifted their production sites to right where the immigrants live, giving rise to a new pattern of ethnic concentration and segregation. Because most Chinese immigrants work for Chinese employers in what contemporary scholars have labeled "ethnic enclaves," their situation is even more isolating: they live, work, and socialize without ever having to leave the enclave, where the initial adjustment to their new country is easy and command of English is unnecessary.

The ethnic enclaves, however, are a trap. Not only are the immigrants doomed to perpetual subcontracted employment, but the social and political control of these enclaves is also subcontracted to ethnic elites, who are free to set their own legal and labor standards for the entire community without ever coming under the scrutiny of U.S. authorities. And while this allows businesses operating within the enclaves to ignore standard American labor laws, law enforcement officials often claim that they have no choice but to deal with local elites because of the impenetrable social structure of the ethnic enclaves and the difficulty of dealing effectively in a language comprehended by only a handful of officials.

More significantly, this non-intervention attitude of the U.S. authorities, while convenient and practical, has helped spawn a new ideology for a downsized America: the belief that new immigrants, traditionally hardworking and self-reliant, now have their own ethnic networks to help and support them, making them independent of public assistance. Because they are doing fine, the theory goes, they should be left alone. Moreover, their cultural values should become the model for others, particularly the traditional native minorities, who are too dependent on government aid for solutions to their problems. Such minorities would do best to adopt the immigrants' work ethic, their strong family ties, and their rugged self-reliance.

The aim of the "model minority" school of thought, with its emphasis on so-called "cultural values," has been to separate immigrants of color from native African Americans by establishing a new type of classification for Asian and Latino immigrants. Asian immigrants have thus been dragged into the middle of this historically black–white debate; and, sad to say, many Asians have readily accepted the myth promoted by American neoconservatives crediting specifically Asian cultural assets for their economic success and social mobility. As with any myth of classlessness, the myth of Asian cultural exceptionalism bluntly ignores vast inequalities within the Asian community. Its proponents have, naturally, kept the unpleasant problem of illegal aliens away from public discourse.

However, only thirty years ago, Asians were barred from legal immigration through a series of exclusion acts—the Chinese Exclusion Act of 1882, the Gentlemen's Agreement of 1907 restricting the Japanese, the creation of the "Asiatic Barred Zone" in 1917; and in 1924 as part of the general restrictions, the Congress enacted the Oriental Exclusion Act that virtually banned all immigration from Asia.[5] The Asians that were in the country, like African and Latino Americans, were all part of the "colored minorities" and were forced to live in segregated neighborhoods and relegated to low-wage, unwanted jobs. In fact, many could not even get work in the American labor market because of the objection of whites to working alongside them.

It was only after the successful struggles on the part of African Americans leading to the passage of the Civil Rights Act of 1964 that Asians (along with all colored minorities) were able to enjoy legal equality. As part of the same liberal and enlightened vision of making America a color-blind society, the Congress passed the 1965 Immigration Act, one year after the Civil Rights Act. The 1965 act eliminated explicitly racial clauses restricting colored immigrants. Ironically, the subsequent massive influx of newcomers from Asia and Latin America since has buried this shared history of the "colored minorities."

There is no doubt that the continued influx of cheap and exploitable illegal labor degrades the position of American workers. The impact is disproportionally felt in the African American community, where a large percentage of unskilled labor suffers from higher than average unemployment rates. Illegal immigration negatively affects the economic opportunities of many African Americans, and should be studied in this context very seriously—particularly in view of the impact legal European immigration has had on their opportunities in the post-slavery era.

After the end of the Civil War, African Americans needed more than emancipation from slavery and guarantees of the political rights available to all American citizens. They needed concrete means to make a living—land and jobs to get started. The federal government enacted the "Reconstruction" programs to address these issues. There were millions of acres of fertile land to be settled as the frontier moved west across the Mississippi River; labor was needed for the completion of trans-continental railroads and the major industrial expansion in Northern cities. Yet this was not to be the promised land for former slaves. With mass immigration from politically and economically troubled parts of Europe, the federal government barred African Americans from settlement while offering free land to European immigrants, who were also sought by the new Northern industries to fill the factory jobs. The former slaves were forced into sedentary agricultural work in the South,[6] particularly with the end of Reconstruction, and their opportunity to be part of the mainstream American society was dashed. African Americans were only recruited to work in Northern industries after World War I, when European immigration slowed, but by then the good jobs had already been taken and labor unions were organized by European immigrants to make sure that black workers were shut out. White Americans in fact blocked African Americans from reasonable access to better-paid jobs until the 1964 Civil Rights Act.[7]

The 1964 Civil Rights Act eliminated legal discrimination based on race and African Americans were promised opportunities for economic mobility through a series of social and affirmative action programs. Yet once again their progress into the American mainstream was hindered by the arrival of new immigrants. With the passage of the 1965 Immigration act, a new wave of immigration swept across America, this time from Latin America and Asia. Partly because of the immigrant selection process, these new immigrants have been highly competitive and have been able to move ahead while, sadly, anti–African American racism continues. Again and again surveys confirm that white employers prefer new immigrants of virtually any nationality or ethnicity to African Americans.[8]

By their sheer presence, these new immigrant groups have been drawn into the black–white debate. Pro-immigrant groups argue that immigrants are more productive and have a better work ethic than many Americans and should therefore be welcomed. On the other hand, some argue that the influx of immigrants takes the jobs away from African Americans and the poor. Asian and Latino immigrants have been pitted against African Americans and find themselves in an awkward, impossible situation. But they are here, and after decades of racial exclusion from the predominantly white America, Latinos and Asians have as much a right to be in this country as the European immigrants and all those who came here before them.

Asian and Latino immigrants are being used as a tactical weapon to restructure the American economy. Nativist reaction to immigration and the curtailment of the rights and benefits of both illegal and legal immigrants in reality help to further segregate American labor along ethnic and racial lines, forcing more and more people to survive in insecure pockets of an underground economy, in the end better serving capital's interest.

Attacking the immigrants only shifts attention away from the real problem. It contributes to the further deterioration of American society in more ways than one: such isolated, unregulated ethnic enclaves bring the lowering of work and living standards, undemocratic political structures, and organized crime to our society at large. It was precisely this type of anti-immigrant sentiment one hundred years ago that led to the exclusion of Chinese from immigration into the United States and their forced segregation into isolated ghettos that deprived them of equal rights and job opportunities. This history of exclusion has set the conditions for the continued isolation of Chinese new immigrants inside their ethnic enclaves even to this day, allowing ultimately for the development of the Fuzhounese indentured labor system.

The issue, therefore, is not to divide Americans into legals and illegals or immigrants versus native-born. We have to understand each other and work together. Latino and Asian immigrants should be sensitive to America's unique history. Their arrival has in many ways complicated the resolution of an essentially biracial conflict. They are not responsible for the tragic legacy of American slavery, but they have been enjoying the results of the 1964 Civil Rights Act, which ended legal discrimination against *all colored people,* and it is important that they appreciate the efforts of African Americans, who are largely responsible for its passage.

Asians, most of all, should not see themselves separated from the American class conflict. A significant segment of the Asian American population is unskilled, less educated, working in dead-end jobs, and living in ethnically concentrated Chinese, Filipino, and Southeast Asian ghettos. The Fuzhounese are merely the most extreme example. In fact, the influx of the Fuzhounese may have peaked already, but their condition has spread. Other Chinese groups will follow. Authorities in Elmonte, California, recently arrested nearly forty illegal seamstresses from Thailand found living and working in virtual slavery in a makeshift garment factory; the smuggling fees for East Indians were reported to have reached $28,000 in 1996.

Ultimately, the presence of Fuzhounese and other indentured servitude in our community is an indication of a decline in the American labor movement. Capital counts on labor's traditional racism and exclusionary practices, for it recruits precisely those whom organized labor excludes. Today, the well-being and living standards of all Americans depend on a successful labor reform movement that rises from a broad, from-the-bottom-up mobilization campaign encompassing the entire working class: the people of color, the immigrants, and the illegal aliens. Inclusion of Fuzhounese immigrants in the ranks of American organized labor will be a test of organized labor's viability in the future. Protecting the most vulnerable segment of the working class from brutal exploitation would signal American labor unions' commitment to moral accountability. And, while showing America's commitment to the principle of equality, it would also save American society from the downward slide in working conditions that will eventually affect us all.

CHAPTER 1

The Pig Trade: The Contemporary Version

EAST BROADWAY, ON MANHATTAN'S LOWER EAST SIDE, IS LOCALLY known locally as Fuzhou Street. It is considered foreign territory by most residents of Chinatown. The people on Fuzhou Street think and act very differently from Chinatown's dominant group, the Cantonese (individuals from Guangdong Province). Known to outsiders as hard workers themselves, the Cantonese often accuse the Fuzhounese people of being interested in making money to the point of recklessness. They call them *gan-she-gui,* the "fearless ghosts," who don't shrink from operating take-out restaurants in the worst and most dangerous ghettos.

The "fearless ghosts," many of whom are undocumented immigrants known as "snake people," have brought unwelcome attention to the Chinese community, according to the old Cantonese residents. So many illegal Fuzhounese have settled in Chinatown in the last ten years that, residents say, they have taken over everything. They are now being blamed for all the wrongs in the community: the unfair job competition, the overcrowded housing, the filthy and congested sidewalks, and the increase in violent crime. Besides, they speak a different language, incomprehensible to the Cantonese.

For more than a century, the Chinese communities across the United States have been ruled by the Cantonese—people from Guangdong Province, or more specifically, from the eight counties surrounding the City of Canton (Guangzhou) along the Pearl River. In New York's Chinatown, people from Toishan County have always constituted the majority, and to navigate effectively in Manhattan's Chinese community you needed to speak Toishanese, which has stronger nasal tones than the more urbane official Cantonese dialect spoken in Canton and in Hong Kong. The group was so dominant that the ability to speak Toishanese was a long-standing requirement for the post of the Consul General of the Republic of China in New York before the 1960s.

Today, speaking either Toishanese or Cantonese is no longer critical for conducting business in Chinatown; now it has become acceptable to communicate in Mandarin, the official dialect in both Taiwan and the mainland. The established community resists the growing influence of the Fuzhounese nonetheless. Not only do the Fuzhounese crowd into the already overcrowded precincts of New York's traditional Chinatown, putting an enormous strain on overextended social services, they also blacken the image of the Chinese who are already here. Already stereotyped as being embroiled in gambling and *tong* wars, the Cantonese see the Fuzhounese as bringing extremely violent forms of street crime, kidnapping, and torture to the new country.

Scorned and shunned by the rest, the Fuzhounese have developed their own community on the outer edge of Chinatown, around the three-block area on East Broadway under the Manhattan Bridge. This is where they eat, shop, socialize, and where their Fukien-American Association (Fukien is the old spelling of Fujian) is located. This is where several of their own Buddhist temples and a number of Christian churches are to be found. It is Chinatown's ghetto—an area rarely visited by the non-Fuzhounese. The incorporation of Fuzhou Street is a relatively new phenomenon, which happened within the last ten years. Previously, this section along East Broadway was occupied by Chinese immigrants from Vietnam and Malaysia.

On a typical day in the mid-1990s, Fuzhou Street is dynamic and bustling. Unlike older sections of Chinatown, here the business facades have not been improved to attract tourists, and the street resembles in many ways its turn-of-the century self. Food vendors sell fish balls and fried taro-root cakes from under tin-lined cardboard roofs splattered with grease, just as they do in rural Fuzhou.

The clothing worn on the street betrays the recent immigrants: men wear mainland-Chinese-designed bleached-out blue jeans, T-shirts with moronic English captions, and off-brand sneakers; women favor silk blouses and brightly colored knee-length skirts, which they always wear with dark, knee-high nylon stockings. Storefronts look

seedy, and often have a transient air about them: one finds an inordinate number of *fuwu gongsi* (service companies) offering help in
applying for political asylum, acquiring temporary work permits, or
procuring essential U.S. documents, such as driver's licenses, social
security cards, or legal birth certificates. Dozens of travel agencies
offer discount fares to Fuzhou, or specialize in *pao-ban*—special tasks
for a family, such as taking complete charge of newborn babies being
sent back to China, or purchasing tickets to enable a relative from
China to emigrate. *Pao-ban* also involves shipping televisions and
refrigerators back to Fujian Province.

And then there are all the Chinese herbal stores, which double as
Western medicine counters, usually under a small sign in Chinese
announcing "in-house well-known medical specialist available." The
crowds bump into hundreds of street vendors along East Broadway as
they patronize Fuzhounese-run restaurants, beauty parlors, general
and electronics stores, all speaking exclusively the Fuzhou dialect.

This new Fuzhounese community within Chinatown happens to
be flourishing in what was historically the area of early Jewish settlement, under the shadow of the old *Daily Forward* building and the
nearly abandoned Eldridge Street Synagogue. The old flavor of the
neighborhood—the smell of hardship, poverty, and sweat—is still
there. The passing years add little more than new layers of grease and
soot to the dilapidated facades.

The Fuzhounese population is expanding so fast that it is already
spreading south of the old Jewish neighborhood toward the East
River, around the old headquarters of the *New York Post* and into
parts of an old Italian neighborhood connected to the South Street
Seaport. Others have moved to the Eighth Avenue area of Sunset
Park in Brooklyn, an old Norwegian immigrant neighborhood,
where they can rent larger spaces for less money. The new immigrants
call it the "Sunlight District" because even those who read no English
know that after the N train leaves Chinatown, if they get off as soon
as they see the sunlight, when the subway emerges from underground
at the Eighth Avenue stop, they are in Sunset Park. This area, too, has

dramatically expanded in the past ten years, and now bustles with Chinese groceries, travel agencies, restaurants, street vendors, and nonunionized garment factories.

LIFE IN THE OLD COUNTRY

One thing you notice almost immediately when strolling along East Broadway is the extraordinary number of establishments that like to use the word *Fu* in their names. *Fu* means "fortunate": a grocery named *Fu An* means "fortunate peace"; a restaurant named *Fu Shing* means "fortunate renewal." *Fu* is the first character in the name of Fujian Province, which means "fortunate establishment." It and the adjacent Guangdong Province just to the south are the fastest-developing regions in China today. And both have long traditions of involvement with the West.

Fuzhou, a city of five million, is the capital of Fujian Province. It is on the northern coastline of the province and has always been known as a major Chinese seaport, just as its people have been known for their seafaring skills and cosmopolitan savvy. Marco Polo visited there in the thirteenth century, during the Yuan Dynasty. He noted that the towns and villages around the Fu-gui were in "an area where the necessaries of life are in abundance . . . and the people . . . are engaged in commerce and manufactures."[1]

Almost 90 percent of the recent Fuzhou immigrants to America have come from the three rural counties outside the city of Fuzhou: Lianjian, Changle, and Minhou, which all lie at the mouth of the Min River. Because of the area's proximity to the sea, its excellent natural harbors, and hundreds of remote islands and coves, the population of these counties has long engaged in fishing and overseas trading. Some have called them "the Jews of China" because of their penchant for overseas travel and adventure. They were among the first settlers of the island of Taiwan, perhaps as early as the seventh century. Traditionally, the Fuzhounese are viewed by their fellow Chinese as very close-knit (even by the standards of the traditional Chinese family), grasping, and uncultivated. And much of their history has conspired to give them that reputation.

Fuzhou is surrounded by a series of rugged mountain ranges, which cut it off from other parts of China except by sea; the port itself is even cut off from the more developed southern parts of the Fujian Province near Amoy (Xiamem). This geographic isolation contributed to and is reinforced by the unique language the people of Fuzhou speak—a dialect not only different from any spoken elsewhere in China, but even distinct from the Southern-Min dialect dominant in Southern Fujian around the city of Amoy and on the island of Taiwan. It is entirely incomprehensible to all but a tiny fraction of the Chinese people.

The first mention of the original inhabitants of Fujian is made in imperial records as early as the Chow Dynasty, where they are referred to as Min. The character for Min in Mandarin is made with a "snake" under a "gate" radicle. It is assumed that the original inhabitants there belonged to a snake-worshiping tribe. The Chinese Han majority usually used radicles based on animal forms to designate foreigners in order to show their contempt for barbarians.[2] Referring to the Fujianese in such a way reflected the latter's marginal status in the larger Chinese civilization.

Cheng Ho, the best-known admiral in Chinese history, led seven expeditions into the Indian Ocean between 1405 and 1433, during the Ming Dynasty, reaching Java, Sumatra, India, and even as far as the Strait of Hormuz at the mouth of the Persian Gulf before returning by way of Mozambique in East Africa. These expeditions boasted the largest fleet of the times and made China an unchallenged naval power in Asian waters.[3] Fuzhou was one of the main bases for Cheng Ho's operations, providing maritime supplies, logistical support, and repairs.

When the Manchu overthrew the Ming in 1644 and established the Qing Dynasty, many Ming loyalists from Fuzhou fled to Taiwan and Southeast Asia, which they used as a base for periodic attacks on the South China coast. To prevent these expatriates from gaining new recruits and agitating for rebellion, the Qing announced that "all those who clandestinely proceed to sea to trade, or who remove to foreign islands . . . shall be punished according to the law against communicating with rebels and enemies, and consequently suffer death by beheading."[4]

The Fuzhounese never stopped their clandestine activities of the Ming era; the fishermen here were in constant contact with pirates from Japan. From 1549 to 1562, these pirates actually took control of several Fuzhounese port cities, carving out locally autonomous fiefdoms completely independent of Beijing.[5] The loyalties of the Fuzhounese continued to be suspect under the Qing Dynasty. Koxinga, the son of a Ming official who had raised a rebellious army to overthrow the Manchu government, made Fuzhou his command center in the late 1650s.

From the eighteenth century on, Fuzhou was the port of call for merchant clipper ships from Britain and New England loading the renowned Wu-I tea. After China's defeat in the Opium War of 1842, the city became one of the five treaty ports ceded by the Qing imperial government to the Western colonial powers as "free trade" zones. The international trade for Fuzhou was, of course, in tea. One Western observer commented that, so picturesque was that trade—with the harbor of Pagoda Anchorage filled with famous American and European clipper ships, racing for high stakes and greater honor with their cargoes of tea around the entire globe, with individual fortunes made and lost on a single journey—that the other ports of China and the country's other products remained as yet undeveloped.[6] When the trade was at its peak in 1903, Fuzhou shipped over 40,000,000 pounds of tea.[7]

During the early part of the nineteenth century both Britain and the United States had carried trade deficits with China. It wasn't until the two English-speaking powers started selling opium to the Chinese in exchange for silks, porcelains, nankeen cotton cloth, and, above all, tea that the balance was redressed.

Americans found opium to be the ideal product for exchange.

Excluded for the most part from the major sources of supply in India, they located an alternative source in the Turkish port of Myrna. Though inferior in quality to the British version, the Turkish drug could be consumed by less discriminating smokers. Philadelphia- and Baltimore-based ships took advantage of this trade as early as 1804.[8] The clipper ships were built for fast passage from North America to Turkey, where they were loaded with opium. They then sailed back out of the Mediterranean Sea through the Straits of Gibraltar, around Africa's Cape of Good Hope, and thence to China's southern coast, where the opium was exchanged for tea; from there they sailed across the Pacific, around the tip of South America, and on to Boston or New York.

With the defeat of the Chinese in the Opium War, the way was cleared for American missionaries. First came the American Board Mission in 1847, then the Methodist Episcopal Mission in 1848, the Church Missionary Society Mission in 1850, the Young Men's Christian Association in 1905, and the YWCA in 1914. Western Christian missionary activities in Fuzhou were so significant that it was chosen as one of the handful of cities in China for the establishment of an institute of higher learning, the Fukien Christian University. Soon there was a Kushan Monastery, the largest in South China, for the most seriously devout among the native population. The Fuzhou Christian community remains active even to this day. According to local accounts, many of the Christian congregations have never interrupted their services during the present Communist rule.

In any event, Fuzhou City has a long history of international exposure. Their seafaring reputation echoes even today in its citizens' smuggling activities, which include ferrying contraband across the Taiwan Strait on their fishing boats in defiance of government restrictions on both sides.

At times, Chinese governments have tried to tap the seafaring skills of the Fuzhounese. After numerous defeats at the hands of the European powers, the late Qing government, for example, decided to establish a naval academy, a modern shipyard, and a merchant marine college on Mawei Island, just outside of Fuzhou City, as a way to both initiate reform and catch up with the West. A great number of the graduates from these institutions became highly decorated admirals, captains, and naval officers of the Qing and Republican periods. Sailors were recruited from precisely the counties that the present immigrants to New York hail from.

Those with ambition used their connections and training to join the merchant marine on foreign vessels, hoping for better opportunities elsewhere. Some migrated to Hong Kong to be near the Western shipping employers. Others moved on to overseas trading posts in Southeast Asia. Today, Fuzhounese financial and trading blocs are well established and well respected in Indonesia, Malaysia, and the Philippines. Liem Sioe Liong, the world's wealthiest expatriate Chinese and one of the twelve richest bankers in the world, is from Fuzhou. His Salim Group, with its stable of some four hundred-odd companies, accounts for roughly 5 percent of Indonesia's gross domestic product.[9] The Fuzhounese presence in the Philippines dates back to the Ming Dynasty's designation of Fuzhou City as China's official trading port for the Pacific Islands. Ex-president Corazon Aquino's family originally came from Fuzhou, and she visited her ancestral home there during her presidency.

THE RISE OF THE FUZHOUNESE HUMAN SMUGGLING NETWORK

The profound Fuzhounese feeling of marginalization—brought on by the combination of their geographic isolation, distinctive dialect, and seagoing vocation—all contributed to the equally profound Fuzhounese spirit of independence and political autonomy. When the Communists took control of China in 1949, for instance, they trusted the locals so little they imported the region's entire top political leadership from outside. Local Fuzhounese were only assigned to posts at the deputy level.

Since 1949 and the beginning of Communist rule, the government has exercised tight control over the movement of people within China itself, and made emigration to a foreign country extremely difficult even for those who had relatives overseas. Families with members abroad could at any time be accused of "spying" for foreigners, particularly during the Cultural Revolution in the late 1960s. In fact, during the Cold War as a whole, emigration to a Western country was viewed as tantamount to treason. Even a group as isolated and independent as the Fuzhounese would not challenge this state policy.

But the Fuzhounese sense of independence is balanced by their strong ties to families and clans. Throughout their history of overseas wandering, they seem never to have forgotten their families in China, sharing jobs and opportunities wherever they found them with home folks whenever they could. Clan and family loyalty is the primary axiom of their lives, as the extent and the speed of recent Fuzhounese migration would seem to bear out. "Fuzhounese are loyal to their own people," says a Fuzhounese community leader in New York City. "They would loan a couple thousand dollars to their village kin without even thinking twice—and that's not to mention what they would do for their own relatives."

Yet for all their prowess and prestige in China as world travelers, very few Fuzhounese came to the United States before the late twentieth century. The first record of their presence involves a few hundred Fuzhounese seamen who worked on American merchant marine vessels during World War II, ferrying supplies across the Atlantic from New York to England and the Soviet Union. Those were dangerous and deadly missions, for the Liberty cargo ships were under constant threat from German U-boats.[10] After the war ended, many Fuzhounese gained residence in the United States as a reward for their service, and most settled in New York, still one of the busiest ports in the world in those days. The community was large enough to establish a Fukien-American Association in New York's Chinatown.

A much larger contingent appeared on U.S. borders in the early 1970s, when Fuzhounese seamen who worked on foreign vessels started jumping ship in New York harbor. The situation became so serious that, after repeated complaints by the shipping companies against their delinquent employees, the Immigration and Naturalization Service (INS) responded by deploying regular raids on Chinatown restaurants and barber shops. The agents would smash into an establishment, demand that all present—customers as well as employees—show their immigration papers, and then ostentatiously search the front, the back, and the cellar, even probing into crawl spaces above the ceilings, in search of illegal seamen. Even those with legal status were regularly harassed. These high-handed tactics so terrorized the community that they led to a storm of protests from Chinese civil rights organizations, and may well have set the pattern for Fuzhounese attitudes toward U.S. legal authorities for well into the next century.[11]

The Fuzhounese seamen who arrived in New York in the 1970s were single men without legal status. Few could become legalized residents. A handful arranged phony marriages with ABC (American-born Chinese) girls, paying them $3,000 to go through the ritual of a bogus marriage. In order to avoid suspicion, the couple had to prepare a shared apartment (where they each kept a set of clothing), obtain a joint bank account, file joint tax returns, and list both names on telephone and electricity bills.

With or without legal status, however, as soon as the seamen became established economically, they started bringing members of their families from China. This was the beginning of the Fuzhounese human smuggling network: a few primitive, simple schemes concocted by enterprising travel agencies to exploit this eager market of merchant mariners. The main challenge was transporting the relatives from Hong Kong to New York.

In the late 1960s, at the height of the Cultural Revolution, the Chinese Communist government opened the border between China and Hong Kong, thinking it might destroy the British colony by flooding it with penniless refugees. Many Fuzhounese with family connections in New York seized the opportunity of this chaotic period to go to Hong Kong, some by swimming across the Shenzhen

River. Once in Hong Kong they gained refugee status and were thus entitled to exit visas.

The travel agencies' task was to obtain, usually through bribery, entry visas for the refugees to countries like Bolivia, Guatemala, or Mexico. When they arrived in those countries, the refugees were then escorted across the Mexican border into the United States. During the days when the border controls were at a minimum, the smuggling fee was a mere $1,800.

This route via South America was already well traveled by Taiwanese criminals—often tax cheats, but occasionally more serious offenders, including embezzlers and violent criminals—in the 1970s. In fact, the very first illegal Fuzhou emigrants used phony Taiwanese passports. This Central American option became even more popular after 1978, when Deng Xiaoping initiated the liberal "open door policy," and thousands of Fuzhounese arrived illegally in New York.

The modern era of human smuggling began with the passage of the Immigration Reform and Control Act of 1986 (IRCA). The act contained an amnesty provision granting legal status to all those who could prove that they had resided in the United States as undocumented aliens before January 1, 1982. IRCA was a bonanza for the Fuzhounese illegals already in the United States. With a stroke of the pen they became legal. Even the would-be illegal immigrants who were still in China could become legal if they arrived in time to hand in their application by November 1988. There were plenty of crooks in Chinatown willing to provide them with the back-dated employment records and tax receipts needed for the application—if they could come up with $500 to $600.

The result was a mad rush. The Taiwanese crime syndicate, which had made most of its money in the past through heroin trafficking, suddenly realized the profit potential in cash-rich, recently legalized Fuzhounese Americans, who were willing to pay almost any amount to get their relatives out of China before the deadline. The syndicate immediately dispatched agents to Fuzhou to build up smuggling networks by hiring locals as recruiters. These local Fuzhounese re-cruiters, called "snaketails," are in charge of signing up the would-be migrants, working out the cost of the smuggling, the method of payment, and providing the syndicate with all the details concerning the immigrant's sponsor, family assets, and risk-worthiness.

Soon the syndicate had muscled in on the operations of the ex-isting small-scale travel agencies in Chinatown, adding its own fa-cilities and sophisticated, worldwide smuggling network to transform illegal immigration into an international corporate enterprise. It was a low-risk and high-profit operation for the syndicate, which quickly raised smuggling fees tenfold to $18,000 per person—the origin of the New York City street nickname for a Fuzhounese illegal: "The Eighteen-Thousand-Dollar Man."

Suddenly, going to America became the only topic of conversation in Fuzhou. Stories of this or that lucky neighbor whose relatives in the United States cared enough to pay the smuggling fee spread like wildfire. People knew that if their relatives acted fast enough, they too could get legal resident status. The desire to leave was only whetted by the behavior of the expatriates who came back to visit. They showered their relatives with money, color television sets, and wash-ing machines; they threw banquets for the whole village, built granite mansions with cast-iron gates for their families, erected temples in honor of their ancestors, and donated funds to establish elementary schools with a special emphasis on teaching the English language. The natives in Fuzhou were particularly impressed by the con-struction of a beautiful senior citizens' home with modern toilets, air conditioning, and a thirty-six-inch color television with huge antennas that could pick up the Taiwan soap operas across the Taiwan Strait.

Local officials showed reverence for returnees, treating them as honored guests and patriotic countrymen. The returnees' family members now lived like nobility, walking around with cellular phones and cruising the streets on Honda 125cc motorcycles. Many were partners in their relatives' joint-venture manufacturing companies, set up in Fuzhou's special enterprise zone. Going to the United States soon became not only an aspiration of most Fuzhounese, but also a matter of personal pride. Only the elderly and small children would stay behind; if you were in your prime and were still in Fuzhou, you were considered lazy and stupid.

America, however, is not the only destination. They can choose to go to Australia, Holland, or Argentina, as well as Japan. A young female taxi driver in Fuzhou had attempted to enter Japan at Narita Airport three times with phony passports provided by the snake-heads, but was turned back each time, at enormous financial cost. Then she tried to smuggle herself into the United States in a trunk hidden under the deck of a cargo ship, but was discovered and returned after four days at sea. Undaunted, she is trying to get out of China again. "If you want to make something out of yourself," she confided when we met her, "even if it is just to find a good husband, you've got to get out."

Of course, some of the returnees who came back to Fuzhou for a visit and acted like big shots actually worked seventy-hour weeks as kitchen help for a meager salary of $1,000 a month in New York, where they lived in basement cellars. But no one in Fuzhou knew this, or cared. Naturally, those who did not make it were less likely to go back. A Fuzhounese waitress in New York whose husband is also a waiter grumbles that she will never go back home again, for when she told her relatives what she did, they only laughed at her, saying that she was stupid for not starting her own business. "How many Fuzhounese are lucky enough to own their own businesses anyway?" she asks.

As the Chinese saying goes: If you win, you are king; when you lose, you become thief. The Fuzhounese have elevated their success into legend. The Chinese character *Min* (nickname of Fujian), they like to point out, symbolizes a snake inside a gate. Once the snake is finally able to get past the shut gate (meaning China), so the my-thology goes, it will turn into a dragon.

In the aftermath of the Tienanmen Massacre in 1989, President

George Bush compromised with China's critics by issuing an executive order permitting all Chinese students in the United States to adjust their immigration status so that they could not be forced to return if they faced political repression. Some suspected that Bush acted to protect China's most favored nation status in Congress, then up for a routine vote, at least in part to shield his brother's thriving business in China.[12] In a later Executive Order 12711, the president instructed the State and Justice Departments to give "enhanced consideration" to individuals who expressed fear of persecution related to forced abortion or coerced sterilization. The new order extended the promise of legal status to almost all Fuzhou immigrants, who could now be classified as refugees, fleeing past or threatened persecution by forced abortion and sterilization.

The 1986 IRCA, together with the 1989 and 1990 Bush executive orders, not only gave a huge number of Fuzhounese illegals the opportunity for lawful existence in this country, but also assured their relatives of the option of legal immigration. The Fuzhounese evidently had enough seed population to grow through this legal process. But some relatives who could come legally did not want to wait the usual period—which, for, say, the wife of a permanent resident, could be three to four years. For a sibling it could be as long as eight years.

Those who did not have relatives to sponsor their legal immigration were given the hope that once they arrived on American soil they could apply for political asylum based on Executive Order 12711's provision construing China's one-child policy as "persecution." The information provided by the smuggling network was that the asylum application process would take a long time; once in the country, even those denied asylum could still appeal and easily evade deportation indefinitely. While waiting for their hearings and appeals, the asylum seekers could get legal work permits and a job. Most of the would-be immigrants who ended up in detention after the *Golden Venture* was discovered off Queens in 1993 were using exactly those grounds in their appeals to remain in this country.

Thanks to such convenient legal decisions, the smuggling operation kept expanding. The largest number of Chinese illegals ever entered the United States between 1988 and 1993. During this period, a dozen new routes opened a variety of new staging areas in Central America, Eastern Europe, and the Caribbean.

And yet the human traffic has been so heavy that bottlenecks develop periodically, causing long delays in transit. The most common problems plaguing the trade have been the recurrent shortage of stolen—or "rented"—legitimate Taiwanese, Hong Kong, and Japanese passports, which are used by the Fuzhounese would-be illegal immigrants to pass various checkpoints. The trade has also been stymied by the breakdown of aging ocean vessels and the sudden, unpredictable tightening of certain border checkpoints. And the cost of smuggling keeps growing: it had reached $22,000 per person in 1988, and $35,000 in the early 1990s.

And as more and more Fuzhounese arrived and started looking for ways to pay off those spiraling debts, life in their promised land got tougher and tougher.

THE MEAT MARKET

The Fuzhounese may have been rushing to immigrate to the United States at any cost, but once arrived, they have not found the situation exactly as advertised. The promise contained in the character *Fu* notwithstanding, the experiences of recent arrivals from Fuzhou seem to show the snake turning into a worm and not a dragon.

The American experience of an illegal immigrant from Fuzhou begins at the intersection of East Broadway, Eldridge, Division, and Market Streets in Manhattan, where dozens of employment agencies are located. Hundreds of young males mill around this street corner at all times of the day, poking in and out of employment agencies, looking for work. On some mornings, lines form outside the storefronts of a few larger agencies, like Mei Mei, Hong Kong, or Atlantic.

A typical employment agency is a simple one-room affair, divided in the middle by a high counter and barred with iron grillwork up to the ceiling, reminiscent of the setup in ghetto liquor stores. On one side of the barrier dozens of workers stand in clusters, chatting and smoking, anxiously waiting for their numbers to be called. On the other side female clerks sit like imperial officials. They are busy taking phone calls from employers looking for workers. As a clerk jots down the details, she shouts through the loudspeaker: "Number 14! Uptown dishwashing job."

Zhen, a schoolteacher from Changle County, outside the city of Fuzhou, who arrived just before the *Golden Venture* mess in 1993, responds. He pushes through the crowd towards the counter and tries to find out more details about this job, like the pay, for instance. The clerk barks: "$600 a month! Why are you asking so many questions? This is not your first time doing this anyway. Don't be *lo sow* (troublesome)!"

Zhen pleads: "Elder sister, I am not *lo sow*, you know I'll take any job, just that . . ."

Before he can finish, the "Elder Sister" cuts him off. "That's right!" she says. "The *Lao fan* (Old Barbarian, meaning foreigner, i.e., Westerner) boss is waiting for you, and you better be there by four. When you get there just ask for Bald Head Li, the Chinese who works there. [He] will tell you what to do. Here is the address."

Zhen takes the address, written half in Chinese and half in English (although he cannot read a word of English), and walks towards the back wall of the office to look at a New York City map annotated with Chinese characters scrawled in blue felt-tipped pen. Others who are waiting gather around to help him find the place. A mild disagreement ensues—some advise him to take the A train and transfer to the C, others suggest taking the N train. Finally Zhen gives up, raises the slip of paper in his hand and says, "I'll just ask somebody after I enter the Canal Street subway station."

This is the sixth job Zhen has had in as many months. They have all been "temporary." Each time the work runs out Zhen, like all the other illegals looking for work, comes back to East Broadway to queue up in employment offices for another one. Job announcements written on slips of paper are posted on the walls. Typically, they read: "Seeking Fuzhounese to work as take-out delivery man, $50/week plus tips, worker provide own bicycle, Uptown," or "Nanny, $800 a month, New Jersey," or "Fuzhounese, construction work, no skill necessary, Long Island, transportation provided, $40/day." All these are standard ten-hours-a-day, six-days-a-week jobs. They offer no benefits. When they do, a character *fu*—the same fu that means fortunate in Fuzhou—is marked on the slip. But only one in fifty has such a notation.

It is a well-known fact among short-term labor employers' circles that agencies around East Broadway specialize in undocumented Fuzhounese workers. The posted employer requests come from all over the East Coast, including New Jersey, Connecticut, and Maine, even from Ohio and North Carolina. None of the ads bother to give the specific cities or towns where the jobs are. As far as the workers are concerned, it matters very little anyway.

Most of the available jobs are restaurant related: a cashier in North Carolina, dishwashers or kitchen helpers in Chicago. Higher-wage jobs are also available, such as assistant to a sushi chef in a Japanese restaurant in New Jersey, nurse's aid for a "western" infirm senior citizen in Connecticut, or housemaid in Philadelphia. The last job pays $1,000 a month. But all these better-paying jobs require some command of English—a skill very few Fuzhounese have.

Almost all of the jobs available through the agency are for men. Women find their work as seamstresses in garment factories or as dim sum restaurant pushcart ladies through word of mouth. Others work at home as bean stringers or food preparers, making soy sauce chicken, barbecued pork, or pickled ducks' feet for restaurants and supermarkets. Some are able to find waitressing, house-cleaning, baby/elderly-sitting, and cashier jobs through agencies.

Securing a Fuzhounese workforce is as easy as ordering a Domino's pizza. All you need is the name and telephone or fax number of an agency, both easily obtainable from a Chinese-language newspaper. I called up one agency and told the clerk that I was looking for two busboys to work in my restaurant serving continental cuisine. Without bothering to inquire about any details, the clerk suggested a three-dollar hourly wage. As if to encourage my acceptance of the deal, she volunteered that the agency fee would be of no concern to me; the workers themselves would pay it, by remitting 15 percent of their first monthly paychecks. That meant the busboys would be making only $2.55 an hour that first month.

When I inquired about the workers' legal status, the clerk said, "You need not worry, they all have temporary work permits" (a privilege given by the INS to those arrested as illegals but now out on bail, awaiting deportation hearings and to those applying for political asylum awaiting hearings). Then she wanted my address and the time the workers should arrive.

The employment agencies target the Fuzhounese because they are undocumented. This labor market is not open to other Chinese, unless they too claim to be undocumented. If they are detected, usually by their accent, the clerk will not place them.

In the past five years, undocumented Fuzhounese have penetrated deeply into the garment, construction, and restaurant trades in New York. Many of their employers are not Chinese. Non-Chinese-owned small electronics factories in New Jersey, construction companies specializing in loft renovation in Soho, and Long Island farms alike use Chinese employment agencies to find Chinese labor contractors who will take care of selection, transportation, payment, and management of their workers. In fact, if one looks into the kitchens of most mid-priced continental or American restaurants in Manhattan, one is likely to find a number of Fuzhounese working there. When a construction company can hire a skilled carpenter for $50 a day and an unskilled one for even less, why should it matter what kind of conditions the workers are laboring under?

There is really no accurate estimate of the Fuzhounese population in New York City. A significant portion is already legal, and some are full citizens. More of them, however, came in the last seven years, and the vast majority of that population is undocumented. According to Paul Smith, an immigration expert at Pacific Forum, an academic think tank, during the period between 1988 and 1993, Chinese illegal entry to this country was about 25,000 per year. That would put the overall illegal Fuzhounese population at least around 150,000. However, Smith's claim is difficult to confirm—there is no census count nor do the illegals live and work in any one area for easy counting. The only thing that is certain is that the wage level in Chinatown has dropped significantly since their influx began.

Another way to appreciate their explosive growth is by measuring the percentage of Fuzhounese children among Chinese youth in the Chinatown-area public schools. Their number has leapt up in several of the schools on the Lower East Side: Fuzhounese are now the overwhelming majority of new Chinese students at P.S. 42 on Hester Street and P.S. 134 on Grand Street. Over 50 percent of the student body at Junior High P.S. 105 in Brooklyn are new immigrants from China, mostly from Fuzhou.

WE ARE THE MODERN-DAY COOLIES

Some of the Fuzhounese leaders claim that the reason the services of the Fuzhounese are so much in demand is because they are the hardest workers. "We have the Cantonese beat!" they say. "They can't work as hard as we do!" A Fuzhounese travel agent proudly asserts, "We are willing to operate in places where other Chinese have never been—in ghettos, suburbs, and small towns in the middle of nowhere. And we are willing to work with and for the non-Chinese. Look at all the Western restaurants around midtown. *Lao-fan* owners love us, that's why we are working there, as busboys, dishwashers, even as chefs and assistant chefs." Employers, of course, prefer Fuzhounese because they are cheaper. And because they must accept almost any conditions in order to pay off their debts to "the snake-heads."

In addition to promising to pay the current price of emigration to America—between $30,000 and $35,000 (depending on the route taken)—would-be illegals have to put down a deposit of between $1,000 to $5,000 before they can begin their journeys. That's a hefty sum, considering that the average yearly income in China stands at $400.

Then a snaketail in China acquires the names, telephone numbers, and addresses of a potential "snakeperson's" relatives in New York and in Fuzhou. The rest of the sum owed the smugglers is to be paid by the relatives within seven days of the illegal's arrival in the United States. Typically, the newly arrived illegal immigrant pays off the relatives within three years, at 3 percent interest. Paying off $30,000 in three years means paying approximately $10,000 a year, or $800 a month—uncomfortably close to the monthly income of the average undocumented worker.

To pay their debts, the Fuzhounese accept any job, and stack them crazily on top of one another. They work a six-day week on a "regular" job, and they also work on the seventh day, euphemistically called the "cigarette day," because the income from that day's labor is meant to be spent on luxury items like cigarettes and movies. Only, the Fuzhounese work on the seventh day to survive.

Zhen wishes that there was an eighth day. "I hate to owe people money. These debts are hurting me like nails stuck into my body," he says. Actually he has two jobs: he works ten hours as a dishwasher in a Manhattan restaurant, then six hours as a night watchman in an office building on Canal Street. "I just find time here and there to lay my head down," he says when asked how he found the time to rest.

Zhen lives a Spartan life. He left his wife and a daughter in China. Here he shares a windowless, one-room apartment on Allen Street with nineteen other male bachelors. A kitchen—rather, a hot plate on a wooden table—is located in one corner of the tiny bathroom. The small, 300-square-foot space is jammed with triple-decker bunk beds. All Zhen's worldly possessions are squeezed into one bundle at the end of the bed next to his pillow, which covers a tape recorder to learn English vocabulary with. His bunk costs him $90 per month. Some of his roommates rent their bunks out for a portion of the day to cut down the cost. Dozens of rooming houses like Zhen's are scattered on Henry, Madison, and Allen Streets, in a mainly Hispanic neighborhood.

Zhen survives by eating *man tou*—northern Chinese-style steamed buns. They are cheap, costing only one dollar for ten, which is enough for two days. Zhen eats them with small sugar-cube-size pieces of a cheese-like, fermented bean curd called *fu yu* ($1 for a jar with fifty cubes), or with pickled vegetables.

There have been so many people coming recently from Fuzhou that their relatives can no longer help, they are so burdened with the debts of others who came earlier. New arrivals have to borrow from the snakehead-controlled underground loan associations, at 30 percent interest. If you make $800 a month, you could just barely pay the interest portion on that loan.

But the debts have to be paid, or the snakeheads will hire "enforcers" to beat it out of the debtors. One favorite punishment is to hit a delinquent debtor on the back, just under the shoulder blades, with a hammer. The injury does not affect his ability to work, but it is extremely painful, particularly when one lays down to rest at night—ensuring the debtor does not forget.

Another favorite tactic is to threaten the debtor's relatives with his imminent execution in order to convince them to come up with quick cash. In 1992, a hysterical Chinese called 911 pleading for police help to save his kidnapped relative, who had just called him while being tortured. The word "kidnapping" was a tripwire that alerted the federal authorities to the case. After breaking into the apartment in Brooklyn where the relative was being held, the police found a half-dead man handcuffed to a bedpost, where he had been beaten with crowbars and burned with cigarette butts.

In some cases, the snakeheads simply have the unfortunate debtor incarcerated. In 1992, the Brooklyn Police Robbery Squad stumbled upon a human smuggling scheme while investigating a youth-gang extortion case. When they broke into an apartment building in the Hispanic section of Sunset Park, they found thirteen undocumented

Fuzhounese, some of whom had been incarcerated in the cellar for as long as fourteen months.

The victims were all unable to pay off their smuggling fees. As a result, they became virtual slaves to the enforcers, who were members of the Fuching (Fujian Youth) gang. During the day, the victims worked at restaurants and laundries affiliated with organized crime. At night, after they were brought back to the cellar where they were locked up, they handed over all the money they had earned that day. At the time the Robbery Squad broke into the cellar, the gang members were planning to execute two of the debtors to better terrorize the rest.

As the smugglers get greedier, even those who have already paid are sometimes forced to pay more. These days Fuzhounese in New York rarely give out their home address or telephone number, use only pay phones, and rent commercial post office boxes to receive their mail. Most of all, they don't want to talk to anyone they don't know.

Incredibly, Zhen is not bitter. He only says that the snakeheads may be a little "too greedy." His snakehead comes from a village next to his. "We know everyone in his family," Zhen says, and then explains: "He has to make a living, too. Besides, none of us would be able to come without his help." Zhen is much more concerned about his ability to pay back the "transportation fee," as he calls it. "I am not afraid of hardship," he insists, "I am only afraid of not being able to find a job." Zhen cannot be bitter against his snakehead, for he still needs the smuggling service in the future. He is dreaming of the day when he will save enough, after his own debt has been honored, to pay for his wife and daughter to come.

The majority of Fuzhounese are honest and hardworking. But their situation in America is difficult: they are exploited by their employers, mistreated by the snakeheads, misunderstood by their fellow Chinese, unwelcomed by the Americans, and unprotected by the law. Even with their close-knit family networks, the Fuzhounese are unprepared to face this complex situation. Everyone is just struggling for survival. There is no organization to give them a voice. The

Fukien-American Association claims to be doing that, but its leaders spend most of their time accusing the media of maligning their good names. They themselves have been repeatedly identified by law enforcement authorities as involved in the human smuggling trade.

GOING HOME AGAIN

Almost every single Fuzhounese person I have talked to regrets the decision to come to the United States. Mrs. Lin and her husband arrived five years ago. Their passage to New York included a forty-five-day trip across the Pacific on a hundred-foot, unseaworthy fishing boat, which almost capsized before reaching the Mexican coast. The journey was horrific. Some 217 people were squeezed under the deck, lined up head to head with barely enough space to lay down. Most passengers suffered from seasickness as soon as the ship sailed into open water, but there were no adequate bathroom facilities. They were not allowed to get fresh air on deck because the snakehead enforcers feared detection and escape. They were given only a few mouthfuls of rice, some pickled vegetables, and a small glass of water a day. The enforcers charged exorbitant prices for anything requested in addition to that.

Fortunately, both Mrs. Lin and her husband survived the ordeal. Once in New York, they went immediately to work, without one day of rest. Mrs. Lin's husband, whom she now rarely sees, could only find a job in a Chinese restaurant in New Haven, where he works twelve-hour shifts and sleeps on the kitchen floor at night. Mrs. Lin lives in a one-room apartment in Chinatown with her in-laws. She puts in fourteen hours of work a day as a seamstress at home. She would work more if the in-laws didn't complain about the noise after midnight.

After four years, the Lins have only paid off half of their debts. "We are the piglets—*zhu-zha*—of the twentieth century," Mrs. Lin says, bitterly.

She is referring to the commonplace term for Chinese labor during the nineteenth century, when the first Chinese to come to the New

World found working conditions that were often worse than the standard of care for livestock. By the first half of the nineteenth century, the European colonial powers had an urgent need for a large supply of labor to develop and extract resources from newly acquired areas in North America, the Caribbean, and Latin America. Non-European slaves, especially Africans, were used extensively for this purpose, but in the early nineteenth century, with the outlawing first of the slave trade and then of slavery itself, other sources of cheap, diligent labor had to be found. After the British conquest of India, East Indians began to appear in British territories as contract labor. Chinese labor was not available at first, for China during the Qing Dynasty continued to refuse to trade with the West and maintained strict anti-emigration laws.

China's closed door was finally smashed open by the Nanking Treaty in 1843, which ended the Opium War. China ceded Hong Kong to the British and opened five additional Chinese seaports to trade (Fuzhou was one of them). With these ports open, the Chinese government could no longer control the movement of its nationals. Now the recruitment of laborers could begin in earnest, and it has been estimated that during the period of 1847 to 1874, between a quarter to half a million Chinese laborers were shipped from Amoy, Canton, and Hong Kong to the plantations in Cuba, Peru, Chile, and the Sandwich Islands alone.[13]

Most of the laborers were hired through a contract system that obliged them to work for the employer who sponsored them for a period of seven years. The laborers, called "coolies" (the origin of the term is not clear. It might come from the Tamil word *koli* to "hire" or a Hindi word for hired servants, adopted by the Europeans to describe workers doing heavy labor and then translated phonetically into Chinese characters meaning "bitter labor"—a person subjected to hard and exploitative labor), were recruited by Chinese brokers who collected the equivalent of $7 to $10 per head from traders or plantation owners.

The coolie traders erected fenced-off compounds—pigpens—to

hold the Chinese laborers. They were stripped naked, scrubbed clean, and then stamped with a sign on their chest denoting the destination of their voyage. Chinese brokers often pressed unwilling workers to fill their quotas, perhaps by taking prisoners in interclan fighting and forcing them into signing contracts, or tricking others into gambling losses and obliging them to pay their debts by surrendering themselves. Some were simply kidnapped outright. Peasants might come to cities such as Shanghai to sell vegetables and then be forcibly abducted. They were thrown into a pigpen and "Shanghaied" onto a ship. The brokers of such trade eventually gained the name "pig stealers." The victims were called *zhu-zha* ("piglets" in Cantonese), meaning those sold to be slaughtered, and the whole labor trade was called "the pig trade" in China. In America it became known as the coolie trade.

The Chinese so feared the coolie recruiters that in 1859 a number of violent riots against foreigners occurred in the city of Shanghai when a number of Europeans were seen strolling with their "pig stealers" in tow. The Chinese thought that the stealers were in town to seize piglets, and they reacted in anger because pig stealers could not be prosecuted—they were employees of foreigners, who enjoyed extraterritorial rights in the treaty ports.[14]

The ships used in the coolie trade were as crowded and as filthy, and the human cargo suffered as high a casualty rate as those used in the early African slave business. In fact, many of the African slave vessels were now used for the Chinese coolie trade. Of the first group of Chinese introduced to work on Cuban sugar plantations in 1847, 28 percent died soon after arrival.[15]

The American ship *Waverly*, bound from China to Peru with 450 coolies aboard, hove to at Carito, Philippines, on October 27, 1855, to make preparations for the burial of its captain. The coolies thought that they had arrived in America, and wished to go ashore. The new captain fired at them with his pistol. After a short struggle with the fully armed crew, the Chinese were driven below deck and the hatches locked. Some twelve hours later, when the hatches were opened, they found that nearly 300 of the Chinese had perished by suffocation.

Coolies who could not endure such treatment either committed suicide or instigated mutinies. Take the case of the Chinese on board the American-registered ship *Robert Browne* bound from Amoy to the United States in 1852. When the 400 Chinese emigrants discovered that they had been deceived and were to be carried into contract bondage, they killed all the officers. Afterwards, they testified in court that they had been promised they would be hired laborers and not contract coolies.[16] Then in 1870 there were coolie insurrections in Peru against the callousness of the hacienda masters. According to one report, the uprising spread and "in one town, whose citizens took refuge in the church, the women suffered a terrible fate, their persons were violated, and their bodies cut into pieces, their heads cut off and placed on poles."[17]

When coolies arrived in the New World, they were either auctioned off to the highest bidder or allotted to various employers who held them as virtual slaves for as long as seven years. Chinese immigrant laborers were in many instances treated no better than slaves.

From 1847 to 1862 American shippers, too, engaged in an extensive coolie trade, until an act of the U.S. Congress in 1862 prohibited such trade on American vessels and at American ports. But after California became part of the union, American employers wanted to make sure of a steady supply of cheap and docile labor from China, and in 1852 California State Senator George B. Tingley introduced a bill legalizing the enforcement of contracts binding the service of Chinese laborers. The bill allowed Chinese workers to sign contracts for up to ten years of service at fixed wages and then make the state government enforce the contract.[18] It was defeated, but only after bitter debate.

The issue of contract Chinese coolie labor was simply too explosive to be raised at a time of emotional national debate involving the emancipation of black slaves in the South. Nevertheless, in 1873, members of the Chinese Six Companies (a Chinese merchants' confederation in San Francisco) admitted that they had imported workers as coolies in the early years of the Gold Rush in the 1850s. By 1862 there was an estimate of 48,000 coolies in the United States and most of them worked in the mines.[19] As late as July 1869, a Chinese Labor Convention held in Memphis, Tennessee, proposed preserving the traditional Southern labor system by substituting Chinese hands for black slaves.

An editor of the Mississippi's *Vicksburg Times* reasoned, "Emancipation has spoiled the Negro, and carried him away from the field of agriculture. Our prosperity depends entirely upon the recovery of lost ground, and we therefore say let the Coolies come, and we will take the chance of Christianizing them."[20]

Still, whether slavery actually existed after 1862 in the United States is difficult to establish, since many of the Chinese labor contracts were set up by Chinese contractors and were enforced through the informal political system within the Chinese community, usually unbeknown to American authorities. Certainly, opposition to the coolie trade was one of the most important reasons given in the late 1870s for excluding the Chinese from the United States.

But the sorrow and hardship experienced by the nineteenth-century piglets were rarely appreciated by their compatriots in China, who thought they had gone to the "Golden Mountain" and were achieving wealth and prosperity in America. Today, Mrs. Lin tries to explain her sorrow and hardship to her relatives back home, but no one listens. She has tried to dissuade relatives from coming; she cries on the phone, pleading with them. But she knows it is no use. "They only think I am coldhearted and unwilling to help them to come," Lin says. "They keep repeating, 'Is it true that you only need to work for two years to pay off the debts, then you can make all the money you want?'—implying that I am lazy and useless for complaining like that."

The greatest cause of Mrs. Lin's anxiety is her inability to gain legal status. After several years of filing and appealing, even her lawyer is telling her that there is no hope. Her circumstances are actually quite similar to that of the coolies of the last century. Then the Chinese laborers were so appreciated by their U.S. employers that the government signed the Burlingame Treaty with China in 1868 to ensure that the Chinese government would "cordially recognize the inherent and inalienable right of man to change his home . . . and also the mutual advantage of the free migration." This was to encourage an easier exit from China for the Chinese willing to come. But during the treaty's ratification, the U.S. Senate imposed an amendment which states, "Nothing herein contained shall be held to confer naturalization . . . upon the subjects of China in the United States."[21]

Nonetheless, Mrs. Lin's relatives are determined to come, because all is not well in China. How else can one explain that during a news conference in 1996 (before their release in 1997), 37 remaining *Golden Venture* would-be immigrants imprisoned in the federal detention facility in York, Pennsylvania—already more than three years behind bars—vowed collectively that they would rather remain in a U.S. prison for another twenty years than be forced to return to China?

CHAPTER 2

Going to America

LUCK DESERTED MR. WANG FROM WENZHOU IN JUNE 1993. WHEN THE *Golden Venture* rammed into the Queens shoreline on that chilly spring morning, Mr. Wang began his career as a jailed man. Yet he was the envy of his fellow inmates at the Metropolitan Detention Center in lower Manhattan—his attractive wife came to see him every day during the prison's visiting hours.

Mrs. Wang came to America illegally in 1990, and understood right away that America was not what it was cracked up to be. The low wages, harsh working conditions, and the unbearable pressure of paying off her $30,000 debt to the snakehead (or "buffalo-back," in the local dialect of Wenzhou) within three years seemed insurmountable. She advised her husband to hold off on his plan to come; he took that to mean that she had found someone else. Mr. Wang decided to leave their daughter in his parents' care and started his own journey to the States, first by bus to the China–Burma border, then on foot through the jungles to Thailand. Mrs. Wang heard about his undertaking only when he cabled from Bangkok asking for $1,700 to pay for continuing the journey. The snakehead had promised passage by plane to New York; instead Mr. Wang boarded a ship, which took him to Singapore and then to the Mauritius Islands in the Indian Ocean before finally landing in Kenya. There he waited for six months before embarking on the ill-fated *Golden Venture* with 285 others.

Mrs. Wang, devoted wife, retained the services of a lawyer and lobbied (despite no knowledge of English) various human rights and church groups to fight for his release. It has not been easy. She works eleven hours a day as a seamstress in a Chinese-owned garment factory on Seventh Avenue, then travels back to her Queens apartment, which she shares with five fellow undocumented immigrants from Wenzhou. After dinner, she spends two more hours on her own sewing machine to complete pieces taken home from the factory.

With all the unanticipated expenses involving her husband, she has yet to pay off half of her "transportation fee." "Hundreds of illegals are still coming from China every week," she noted, somewhat bitterly. "So why is my husband still in jail? We are, after all, law-abiding and decent people."

She urged me and two other American journalists—Jon Alpert, a freelance documentary film maker on assignment with NBC, and Ying Chan, a reporter for the *New York Daily News*—to visit her families in Wenzhou and see for ourselves, since we were already planning a trip to China to do an investigative report for NBC News on human smuggling. Originally, we had contacts only in Fuzhou, where we intended to visit the "Snakehead Capital of China." But with a good contact in Wenzhou to help us, we decided to add Wenzhou to our itinerary.

The Wang family lives on the rural outskirts of the port city of Wenzhou, which is in Zhejiang Province, eight hours south of Shanghai and approximately the same distance north of Fuzhou city. Wenzhou people, similar to the Fuzhounese, are known for their commercial and seafaring heritage, which was clearly visible in the vigorous boatbuilding yards along the shores and the elaborate canal system crisscrossing the old city.

Wenzhou, like Fuzhou, is isolated geographically from other parts of China by surrounding high mountains. Wenzhounese, too, speak a dialect different from that of the nearby Shanghainese. They are better known for their long tradition of migration to Europe, especially to France, Italy, and the Netherlands. In recent years, fueled by investments from the overseas Chinese in Taiwan and Hong Kong, Wenzhou has become part of the booming economy of southern China that has received so much attention abroad. Wenzhounese are well known in China as tailors, particularly for their skills in making leather products such as shoes and jackets. The city of Wenzhou claims to be the "button manufacturing center of the world." It is also the second-largest source of illegal migration from China to America, after Fuzhou.

Once in Wenzhou City, we took a ferry, a bus, and finally a pedicab to get to Mr. Wang's village to visit his parents. We set up our equipment and showed our videotape of Mr. Wang in his yellow prison garb, and his mother choked back tears. Wang's leg had been injured aboard the *Golden Venture* and, according to him, prison authorities had not provided the treatment he needed on his arrival. Consequently, one leg is now shorter than the other, and he walks with an awkward limp. "He has aged so much—all skin and bones," she sobbed. "I can't believe that's him. We always thought America was a humane country. How can you lock him up like an animal for so long?" Her anguish brought on an asthma attack.

We explained to the grieving family that the Clinton administration found itself in a public relations dilemma. It cannot release the *Golden Venture* inmates lest it encourage more illegals to come, causing spasms of protest from anti-immigrant groups eager to invoke the specter of the "Yellow Peril." On the other hand, by dealing with them harshly, it faces reproach from humanitarian groups and those critical of the Chinese government's record on human rights, including conservative right-to-life organizations who are critical of China's "one-child" policy (the basis on which the *Golden Venture* inmates are requesting political asylum). We suggested that their son would be released, or at the least returned to China, when public attention drifted away from the issue.

Mother Wang leapt up in alarm at the last suggestion. "No! No! They cannot send him back! That would be the death of this family. I'll commit suicide." Her daughter disclosed that her parents had already borrowed the initial $1,000 as down payment for Mr. Wang's trip. Because the family had no rich relatives abroad to foot the bill, they had to secure it from a local loan shark at a 30 percent interest rate. The loan was expected to be paid off as soon as Mr. Wang started working in America.

Now that he was in prison, they had to borrow more to pay the interest on the loan. If he were sent back to China, there was absolutely no way that Mr. Wang could return that large a sum based on the Chinese wage scale, not to mention the fines and imprisonment the Chinese authorities might impose on him. The normal punishment for illegal emigration is one month's imprisonment, a fine of 10,000 yuan (approximately $1,200 U.S.—a prohibitive sum in China), plus the cost of room and board at the prison.

The Wangs are not the only family in the village facing such a dire predicament. As the news of our presence spread, other families who had relatives on the *Golden Venture* began to appear. Of the 286 *Golden Venture* passengers, forty were from the Wenzhou area (the rest were from Fuzhou), and of them, twenty-five were from Mr. Wang's village and neighboring Jiudu Island. Quite surprisingly, almost all of the area's few thousand residents are Christians. We were told that the local congregation has a sixty-year history, predating the socialist revolution.

On our first evening there, a Sunday, the minister of the church invited us to attend a special prayer service for the *Golden Venture* passengers. Three hundred people attended, including all the relatives. The sobs and prayers of the congregation made it clear that the community had suffered a major calamity.

Relatives back in Wenzhou have no contact with American authorities, and the Chinese government has maintained strict silence on the matter. Sixty-six-year-old Mrs. Peng, whose only daughter was at that time incarcerated at a Louisiana prison, mourned, "We are totally in the dark."

The helpless villagers looked to us as a ray of hope. The minister in his prayer compared us to "angels from heaven," who were sent to convey the message to the American public that his were honest people, deserving of freedom.

As we started to talk with the local residents, we began to find out the reasons for their interest in leaving for America. Mr. Sun, once a small-time party cadre, now a small-time shoe manufacturer, has four extended family members imprisoned in the United States, including his daughter. "We are simply trying to make a better living for ourselves by going to America." Mr. Sun explained, noting that while

Deng Xiaoping's reforms initially improved conditions in the countryside, as witnessed by a number of small-scale factories dotting the rural landscape, the benefits did not last. As an increasing number of people got into making shoes and clothing, the profit margins declined and the markets dried up. Besides, village enterprises like Sun's own simply could not compete with the newer, urban ventures equipped with modern machinery and backed by foreign investment.

"We are left to fend for ourselves in a highly risky business," Mr. Sun says. "Without government connections, we cannot get into the more lucrative export markets. Where can we sell our products?" At the time, Mr. Sun's son was desperately attempting to make contacts in Manchuria in order to clear a warehouse full of men's dress shoes. He was told of thriving black markets just this side of the Russian border, but traveling all the way out there could still be a bust.

Many studies confirm Mr. Sun's description of the problems facing rural industries in China. Deng's reforms initially brought remarkable gains in rural productivity. Between 1978 (the beginning of the reform) and 1984, the gross output in the countryside, including rural industries like the Suns', grew at an impressive annual rate of 9 percent. Some economists, including Carl Riskin of City University of New York, argue that this spurt in output resulted from technological and infrastructural improvements of the collective era (pre-Deng reforms) that were not fully exploited then.[1]

The rural output slowed down noticeably in contrast to growth in the urban area around 1985. China's own studies show that while the rural population, some 80 percent of the nation's population consumed 65 percent of all the goods and services in early 1980s, its consumption declined to 42 percent in 1985 and even further to 37 percent in 1992. Some analysts suggest that once peasants abandoned grain production for the more profitable cash crops and rural industries, they soon fell victim to the cyclical process that begins with heated market competition and leads to the shortage of raw materials, price inflation, and finally overproduction and glut.[2]

That's why Mr. Sun and the elders in the family raised the money to send Sun's brother-in-law, who was young and the most capable in the family, with a talent for figures, to America. The brother-in-law did not disappoint. After only four years in New York, Mr. Li paid off his debts and became the manager of a small garment factory. He agreed to send for his wife, his nephew, and two nieces (all three of Mr. Sun's children) if Mr. Sun raised $4,000—an incredible sum for any Chinese—to pay the snakeheads for the journey to America.

To Mr. Sun, it seemed a worthy investment. "We thought it would be easier to make money in the U.S. Once they get there and make enough money to send home, the elders can retire from the fields, the family can build houses and pay for daughters' weddings. As members of an 'overseas family,' we also gain respectability." This family plan, inspired by a Chinese version of the American dream tinged with filial piety, turned into a nightmare when the *Golden Venture* went aground in New York harbor with four young members of the Sun clan aboard.

Mr. Wang's parents still live in the oldest and smallest house on their block. (Wang was released on humanitarian grounds about a year and a half after we returned from China and brought his family's message of support and hope to him. He now lives with his wife in New York City, and his children have already joined them.) The Suns were forced to rent part of their family compound to a local factory, and the head of their household, a great-grandfather nearly eighty years old, had to harvest and thresh rice under the beastly July sun. Mrs. Peng, who lost her only daughter, the only source of income and labor power, has to do all the heavy field work and feed the pigs by herself.

No one in the village feels that they did anything wrong. As Mr. Sun puts it, "If we had the connections to get to America *legally*, we would. But we don't. This is the only way." Mr. Wang's younger sister, Mai, was working in a dilapidated, airless, county-run sneaker factory, toiling forty-eight hours a week for $20 a month. She was not troubled by her brother's predicament. She confided that she was planning her own escape, and that she would get a much better snakehead than her brother.

THE OUT-OF-PROVINCE PEOPLE ARE DESTROYING EVERYTHING

When we got to Fuzhou to visit the family of Xiao Lin, another *Golden Venture* inmate at the Manhattan Detention Center, we found exactly the same sentiments in his village as we did in Wenzhou. The one difference is that in Fuzhou the smuggling activities are much more extensive. Many villages, their able male population already gone, are left with only children, women, and the elderly. One sees almost exclusively women laboring in the fields, the few men in evidence being from villages elsewhere.

Without overseas relatives, the Lins belong to the poorer section of the village. The senior Lin, a butcher (not a respected profession in China), was ashamed of his trade and had never permitted his son to visit him at work. He usually starts work at the slaughterhouse at two in the morning. He works with a team of four, using primitive tools right on the cement floor, in a room lit by only one bare, forty-watt bulb. The men first hold the squealing pig down by their bare hands and cut its throat, then they skin it, clean the innards, drain and finally gel the blood into blood pudding. By four A.M., before sunrise, Mr. Lin loads his portion of the meat onto the back of his bicycle and rushes to the market to await the arrival of customers. He usually packs up to go home around noon, after all the meats are sold. For this disagreeable work he gets an average of five dollars a day.

Mr. Lin had slaved away for years just to be able to send his son to America. Now with Xiao Lin in prison, senior Lin has to grind on to keep the snakeheads at bay. The mood of the family when we visited reminded us of a wake. Xiao Lin's wife sat motionlessly in the corner of the living room with her three-year-old daughter in her lap, staring blankly ahead. Only sympathetic neighbors dropped by to break the silence. "The American government should really set Xiao Lin free," one young woman from next door, whose husband was in

New York at the time applying for political asylum, said, "because we are all victims of China's one-child policy."

She went on to explain that every three months, members of the birth control brigade checked all women of child-bearing age to make sure that their IUDs (intrauterine devices) were in proper position. Upon examination, they stamped the women's red Health Certificate booklet with dated seals. If anything was amiss, the woman could be forced to abort, fined, and possibly imprisoned.

As we were trying unsuccessfully to explain the intentions behind President Bush's original Chinese "pro-life" political asylum program and President Clinton's subsequent change of position, Xiao Lin's sister, quiet all along, suddenly burst out shouting. "If you Americans don't want illegals, why don't you enforce the law strictly, so nobody would come in the first place?"

To deflect the rising emotions in the room, I ventured to suggest that the family might be better off by sending Xiao Lin to work in Fuzhou City, considering how dynamic its development had been, with all the new high-rise construction going on and hundreds of foreign-owned companies opening up factories in the mammoth free-enterprise zone.

Mother Lin sneered at the idea. "That's for *wai sun ren* [out-of-province people], we can't do that. First of all, it is impossible to get residential registration (*hukou*) in the city," meaning that one would not be able to find legal housing there and would thus be living there illegally. "Besides, these are not good jobs. You have to work like a slave—digging ditches, carrying bricks, loading trucks and building roads—for almost nothing."

These types of jobs are only attractive to people from China's interior, where a market economy has yet to develop and cash income hardly exists. In the early 1980s my cousin, a chemical engineer in a state fertilizer factory in Shanghai with a salary of less than $50 a month, hired a maid—or a distant relative, as my cousin liked to call her—to help out with housework and care for her sick mother-in-law in the hospital. This fifty-year-old lady from a village six hours by train from Shanghai did all the cooking, washing, and shopping. She ate the leftovers, bathed in luke-warm sully water used by everyone else before her, and at the end of the day slept under the mother-in-law's sick bed at the hospital to be on hand in case of an emergency. For all this service the maid got ten dollars a month. She, who had not been home for two years, was saving money for her son's wedding, which was to cost $300. It might take several more years of working at my cousin's, but her own village had yet to develop jobs that would give her any cash income at all.

Most of China is still like this. Much of China's most dynamic expansion has occurred in sectors predicated on export, and their development was mainly financed by foreign investment, largely Taiwanese and Hong Kong capital. Thus, most growth is concentrated in the southern coastal areas near Hong Kong and Taiwan. Cities like Wenzhou and Fuzhou are inundated with "out-of-province people," waiting at street corners, bus stops, and train stations to be hired as day laborers.

China's internal labor migration is encouraged by factory owners, including the foreign ones, who prefer the rural out-of-province workers for being "less demanding and working harder." The highly profitable Reebok shoe factory in the city of Fuzhou, located in a huge, impressive complex within the free-enterprise zone, attracts few local workers precisely because of its low wages and long hours. Some factories recruit only young out-of-province girls, who work and live in barracks-like sweatshop conditions. Still, workers from Sichuan Province—once the rice bowl of China and now fallen on hard times because it did not benefit from foreign investment and new market developments and was further devastated by recent floods—are competing for these jobs, because whatever they make here is far more than is available at home. In many areas of the Pearl River Delta region near Hong Kong, *wai sun ren* equal and even surpass the local population in numbers.

According to the Chinese government's own "white paper," there are over 60 million *yuming*—"floating people"—roaming around the country looking for jobs.[3] Unaccompanied teenage girls and boys sleep in the open air and sell their labor and bodies in city markets to anyone willing to pay. Some of them become street urchins, barefoot and dressed in rags, scabby-headed, with flies gathering in the corners of their eyes. Their presence recalls the human deprivation of the pre-1949 China.

The Chinese government has taken to labeling these people as *meng-liu,* meaning "the blindly floating." They float in two main currents: one goes north to Beijing; the other moves south, to the Guangdong and Fujian Provinces. This rural-to-urban, north–south migration has brought inflation, overcrowded housing, open sewage, street congestion, depressed wages, high unemployment, petty crime, and general social disorder to the cities.

People like the Lins have no incentive to compete with the floating population in Fuzhou City, and prefer to find their future in New York. Ironically, just as people in Fuzhou City complain that the *wai sun ren,* outsiders, are at the root of all the problems in their city, so the Cantonese too blame the Fuzhounese for all the problems in New York's Chinatown.

FLOATING OUT TO FOREIGN LANDS

Chinese desire to emigrate at times of economic expansion at home is not unusual. It is generally recognized that economic development in the short run does not reduce the pressure on migration, but rather increases it.

Both Taiwan and Korea began their phase of economic expansion in the 1960s, and since then close to two million legal immigrants from those two countries have arrived in the United States, thanks to the 1965 Immigration Act. The emigration pressure in the two countries only began to ease in the 1990s, when their economic development created enough jobs to retain their citizens.

The pressure created in China is much greater. The combined population of Taiwan and Korea is 66 million. As of 1985, the population of China was 1.1 billion; in the last ten years it has grown by 100 million to 1.2 billion. For the next five years China's population is projected to grow by 15 million per year, accelerating to 17 million a year during the following five years as the large cohorts of women born during the Maoist era of the 1960s and 1970s reach their peak childbearing age. Thus, by the year 2005, China's population is likely to reach 1.36 billion.[4] Other experts claim that China's population has already reached 1.4 billion.[5] Much of this population growth is occurring in the poorer, more rural regions of China.

China's worrisome population growth is taking place despite the much-trumpeted one-child policy. That policy has slowed the growth rate, but it has not met its target because of local resistance. Elders in rural areas like Xiao Lin's village, now without the safety net once provided by people's communes, expect their sons to support them in their old age. The one-child policy raises the question, "What's the use of a daughter, when she marries into another family?" Besides, the traditional attitude in the rural countryside has always been that the more people in a family, the more things get done, and the higher the family income.

It is not surprising that China's one-child policy is honored more in the breach than the execution. Researchers have found several villages in Shanxi Province where the birth rate is low, and the male/female birth ratio is extraordinarily high, reaching 1.33 males to one female.[6] Twenty-five percent of all female births appear to be missing—not necessarily the result of infanticide, as some have speculated, but hidden by sending unregistered female babies to live with relatives or neighbors.[7] With the swelling of a roaming population in China, the missing babies are ever easier to hide.

Deng Xiaoping's reforms have made China's development much more volatile. Mao had pushed for even national development, fearing that concentrated industrial development in urban centers would create gross inequalities between the urban and the rural, between coastal and interior regions—not just in terms of wealth, but also in social, cultural, and educational levels. Mao insisted on decentralized development: each region was to maximize its economic potential by utilizing its own labor supply and its local resources. Surplus workers in rural areas were to be held in place by being engaged in local infrastructure construction, and by generating small-scale industries and handicrafts. Everyone was registered with the authorities through the system of household registration (*hukou*), and nobody was permitted to change residence without authorization.

Deng Xiaoping, once branded as a "revisionist" and "Number Two Khrushchev" of China by Maoists because of his famously pragmatic view that "It does not matter whether a cat is black or white, as long as it catches mice," abandoned Mao's model by introducing a market economy. The previously "hidden" rural surplus labor, engaged on local construction projects and in local industries under Mao's policy, suddenly found itself either unemployed or underemployed.

At present, China has a rural workforce of approximately 440 million. At the current rate of agricultural production, only 200 million farmers are needed.[8] In the early 1980s, the newly sprouted village and township enterprises like Mr. Sun's shoe factory in Wenzhou alleviated this unemployment temporarily, until the more efficient city enterprises with larger capital investment put them out of business. Even so, by the end of 1995, village and township enterprises were providing work for 126 million farmers.

This leaves China with some 110 million unemployed, who roam around the country in search of work. This floating population is expected to reach 200 million by the year 2000.[9] China's economic growth, impressive as it has been, is not likely to absorb this surplus manpower unless jobs can be created miraculously by the private sector and by foreign investment. These predictions assume that China's development will move along without having to deal with any political instability.

That's a risky proposition. In the countryside there is a great deal of unrest due to the imposition of heavy and arbitrary taxes by local officials. When the peasants cannot pay, officials resort to confiscation of property and imprisonment. These harsh measures have led to violent revolts in half a dozen provinces, including Fujian. The worst reported incident happened in one county of Hunan Province where the peasants, angered by a variety of unreasonable taxes, demonstrated in front of the county government building. More than ten thousand gathered and would not disperse, even after the police fired tear gas into the crowd. The mob sacked the government offices. Eventually thousands of police and militia were called in from other regions to quell the uprising.[10]

In the urban areas, unemployed workers have reached into the millions because of the Chinese government's drive for privatization of state-owned enterprises. In the first nine months of 1996, there were 1,520 reported incidents of mass demonstrations by threatened and laid-off workers in 120 cities. They marched under unofficial, unsanctioned banners, reading "Unemployment Workers Alliance," "Anti-Capitalist Restoration Association," or simply, "Chinese Labor Association."[11]

HOW MANY MILLIONS OF CHINESE DO YOU WANT?

During times of war and economic instability throughout the twentieth century, many Chinese have taken the path of emigration; it is estimated that there were 12 million ethnic Chinese living overseas in 1950, 27 million in the 1980s, and 35 million in the 1990s. Most Chinese have been emigrating to Southeast Asia, but in recent years they are moving increasingly to North America and Australia. Total Chinese emigration has reached 180,000 people per year in the last decade.[12]

If the size of China's floating population continues to expand, and even if only a very small percentage of it seeks emigration as an option, we are likely to witness an international problem of serious proportions. Given the present trend of Chinese emigration targeting North America, sociologist Jack Goldstone, in his studies, suggests that it would not be unreasonable to expect the influx of Chinese illegals in the United States to match that of the Mexican incursion.[13]

In 1979, when Deng Xiaoping met President Carter at the White

House, he broached the subject of China's interest in gaining most-favored-nation trading status. Carter reminded him of the 1974 Jackson-Vanik Amendment, passed by the U.S. Congress, which forbids granting of most-favored-nation treatment to any "nonmarket economy countries" that limit the rights of its nationals to emigrate. Unfazed, Deng asked Carter, "How many millions of Chinese does the U.S. want?" While Carter was still caught in the Cold War, anti-Communist frame of mind, Deng had already foreseen the very real possibility of using emigration as a way of solving China's population problem while intimidating world leaders with the threat of an uncontrollable stream of emigrants.

The Chinese government has long considered the overseas Chinese population as a national asset. The more people leave, the less unemployment at home and the more foreign-exchange reserves the Bank of China can claim in remittances from abroad. And in so far as human smuggling is concerned, the Chinese government hardly interferes. Before I visited Fuzhou, I was earnestly told by U.S. authorities that the Chinese government had considerably tightened its control of human smuggling after the *Golden Venture* incident, declaring it be a capital offense. Indeed, the city of Fuzhou was festooned with huge banners and billboards denouncing the crime of illegal emigration and human smuggling. "Illegal Emigration is a Crime," "Resolutely Clamp Down on the Crime of Snakehead Activities and Illegal Emigration," they proclaimed. "Resolutely Eliminate Illegal Emigration; America is not a Paradise for Illegal Emigrants," read another.

However, when Ying Chan (the *New York Daily News* reporter) and I pretended to be helping a local friend to get to the States, we had no problem finding willing snakeheads, or "snaketails," as they are more properly called over there. Just waiting around a cafe and a candy store one afternoon, we met four snaketails offering their services. Their average price was $33,000, with $1,500 down, and the rest to be paid upon arrival in New York.

The snakeheads were selling passages to Japan and European countries as well. We were told that most Fuzhounese preferred Japan, because working there one could save more than $2,000 a month on a strictly enforced eight-hour workday. The smuggling cost was $18,000 (raised to $25,000 in 1997). However, passage to America was the most expensive because staying in the United States was relatively easy, even though one made less under unregulated labor conditions. Once in the United States, the illegals were safe to work without harassment, arrest, or deportation by the U.S. authorities, which regularly occur in Japan and France. The Japanese government routinely deported those arrested back to China after informing Fujian provincial authorities.

Still during the period we were in Fuzhou, we got to meet only the lower-ranking, retail-level snakeheads in this multi-billion-dollar international operation. They circle the city of Fuzhou and travel along China's southern coast, competing for customers in rural communities. Each promised a better deal: entry by plane, money-back guarantee in case of failure, a 50/50 split of the cost of bail and lawyer's fee if the customer gets caught.

I knew from my interviews with illegals in New York that local Chinese Communist Party officials took bribes to issue Chinese passports and exit permits. Other officials are also known to assist smuggling operations: the Chinese Coast Guard conveniently disappears when a Taiwanese fishing vessel comes off shore to pick up would-be illegals.

An INS report states that because of the effective interdiction of illegals at the Mexican border and at U.S. airports, new avenues of illegal entry are being devised. The smuggling networks, for instance, obtain valid exit visas for the would-be emigrés as members of official commercial delegations touring the United States. According to an informant, the delegation members, sporting fancy titles like "plant manager," arrive on the West Coast, then rush to New York, and in a few days re-emerge working in a Chinatown restaurant wrapping spring rolls. The INS estimates that three delegations like this came each day during the summer of 1996. The illegals are expected to have paid Chinese officials in charge $18,000 for this "legal" entry.[14]

A State University of New York campus set up a scholarly exchange program with a university in northern China and twenty-one "scholars," who were mainly from southern China, arrived for the spring session in 1995; at the end of the semester, only five of the "scholars" returned. The rest were officially listed as missing, though several are known to be working in Chinatown and others are appealing for political asylum.

In Fuzhou, we came upon a blatant official swindle. An informant told us that citizens could purchase "legal" visas to go to America through a foreign labor program set up by a division of the Fujian Provincial Labor Department in charge of exporting labor. We spoke to the deputy director of that office, asking his help to engage agricultural experts to work on our farm in New Jersey. The deputy saw no difficulties, as long as we could obtain the U.S. Labor Department work permits, i.e., the H series non-immigrant worker visas; his office would handle all the other details for as many "experts" as we wanted. Furthermore, he offered us $15,000 for every Labor Department H visa we could procure for him. In his words, "We pay you the money and you don't have to worry about the workers at all."

When questioned about the legitimacy of this deal, the deputy director proudly showed us the endorsement of his operation by members of the State Council in Beijing, including a group photo of him with one of the Vice Premiers. "Don't worry," he assured us, "you'll be paid in U.S. dollars from a bank account in Hong Kong. You should do at least one hundred, for a profit of a million and a half."[15]

According to this scenario, his office would sell the permits for $30,000 on the open market. Upon their arrival at Kennedy Airport, the legal "labor experts" would be greeted and grabbed by "enforcers" to make sure they honor their "transportation fees." Similar labor export schemes also exist between various Chinese provincial labor offices and Latin American countries, most notably Bolivia. These cost only $8,000. Of course, those who avail themselves of the Latin American option intend eventually to travel north to the United States.

The Chinese government is itself acting as a snakehead and profiting handsomely from this illegal human smuggling trade. Particularly alarming is the inevitable cooperation between Chinese officials and the underworld crime elements. This, of course, is not new. In the name of deploying a "United Front" strategy to isolate reactionary enemies (usually pro-KMT [Kuomintang, the Nationalist Party] factions) in Hong Kong and other overseas Chinese communities, the Communist government has been cultivating a relationship with various "nationalistic elements." They include members of the triads and *tongs*—secret fraternal organizations that originally formed to overthrow foreign Manchu rule of the Chinese people—who have always claimed to be "patriotic organizations." Though their history goes back to the beginning of the Qins Dynasty, they are much better known for violence and organized crime.

In 1995, the Hong Kong police detected a pattern of crimes in the colony that pointed to the possible cooperation between the triads in Hong Kong and the local commanders of the Chinese Peoples' Liberation Army unit stationed at a border garrison. In fact, the police were particularly alarmed when they found commanding officers appearing in public gatherings with top leaders of Hong Kong's notorious Shin Yi An triad. The Hong Kong police asked for "clarification" from the Beijing government about the matter.[16]

Not only local Chinese officials are taking advantage of would-be emigrés. The latest scandal involved the issuing of "official" passports to Fuzhounese immigrants by the New York PRC consulate office. Illegals, particularly those who arrive in this country by sea, usually do not apply for passports before leaving China. Once they make it to the United States, possession of a passport becomes important, even for an illegal who is in the process of applying for political asylum with a work permit. One needs a passport as identification to open a bank account, to obtain a driver's license, and for a number of other purposes. Illegals from Fuzhou usually obtain "replacement" passports through the help of a travel agent or a *fu wu kung si* (service agency), most of whom have special access to the Chinese consulate. Knowing the irregular circumstances involved, the illegals are willing to put up $2,000 for such documents. The normal procedure is for an illegal to provide all the necessary information to the consulate, and then take a call for an interview by the consulate staff. Weeks later, the illegal will receive a signed passport.

Several individuals with such "replacement" passports decided, after they had settled their affairs in New York and could stay here legally, to visit their families in Fuzhou. They were arrested at Fuzhou airport for possession of invalid passports whose records had not been filed either in the Ministry of Foreign Affairs or in Fuzhou City's police headquarters. They were fined as much as $8,000 U.S. and then released—although, without passports, they now had no way to return to America.

At first, the victims dared not tell anyone. But soon their story leaked out and caused a general panic in the Fuzhounese community. Sure enough, after investigation, they found that a good number of the passports issued from the New York Chinese consulate have no filed records in China. Those who had spent $2,000 for these bogus passports were outraged. Then a *New York Times* story on the subject blew the scandal wide open.[17]

Dozens of victims with similar problems held a news conference in Chinatown and threatened to demonstrate in front of the consulate if the problem was not resolved.[18] In the meantime, a reporter for a local Chinatown magazine mused that there are about 150,000 Chinese illegals from mainland China in this country, and if each paid $2,000 for a passport, then that's $300 million for the consulate.[19]

In any event, the central government of China is also known to have used the Chinese exodus as a political weapon in international politics. In 1989 Deng Xiaoping, angered by Hong Kong criticism of the Tienanmen massacre, was quoted as saying that were the Communist Party to lose control on the mainland, 100 million Chinese would immediately flood into Indonesia, Thailand, and other Southeast Asian countries, including Hong Kong. Vietnamese boat people in the late 1970s created havoc in the international community, forcing it to resettle 1.5 million refugees. The ramifications can still be felt twenty years later, with 40,000 boat people remaining stranded in refugee camps in Asia. In another speech in 1991, reacting to the hostile Western response to the Tienanmen massacre, Deng said: "If the West continues to insist on economic sanctions, we might as well relax a bit in the coastal areas, letting out those who wish to flee overseas to follow in the footsteps of the Vietnamese."[20]

China's ability to play refugee politics is not an idle threat. It has repeatedly shown its readiness to relax the borders whenever dealings with the Hong Kong government were deemed unsatisfactory. It just so happens that we have witnessed a sharp rise in Chinese illegal migration worldwide, and particularly to the United States, since Deng first threatened to relax restrictions.

THE GRAND ESCAPE

The illegals I have interviewed in the United States cite this type of cynical Chinese government politics and official corruption as one of the main reasons for wanting to leave China. Everyone has stories of Chinese governmental corruption to tell. Those in small businesses have to bribe officials at all levels to survive, paying off the health department, the license bureau, the tax bureau, and entertaining the police and members of neighborhood committees. Surviving in China, a Fuzhounese illegal in New York laments, depends on one's ability to deal with officials. Without a legal system, every step is an obstacle. You have to satisfy all the people in charge.

The extent of the problem in the rural areas is revealed in a Fuzhou newspaper editorial:

Certain local leading cadres have resorted to various disgusting tactics to seize land for building houses. Some have paid nothing, or just a little token, for the land they have occupied. . . . Some have not only seized land for building their own houses, but have given cropland to their relatives, friends and people of special relations for building houses. Some have used their public office for private gain. For example, while planning the budget for a collective housing structure, they have included the budget for building their own. . . .[21]

Chinese communist party officials are using their positions to monopolize the most lucrative enterprises for themselves. It is a common complaint that party officials allocate public funds to invest in their private business ventures. According to an official American survey, mainland Chinese investment in the United States has surpassed $7 billion U.S. Most of the Chinese government's money is handled by Chinese officials residing in the United States. Although a majority of these ventures are losing money, the officials are living in plush condominiums and mansions in Westchester county outside of New York City, carrying on like billionaires. And there are worse goings-on. During China's 8th National People's Congress 5th Plenary Session in Beijing in March 1997, delegates castigated the government for its inability to halt the massive exodus of $100 billion U.S. in stolen government funds since 1979. An estimated $17.8 billion left in 1995 alone. The culprits are top managers of national enterprises and sons and daughters of high-ranking officials—known in China as "princelings"—who use their privileged positions to channel state funds to private savings accounts outside the country.[22] Members of the Communist Party have, in effect, arranged for themselves and their children to be first in line to benefit from China's transition to capitalism.

The corrupting environment is so suffocating that the average Chinese—people like Mr. Sun—feel that they have no future in China. Moreover, they believe that continued government corruption and the increasing polarization of classes in China will inevitably lead to another political upheaval, probably much worse than the Tienanmen massacre of June 4, 1989.

YOU DON'T HAVE TO BE POOR AND AT THE BOTTOM OF THE SOCIAL strata in China to want to leave. None of the families of *Golden Venture* passengers, like the Wangs from Wenzhou or Lins from Fuzhou, are bad off by Chinese standards. Otherwise, they could not possibly come up with the $1,500 required as down payment for the illegal trip. In the end, it is not even always for their material well-being that these Chinese want to leave—many simply feel stifled as long as they remain in China.

Most people with means plot to escape. University students in the cities escape by applying to study abroad. College graduates from lesser-known provincial schools, or those with poor grades and non-existent English, normally have no chance to get an I-20 visa to attend an American university. However, for a few thousand dollars down, they can get a phony diploma from an elite Chinese university, a certificate for passing the TOEFL exam (a standard English language proficiency test requested by all American universities), an admissions letter from a major American university, and a letter of sponsorship from a Chinese American with his financial statements attached. Thus equipped, even the most inferior student only needs to pass the hurdle at the American consulate in Canton before he finds himself in the United States legally, working in a Chinese restaurant to pay off his transportation fee.

In all the conversations I had in China with different people, I have yet to convince a single individual that illegals in the United States are facing tough times. Once I said as much to an elderly farmer, who stared me in the eye and said, "Look, I work on four-mu land [less than one acre, larger than the average land holding in China], year in and year out, from dawn to dusk, but after taxes and providing for the family's needs, I make $20 a year. You make that much in one day. No matter how much it costs to get there, or how hard the work is, America is still better than this."

CHAPTER 3

Snakeheads

IN THE AFTERMATH OF THE COLD WAR, THE WHOLE WORLD STARTED marching to the drumbeat of a market economy while singing the anthem of free trade. The unimpeded flow of capital as well as goods and services promised universal peace and economic well-being for generations to come. Yet even as tariffs have been lowered around the world because of the NAFTA and GATT agreements, national borders remain closed to the movement of people. The virtues of unobstructed labor mobility are rarely contemplated seriously in international negotiations. During the NAFTA negotiations, for instance, the Mexican government would have liked to see labor included in a free trade agreement with the United States, but the United States rejected the proposition. The inclusion of a freedom-of-movement provision would have proved to be a "poison pill" that would have killed any chance of U.S. congressional approval of the trilateral treaty.[1] But the people do vote with their feet, moving to places with higher wages and better opportunities. Thousands migrate each day from the developing nations, aided by advanced transportation systems and communications networks, confident that employers in the advanced countries will hire them because they ask for less than domestic workers.

This movement has become so pervasive that illegal migration is no longer limited to those from the poor nations of the south moving north; people are also moving from east to west, from the relatively developed to the most developed nations. The United Nations Population Fund has asserted that international migration has become the human crisis of our age.

Of course, without vast smuggling networks that stretch from one end of the globe to the other, this movement could not occur on anything like the scale we have seen in the past decade. Smuggling has now become a growth industry, to the point that anyone anxious to escape Fuzhou or Lagos or Crakow or Kabul can find smugglers right on his street to guide him to almost any destination around the world. North America and Australia are the most profitable trips for the smugglers to arrange, but they are also willing to move thousands of illegal migrants from Asia, Africa, and the Middle East to Europe along routes that cross from Morocco to Spain, Albania to Italy, Turkey to Greece, the Czech Republic to Germany, and the Baltic states to Scandinavia. The collapse of the Soviet bloc has created many newly porous borders; with the rise of organized crime and the decline of civil authority, the former Warsaw Pact nations have turned into a smuggler's paradise. Russia acts as a holding pen for up to 200,000 Asian illegals awaiting transport to the West at any given time. Romania, Bulgaria, and Albania, three notably Stalinist states in the recent past, now have no visa requirements, and are therefore prime staging points for westward migration.[2]

The oil-rich countries of the Middle East, too, are plagued by the problem: Sub-Saharan Africans try to enter Libya, Pakistanis aim for Saudi Arabia, and Filipinos for the United Arab Emirates. The main target for smugglers in Asia is Japan. It is awash in boat people mainly from China, Korea, Pakistan, and Bangladesh on a weekly basis.[3] In the United States, up to 100,000 illegals each year are smuggled through the Central America–Mexico corridor and from the Caribbean basin through the Gulf states.

The huge profits in the smuggling business have attracted some of the most sophisticated operators in international organized crime, including many previously involved in trans-border trafficking of heroin, stolen Mercedes, Stinger missiles, or counterfeit currencies. According to Jonas Widgren of the International Center for Migration Policy Development, smuggling rings reap profits up to $9.5 billion U.S. per year, earning more than many drug cartels.[4]

The vast scope of the modern smuggling enterprise is usually glimpsed anecdotally, as in the drug trade, through chance interceptions. Italian coastal police trying to evacuate a burning Lebanese ship discovered 160 illegals from India in the hold who were trying to reach Porto Palo, an island off the Italian coast, where they were to arrange transshipment to their final destination in Switzerland; each illegal had paid $1,000 for the journey.[5] Hungarian police stopped a minibus from crossing its border filled like a college prank with dozens of Egyptians trying to get to Slovenia; each had paid $1,500 to traffickers for the privilege. By the time Ukrainian border guards found forty-two illegal Chinese in a sealed refrigerator truck near the Slovakian border, several of them had suffered frostbite or needed serious medical attention. Yet each had also paid handsomely for the experience.[6]

The social and economic impact on the receiving countries of such large-scale migration has generally caused profound misgivings, particularly given the racial and ethnic backgrounds of the illegals and the recent global economic recession. Legal restrictions and other anti-immigrant measures are being instituted everywhere. Argentina blames illegal immigrants for the country's unemployment level and has legislated strict regulations aimed at cutting their number. The Dutch parliament has voted in favor of increasing the prison sentence for people convicted of smuggling workers into the country from one year to four.[7] In France, the immigrant issue has given the far right the crucial popular support to pass a harsh Aliens Law. Lithuania, Russia, and Poland are working together on a trilateral basis to combat illegal migration in their region. The European Conference on Uncontrolled Migration, known as the Budapest Group, began in 1993 to coordinate the efforts of thirty-six governments to gather information and promote coordination among interior and other ministries in Eastern and Western Europe. The group is in the process of discussing the establishment of minimum standards for anti-trafficking legislation.[8] At the 1996 G-7 meeting, one of the top issues on the agenda was the formation of a coordinated policy to combat human smuggling.

It is precisely because of the smugglers' ability to act without regard to state borders that they are seen by most governments as a serious menace. A number of countries consider human smuggling their single greatest national security threat. Many Western democracies now argue that they have been too generous to refugees and illegal aliens, although this generosity has largely been a legacy of the Cold War, when illegal political defections were encouraged as state policy. Cubans floating into U.S. waters and East Germans jumping the Berlin Wall were "freedom fighters" worthy of medals and cash rewards.

Now, just a few years after the collapse of the wall, under a 1993 Clinton executive order, twelve departments and agencies of the U.S. government are working with the coordination of the White House Domestic Policy Council and the National Security Council to stem illegal migration and human smuggling. The CIA, long the leader of the fight against international communism, has now been given the task of developing the ability to identify smugglers and disrupt their operations. The FBI has taken over as chief enforcer of national laws against illegal immigration by land—equivalent to the Coast Guard's role at sea. In a memorandum to the attorney general dated October 1995, the president revealed his continuing concern with the issue of alien smuggling when he authorized $6 million to the Immigration Emergency Fund to be used to cover the costs of repatriating aliens "intercepted en route to the United States when it appears that such persons [sic] are been smuggled by international organized crime syndicates."[9]

The new 1996 Illegal Immigration Reform and Immigration Responsibility Act stipulates that the penalty for human smuggling be increased from five to ten years. It also identifies smuggling as a RICO-predicated felony, and extends the authority for wiretaps and interception of oral communications to such crimes. Much to the dismay of civil libertarians, the new Anti-Terrorism and Effective Death Penalty Act of 1996 permits aliens seeking admission to the United States to be summarily excluded, deported, and their asylum claims administratively determined before a non-judicial officer while they are detained. These harsh laws are made possible by the fact that Americans have begun to identify illegals with terrorism.

Still, it's like playing chess with a handicap: the criminals can move anywhere they want in any manner they want to any spot on the globe, whereas nation-states are limited to moving within their own borders, where they are pretty much reduced to ineffective defensive maneuvers.

THE GLOBAL REACH OF THE CHINESE SNAKEHEADS

Chinese organized crime has developed human smuggling into a truly global business, shepherding some 100,000 people per year to a range of destinations including Taiwan, Japan, Germany, Canada, Australia, the United States, France, England, and the Netherlands. Stories of Chinese-run smuggling rings are ubiquitous. Japanese authorities found Chinese smugglers had been working with the *Yakuza*, the Japanese crime syndicate, to smuggle Chinese nationals into Japan through Tamara Island in the Tokara chain, south of Kyushu. The Chinese snakeheads charge as much as $25,000 to sneak job-seekers into Japan, and their *Yakuza* partners scout out quiet landing sites and use walkie-talkies to help guide the boat people safely ashore. Buses or trucks are awaiting to whisk them off to the cities where they quickly find jobs in the underground economy.[10] Since 1990, Japanese authorities have intercepted some 160 vessels carrying more than 3,000 Chinese illegals. In the same period, the Australian coast guard stopped dozens of ships carrying thousands of Chinese. Austrian authorities uncovered a Europe-wide network of Mafia-like Chinese criminals, responsible for smuggling thousands of people into Vienna.

The Chinese smuggling network operates actively in the Caribbean Sea, taking full advantage of the area's multiple defenseless border crossings. Police on the Caribbean U.S. territory of St. Croix were alerted to the presence of a pack of suspicious, strangely dressed Asians waiting to be served in front of a snack bar. They turned out to be Chinese illegals who had just gotten off a fishing boat from the Dominican Republic, taking a break on their way to the airport to catch a domestic flight to Miami. They were arrested en masse.

In 1996 the Argentine government claimed to have dismantled a

Chinese trafficking ring which had provided 120 illegals with false documents to enter Buenos Aires en route to America. According to a Romanian press report, many private Chinese companies have been set up in Romania, shipping Chinese illegals legally, as their employees to do business in Western Europe. And then there were the early 1994 media reports of a Chinese restaurant in Prague so successful that it employed over 800 people—although it had only eight tables and hardly any business. The kitchen staff was really on its way to Germany.[11]

The profits of the Chinese smuggling network are reported to be in the range of $3.1 billion U.S. per year.[12] It is certainly an elaborate network. Indeed, Chinese transit operations seem to have penetrated every major airport and harbor around the world. According to a China Public Security Bureau estimate, at any time there are a half million Chinese nationals in smuggling waystations around the world—50,000 in Moscow, 15,000 in Ho Chi Minh City, 25,000 in Bangkok, 25,000 in Africa, 10,000 in Brazil, and thousands in other countries, including the Dominican Republic, Mexico, and Bulgaria.[13]

In the past, human smugglers simply provided assistance in border crossing, like the "coyotes" who charge at most a few hundred dollars for sneaking a client across the U.S.–Mexico border. Smuggling services are much more comprehensive today, and Chinese smugglers are among the most sophisticated. Their package includes passage out of China, a transit location or locations as the case requires, and transport to a final destination. Today's smugglers charge much higher fees for their services: anywhere from $18,000 to $50,000 per customer.

The high fee has nothing to do with the actual cost of transportation, but it has transformed the relationship between the smuggler and the client from a simple one-shot deal—paid for up front, before the journey—into a complex financial arrangement that may last for many years. There is usually a complicated payment arrangement to be worked out after the client's arrival that may even require the

smuggler to find them employment. The fee is paid either in installments or through loans from their relatives. The most important
feature of this system is that even if the fees were paid by their
relatives, they, too, have to borrow that large sum from others. The
latter, in turn, expect fastidious repayment or face deadly consequences. In the end, the illegals would still have to work hard and fast
to repay that amount promptly. The heavy debt burden gives the
Chinese operations similarities to nineteenth-century coolie contract
labor.

THE BASEBALL GAME

The most developed and best organized of all the Chinese smuggling
routes leads to the United States. In testimony before Congress in
1994, then-director of the CIA James Woolsey Jr. claimed, according
to his office's study, that some 100,000 Chinese are being smuggled
into America each year. Many are sent first through Belize, Guatemala,
the Dominican Republic, Mexico, or other countries in Central
America and the Caribbean region.[14] But, for most, the road starts in
Fuzhou and ends in New York.

Fuzhou has had a long history of illegal emigration, but the thrust
of recent smuggling activities was sharpened by the United States'
abrupt abandonment of its role in Vietnam. During the Sino-
Vietnamese political crisis in 1978—after the American withdrawal
from Saigon and the exodus of the Vietnamese boat people—almost
one million Vietnamese of Chinese descent were resettled in China.
Most of them were relocated in Guangxi Province, which borders
Vietnam, but some refugees of Fuzhounese descent were repatriated
back to Fuzhou's rural villages.

Unhappy with their relocation, many decided to pull up stakes
and try again, hiring fishing vessels to carry them to Japan. In the
early 1980s, dozens of fishing boats drifted into Japanese waters, and
their passengers appealed for political asylum—rightly—as Vietnamese "boat people." Mixed among the legitimate refugees, however, were others who were less so.[15]

Later, Taiwanese crime syndicates took over the Fuzhounese snake-head business, and the operation underwent various refinements. The basic strategy is to avoid detection en route and, when that is not possible, to look for new alternatives, including bribery. This means gaining the most up-to-date information about police plans in order to respond flexibly. Most of all, however, the syndicate's techniques exploit every weakness of national governments, including their limited reach beyond their borders, their lack of inter-government and intra-government coordination, legal loopholes, bureaucratic incompetence, and official corruption.

Chinese human smuggling is played like global baseball. The sprint to first base is the transfer of would-be illegal immigrants onto small fishing boats in Fuzhou and Wenzhou harbors for ferrying to international waters, where they will be picked up by Taiwanese seagoing vessels. Once fully loaded—shipping companies are paid per head—the ships sail southwest to Thailand for refueling before making a stab for second base. After crossing the Pacific, they land in the coastal areas of either Central America or Mexico, usually debarking aboard small fishing boats or pleasure craft. This sea route south of the United States avoids detection by American reconnaissance satellites, which monitor the U.S. coasts. Once on land, the smugglers use safe houses operated by Taiwanese nationals in La Paz, Bolivia, as the transit point.

The dash to third base is the crossing of the U.S. border by land. If their ship docked in Central America, the smugglers travel through Mexico City, infiltrate the Texas border, and arrive in Atlanta, Georgia, or Houston, Texas. If it landed in Mexico's Baja California Peninsula, they cross the border into San Diego and rest in safe houses in largely Chinese American Monterey Park before flying on to home base, New York.

The route from Baja California is in fact an old Chinese trail. Today's elaborate border controls deterring Mexicans were originally established during the early decades of this century in response to illegal Chinese immigrants, who were banned from legal entry by the

Chinese Exclusion Act of 1882. There is a small fishing village, Punta China, in Baja California, so named for being the favorite landing spot for Chinese ships carrying illegals.

There are dozens of variations on this sea/land route. Xiao Lin, the butcher's son, and several others from the *Golden Venture* took a different road, to Thailand. They were transported by train to Kunming in Yunan Province, southwest of China near the Burmese border, where they transferred to a bus that took them to the border town of Pu-erh. From there they rode on horseback through thick Burmese jungles. It took them two to three weeks of strenuous journeying to reach Thailand and eventually Bangkok. Along the way they rested at Chinese-operated guest houses as they passed through the notorious "Golden Triangle" on the Burma–China–Thailand borders, the world's most important heroin production center. They traveled, in fact, along the principal heroin trafficking route to Bangkok. Intelligence reports suggest that the human smugglers have close contacts with the heroin traffickers,[16] who are controlled by the overseas Chaozhounese syndicate (Chaozhou is in the northeastern coastal region of Guangdong Province).

Some illegals, who came to the United States by land through Mexico aboard chartered private planes, report seeing other private planes on the illegal Mexican landing strip that were used by drug traffickers. So, it appears, Chinese snakeheads have connections with the cocaine cartels in South America as well.[17]

NO FEAR OF FLYING

The most comfortable and the fastest route to America is, of course, by air. It requires, however, that the smuggled individuals have legal visas for transit countries. For 300 yuan ($45 U.S.), one can get an "official invitation" from a Russian company enabling Chinese citizens to obtain Russian entry visas. Once in Moscow, the U.S.-bound illegals begin to maneuver, trying to arrange visas to enter other transit countries. This may take weeks, and the snakeheads have already set up Moscow coordination centers, complete with hostels established just for Chinese illegals. The trick is to get to a transit country whose airport security is so lax or, more likely, so corrupt that it would let Chinese with questionable identification papers board a U.S.-bound plane. The moment an illegal is on a plane headed for the United States, he is virtually home free, for even if his fake documents are detected, he can always request political asylum and stay.

So Chinese illegals wait by the hundreds in Moscow or Bangkok at any given time to get the easily obtainable entry visas to places like Libya or Somalia. Then they purchase a round-trip ticket to that country with a scheduled stop in Madrid or some other location along the Western air trunk routes, where they try to hop on a flight to the United States.

This often means last-minute changes of itinerary. A phone call informing those waiting at Karachi Airport that a "friendly" customs official at JFK in New York will be on duty when a certain United Airlines flight arrives at the airport can mean frantic last-minute booking. Or the phone call could warn smugglers not to try Anchorage, Alaska, but that Singapore Airline's personnel at Madrid Airport will allow passengers flying to Vancouver, Canada, the courtesy of Transit Without Visa (TWOV), so when the plane makes a transit stop in San Francisco the Chinese illegals can get off and grab a plane to New York.

Airline personnel are supposed to prevent this sort of thing from happening by making sure that the passengers follow proper transfer rules. The companies are subject to fines in case of mishaps. Over the last few years, the INS has increased its pressure on the airlines to tighten their security, in part to deter entry by terrorists. But many smuggler schemes play in a different league than airline security.

A surer way to enter the United States painlessly is to obtain a second set of documents—either a stolen or a fake Taiwanese, Indonesian, or Argentinean passport with a "valid" tourist visa for entry to the United States. Several Central American countries' consulate employees stationed in Hong Kong working with smuggling rings provide future aliens with travel papers without requesting identification. Another way to avoid airline detection altogether is to fly to Cuba, the Dominican Republic, or the Bahamas, then board a chartered fishing boat to Puerto Rico or the U.S. Virgin Island of St. John. Once there, New York is within reach via a domestic flight.

With the possibility of putting five or six clients on a flight and so many scheduled commercial flights to choose from, air transport can be surprisingly efficient. Yet the cost per head is higher and it is very chancy. Smuggling by sea is certainly cheaper and is used extensively. Between 1991 and 1993, thirty-two ships with a total of as many as 5,300 Chinese aboard were found by various immigration authorities in the waters off Japan, Taiwan, Singapore, Guatemala, El Salvador, Australia, Haiti, and the United States.[18] Of course, many more went undetected.

During the golden days of Chinese smuggling, before serious U.S. anti-smuggling measures were enacted, ships sailed from Fuzhou across the Pacific directly to U.S. shores. The first such vessel, detected in 1991 off Los Angeles with 131 passengers aboard, was the *I-Mao*, registered in Taiwan. During the spring of 1993, before the *Golden Venture* incident, four vessels were caught carrying almost 700 illegals off the California shore. One month after it went aground in June of that year, three more ships were drifting off the Baja Peninsula south of San Diego under the surveillance of the U.S. Coast Guard, waiting for the chance to unload.

Since that time, the Coast Guard and the Navy have been authorized by the U.S. government to board suspicious vessels in international waters, and the number of interdicted vessels has declined dramatically from 1994 on.[19] Officials familiar with the situation say that this is not necessarily a sign that the smuggling activities are in abeyance. Instead, the smugglers have stretched the Coast Guard's patrol grid far to the southern end of the Pacific, perhaps beyond the limits of their effectiveness.

The majority of the ships used for human smuggling have been of Taiwanese origin. Although Taiwan has a large ocean-going fishing fleet, the ships employed for this purpose are usually on their last legs, crudely converted for their new purpose. Many are unseaworthy. Sometimes they end up drifting for days awaiting repairs, and as a last resort some have even had to send out distress signals. In order to save money, none of the standard safety features or sanitation facilities required for transporting large numbers of people are available on board. The snakeheads even skimp on fuel and provisions. The sea journey, always slow, is now even longer as the ships evade the Navy and moor offshore in international waters, waiting for local snakeheads to arrange for chartered local craft to pick up the passengers.

Snakeheads can be very cruel at sea. When the Coast Guard boarded the disguised trawler *Jung Sheng No. 8* off Hawaii in June 1996, they found 120 men packed into a tight, twenty-by-thirty-foot camouflaged compartment that had been nailed shut without ventilation. The men were naked and had been held between decks for several weeks without showers; they were caged in their own waste, and ate in a mass-feeding area where bowls were nailed to the table. Eight women were held in the converted stateroom on the main deck. Many aliens on the ship suffered from skin and urinary tract infections due to dehydration and unsanitary conditions. One of the Coast Guard officers who boarded the ship recalled: "When we pulled the hatch on the hold, we were overwhelmed with the rush of hot steamy air that smelled of urine and fecal matter"; and that it "just never went away."[20]

The smugglers had recruited enforcers to terrorize the illegals during the voyage. They would hold them down while others beat them, force them to drink sea water, or force them to perform sexual acts. The enforcers tried to extort anything valuable from the passengers to drive them even further into debt. They even came up with the idea of making their captives sign IOUs for phony gambling debts in their own blood, cutting their fingers and pressing their bloody fingerprints onto receipts.

The barbaric conditions—hardly atypical—on *Jung Sheng No. 8* stunned the Coast Guard boarding party. They were scarcely better than those suffered by the slaves brought from Africa in the eighteenth and nineteenth centuries.

THEY ARE ANIMALS

A special feature of Chinese smuggling operations is the extensive involvement of smugglers with the clients after they arrive in the United States. Usually the snakeheads hold the illegal immigrants in safe houses until all their debts are paid. The payment schedule is clearly stipulated in a standard contract, which states that the would-be immigrants had to deliver a down payment before they started the journey to cover the cost of "registration" and their transportation, none of which is refundable. The remainder is to be paid after they arrive in New York.[21]

In the early stages of the human smuggling industry, some snakeheads extended credit, allowing their clients to pay the debt off in monthly installments. However, as the smuggling business grew, keeping track of credit allowances became a nuisance. Also, a lengthy involvement with a freely roaming client made brushes with law enforcement more likely. These days, smugglers insist on the full final payment before releasing the illegals. They prefer to shift the responsibility of keeping track of the debt payments to other enforcement parties, be they relatives, local gangs, local loan sharks, or village associations. Indeed, they often insist that the final payment be completed in China, in order to avoid the need to launder their money in the United States and thus risk detection by the authorities. This means that the relatives of the smuggled aliens have to transfer their funds back to China through illegitimate money-laundering services in Chinatown. An illegal immigrant held in New York is released only after a phone call from the snaketail in China confirms the completion of the transaction.

The worst abuses of illegal immigrants occur in New York safe houses while they wait for their relatives to come up with the final payment. To encourage the relatives to raise the funds by borrowing from various sources more quickly, the smuggling networks contract with non-Fuzhounese youth gangs—sometimes American-born Chinese, other times Vietnamese—as enforcers. Members of the infamous Vietnamese Born to Kill gang, known for their mindlessly indiscriminate violence, were once hired for such services.[22] The enforcers begin to abuse the illegals as soon as they arrive at the safe houses, at times forcing them to talk to their relatives on the phone while undergoing torture.

The police claim that there are some 300 safe houses holding newcomers in New York City.[23] They are usually located in basement cellars, and all illegals have to spend some time in one before being released. The immigrants are obliged to eat, sleep, and urinate in the same place as more than a dozen inmates, all of whom are confined to one room. They are starved, deprived of fresh air and sunlight, and beaten regularly. At times they are ordered to inflict pain on each other. Many are shackled and handcuffed to metal bed frames. Males are told that they could be killed; the females are threatened with work in a whorehouse.

Some men have in fact been killed to set an example to others, and girls have in fact been forced to work in massage parlors for years without pay; others end up locked in during the day and forced to work at gambling joints at night. One thing the smugglers always make sure of is that their victims do not dare to inform the authorities or testify against them in court—not even to talk about their experience with other illegals. They are never allowed to forget that the smugglers control the whole community. They should see no evil, hear no evil, and mind their own business after their release.

THE HEAD OF SNAKEHEAD NETWORK

The success of human smuggling operations depends on the cooperation of hundreds of individuals, including snaketails in Fuzhou, corrupt officials in China, fishermen-smugglers on China's coast, Taiwanese fishing and freight fleet owners, Malaysian shipping crews, safe house operators dotting the globe, and underworld "facilitators" along the smuggling routes from Bangkok, Central America, Mexico, and Texas to New York.

The smuggling network also involves passport and visa counterfeiters in Hong Kong, gangs who specialize in stealing passports in Asia, money launderers in New York who transfer smuggling funds back into China, and financial operators who handle debt payments in China. In New York, the smuggling network relies on Chinese youth gangs as enforcers who oversee the snake people, on lawyers who defend illegals and appeal for political asylum on their behalf, and on members of the Fukien-American Association on East Broadway, who were observed by law enforcement officials placing threatening calls from their offices to Fuzhounese immigrants in New York, demanding smuggling fees.[24]

Parts of the operation are subcontracted out by the syndicate. The U.S.–Mexico border crossings are usually handled by Hispanic subcontractors. Until her arrest in 1996, Gloria Canales, a citizen of Costa Rica, headed one of the largest immigrant smuggling operations in Central America. Immigration officials have estimated that Canales and her confederates had moved yearly at least 10,000 migrants from India, Pakistan, and China from Central America through Mexico to major U.S. cities.[25]

The smuggling business is so profitable that, like the drug trade, it is able to offer high prices to coopt government officials. According to the U.S. inter-agency working group, "Alien smuggling is made possible by staggering levels of official corruption." In Belize, the director and deputy director of the national immigration authority were recently arrested for corruption involving alien smuggling; immigration directors in Panama, Guatemala, and the Dominican Republic were replaced for the same reason.[26]

Evidently, American officials are not immune to the temptation, either. Jerry Stuchiner, a nineteen-year veteran INS agent who was the officer-in-charge in Honduras and the only INS agent based in Central America, was arrested in Hong Kong for possession of Honduran passports he intended to sell to Chinese illegals in 1996. Many criminals have purchased similar passports in the past for $50,000 apiece in order to get into the United States, among them the suspected terrorists in the 1993 bombing of the World Trade Center in New York.[27] And Stuchiner was no ordinary agent. He was the INS's top investigator of Chinese alien smuggling, a position earned through his experience as an agent in Hong Kong. Ironically, he was caught just after playing an instrumental role in the arrest of Gloria Canales, the "queenpin" of alien smuggling in Costa Rica. People familiar with the investigation speculate that Stuchiner tried to use his authority to bust an important competitor at the time.[28]

In a 1996 budget request hearing in front of the House Appropriations Committee, Inspector General of the Department of States Jacquelyn Williams requested more funds to be provided for oversight of State Department operations. She noted that the third-largest category of caseload handled by her Office of Oversight is, in fact, investigation into passport and visa fraud perpetrated by State Department Employees.[29]

Although many of the human smuggling operations are subcontracted out, the Chinese smugglers have to maintain a coordinating command center if they are to transport thousands of migrants across the vast distances separating China and the United States. Taiwan's imprint on the human smuggling network is everywhere: most of the forty smuggling ships interdicted by U.S. authorities have been owned and captained by Taiwanese nationals; a majority of the passports used by the illegals have been issued by Taiwan's consulates around the world. Some of the snake people recall that they were given lessons by "instructors" to walk, talk, and dress more like the Taiwanese—which means with some urban sophistication—while they waited at transit points.

Almost all the major safe houses in Central America are operated by Taiwanese, and the countries whose consulates issue visas used by the illegals are the very few countries that have friendly relations with the Republic of China, such as Panama, Guatemala, Honduras, Bolivia, Belize, and Costa Rica.

Yet no evidence has emerged to this date linking the Taiwan government directly to the alien smuggling trade. The innocence of Taiwan's organized crime cartels and the government intelligence community, however, is less clear. The Nationalist Party (KMT) had maintained discreet ties with Shanghai's infamous criminal Green Gang in the 1920s. Chiang Kai-shek, then leader of the party, was said to be a member of the gang, and the KMT could trace its own origins back to nobler, more patriotic anti-Manchu triads, or secret societies. But most of the old triads long ago degenerated into little more than criminal associations, with their members deeply involved in gambling and narcotics. This did not stop the KMT from using them, even into the present day. The party leadership has not flinched from using criminal syndicates—such as United Bamboo Alliance, a criminal syndicate in Taiwan—to do its dirty work, such as the assassination on U.S. soil of Henry Liu, an American citizen who had published an unflattering biography of then Taiwanese president Chiang Ching-kuo.[30] In other words, the covert branches of the government have a "healthy understanding" with organized crime.

Taiwan's government has lived with this ambiguity for a long time. After Chiang Kai-shek and his KMT cohort escaped to Taiwan in 1949, part of the KMT army retreated to the China–Burma–Thailand border, commonly known as the Golden Triangle, where they were developed into the anti-communist Chinese Irregular Forces with CIA help. The entire region was under the authority of the Intelligence Bureau of the Ministry of National Defense (IBMND). Taipei regularly rotated IBMND agents and military officers into the Golden Triangle. Weapons and cash payments were made available, and hundreds of officers were flown routinely to Taipei for training. The forces were meant to become a part of the worldwide anti-communist insurgent movement, and also the intelligence arm of the Nationalist government in Taiwan.

But over the years these irregular forces extended their operations into the narcotics trade traditionally so prominent in the Golden

Triangle. American drug agents tracked huge transfers of cash from northern Thailand to Taipei and back again, where the funds were said to be used for paying troops and gathering intelligence.

A few American intelligence officials have questioned such claims. "This is widely known there," says a U.S. official familiar with the operation. "Once you get to the Golden Triangle, you find that you can get terribly rich—provided you fabricate enough intelligence." Or, as another American official with long experience in the region, this time with the Drug Enforcement Administration, bluntly puts it: "The KMT intelligence people are involved in heroin up to their necks."[31]

Again, there is no direct evidence the trade has been officially sanctioned by those who run the KMT. However, there are troubling questions. Take, for instance, the case of Ma Sik-yu and his younger brother Sik-chun, who rose from the streets of Hong Kong to the pinnacle of the Southeast Asian heroin business. Beginning in 1970, KMT intelligence used the Ma heroin empire as a spy network. At the height of the operation in the mid-1970s, the KMT was said to be pouring millions of dollars each year into the Ma organization, fielding more than forty agents in a half dozen Asian countries. Along the way the Mas became multi-millionaires, purchasing real estate and the Chinese-language newspaper *Oriental Daily News*, the colony's leading pro-KMT paper. And the elder Ma, dubbed "White Powder Ma" by the press, gained notoriety as the man who helped expand the reach of Chinese organized crime throughout the world, particularly in places along the international heroin transport routes into Western Europe and North America.

By 1977, as a sixty-man police task force in Hong Kong was closing in on the Ma brothers, they fled to Taiwan. The Ma connections on Taiwan shielded them from both jail and extradition, despite loud protests from law enforcement authorities in Hong Kong.[32]

Some law enforcement officials in the United States assert that heroin and aliens are being smuggled by the same people.[33] Willard Myers, a leading expert on Chinese alien smuggling, told the Senate

Foreign Relations Committee in 1994 that Taiwan's military and intelligence communities are profiting directly from the Fuzhounese human smuggling trade, and both are beyond the reach of the civilian law enforcement. In earlier testimony, Myers even identified an unnamed high-ranking member of Taiwan's national police agency as part of the operation.[34]

Several of the illegals who traveled through the Golden Triangle to enter Thailand were told by their snakeheads that if they were not able to pay off all their debts, they could act as "mules" carrying white powder to settle up.[35]

The Taiwanese government has been reluctant to respond to American inquiries about suspected smugglers with criminal records residing in Taiwan, much to the frustration of the American side. Nor has the government arrested and prosecuted those smugglers that American police officials have identified as human smugglers.[36] The government has even ignored U.S. pleas to pass an anti-smuggling law.[37]

DEADLY FUZHOUNESE, TAIWANESE, AND HONG KONG CRIMINAL COMBINATIONS

As the highly profitable human smuggling industry matures, and an ever-increasing number of freelance operators become involved, more mid- and low-level operators in the industries go off on their own, such as the counterfeiters in Hong Kong and the Hispanic coyotes on the U.S.–Mexico border who began to make deals directly with various smaller operators. Consequently, as more new routes get developed, the dominance of Taiwan's syndicate is becoming difficult to maintain.

There are indications that the Fuzhounese themselves are taking over the business. Guo Leong Chi (also known as Ah Kay), a Fuzhounese illegal immigrant himself, paid his debts by working for the snakeheads as debt collector. Eventually, he became the head of the Fuching youth gang, which functions as an enforcer for the smuggling network. Once Guo gained enough knowledge and established strategic contacts within the smuggling network, especially in Fuzhou, he went into business on his own: The *Golden Venture* was one of his operations, and it failed only when his brother, who was supposed to direct the vessel's entry into New York harbor, was killed by rival human smugglers. Guo, however, did not last very long in the business before being arrested in Hong Kong and extradited to the United States.

Yet other Fuzhounese are successful at the game, in part because they have accumulated enough capital and experience; they have the added advantage of operating on their own turf, with all the local interests, including government officials, already involved. Several recent reports are indicative of Fuzhounese local initiatives: In Xiamen, south of Fuzhou, Chinese law enforcement officials have detected smugglers using container ships as a hiding place for shipping illegals to various destinations; at the Hong Kong Airport, authorities have noticed an increased use of the People's Republic of China green service passports by illegals. These passports, which are issued for official purposes, usually come with a letter of invitation by a host country, often forged in China.[38]

Though there are many more players in the human smuggling business, the base of the industry is expanding as well. What is significant is to realize that since the economic reforms in the People's Republic of China, the government's ideological hostility to a free-market economy has evaporated along with its tight control over Chinese civic order. In the past decade there has been a rapid rise of organized crime in China, in prostitution, drug trafficking, gambling, smuggling of goods, and counterfeiting, often with the cooperation and under the protection of corrupt government officials.

Now, with the lessened political and ideological tension between Taiwan and mainland China, organized crime elements in both places are working together in various international operations, including heroin and human smuggling, and have enlisted the additional involvement of the Hong Kong triads. With such a large hinterland as the Chinese mainland as a base, and the combined sophistication of all the different strains of organized crime networks, the potential global growth of the human smuggling business has serious international implications.

CHAPTER 4

The Limits of Kinship Networks

CURIOUSLY, GIVEN THE HUMAN SMUGGLING NETWORK'S SOPHISTI-cated global reach, most of the smuggled aliens have been recruited from Fuzhou. The reason for this cannot be their peculiar economic aspirations—China is full of people with similar drive. Nor is it because of Fuzhou's proximity to the sea, since the entire densely populated coastal belt extending from Manchuria to the Vietnamese border could claim the same. Neither is it on account of Fuzhou's historical exposure to the West, because the residents of China's most cosmopolitan cities, like Shanghai and Tianjing, would make more likely candidates.

Most smuggled aliens are not even residents of Fuzhou City. They come predominantly from four counties on its rural outskirts. Fuzhou has, therefore, produced a textbook example of a rural migration network based on kinship: once an individual arrives in a foreign place, others from his tight-knit village follow. City residents, on the other hand, do not tend to emigrate in large chains because their kinship ties are relatively weak.

All rural Chinese communities have strong kinship bonds that encompass members of the immediate family—spouse, parents, children and siblings—and extend to the in-laws. The kinship ties of the rural Fuzhounese are unfettered by urban experiences and reinforced by their historical self-perception as independent-spirited people. But even with the help of their overseas relatives, illegal migration is costly for the Fuzhounese. It is only feasible if it operates like a "family project," and runs like a relay team. The family first pools all its resources and social connections to send one young, capable, and dependable male abroad. In the beginning, he has to work for others in the United States to pay off his debts. The ideal narrative from here on goes like this: Once his debts are paid, he begins to save to bring other family members over. He familiarizes himself with his new environment and selects a business that is likely to succeed as a "family enterprise" —a take-out restaurant, for instance, as is commonly the case with the Fuzhounese. The migration relay begins. The next in line to be sent overseas may be his wife, but most likely it will be a male sibling who will maximize the family's capital accumulation—a hardworking, "productive" male is preferable. A wife is considered as a prime candidate for migration if the family wants to have a child born in the United States to secure its future legal footing.

Once this early core group, the "seed population," begins to get established—when it accumulates enough savings for a down payment on a take-out restaurant in the Bronx, for instance—other family members are brought over one by one: wives and sisters to help out as cashiers, grandparents to look after the children, and so on. The children will be put to work as soon as they are old enough to act as translators and delivery boys—forming the second generation of the family's "corporate venture."

The migration engine does not stop there. The wives do not abandon their original families—they and their in-laws' family will assist their siblings and parents by linking them into the migration chain. The siblings can then start a new cycle of family migration, thus extending the network to people with different surnames and eventually encompassing an entire community of neighbors and fellow villagers. The chain can eventually include not just the population of a whole village but an entire dialect group.

The Cantonese have exactly the same migration pattern. That's why, before the 1960s, the majority of the approximately 20 million expatriate Chinese in the world were of Guangdong and Fujian origin. All those from Guangdong come from eight small counties (not much larger than Rhode Island when taken together) on the rural outskirts of the city of Canton (Guangzhou). Some 90 percent of the Chinese in the United States before World War II were of Cantonese origin; half of them came from a single county, Toishan. Today's Fuzhounese come from four counties outside the city of Fuzhou.

The strong sense of family and kinship loyalty that underlies group migration should not be seen purely in cultural and moral terms, because it is ultimately informed by an explicit economic rationale. Bringing family members into the migration chain is seen by the Cantonese and the Fuzhounese as a chance to extend their economic power, either by bringing in a relative as a business partner or as cheap labor. To the Chinese in America who came early, Fuzhounese immigrants represent the rock bottom of the economic ladder in the community. They can only move upward if they accumulate some capital, and for that Fuzhounese need cheap and dependable labor. Their kin back home are the ideal candidates.

More than a century ago, after the harsh restrictions imposed by the Chinese Labor Exclusion Act of 1882, and long after their dream of the "Golden Mountain" had faded, the Chinese in the United States retreated to the humble, self-employed professions in restaurants and hand laundries so often associated with Chinese Americans by the mainstream culture. Those Cantonese who had some money tried to bring their relatives to this country, too, to work as "helpers" in their laundries or as waiters in their restaurants to speed up their rate of capital accumulation. However, in the days of exclusion, only scholars, merchants, and diplomats could come into this country legally.

The Cantonese devised three options: first, arriving legally by claiming to be a merchant—a grocery store owner, for instance. That meant applying for entry as a partner to a relative who already had a legitimate business in the United States. This would entail drawing up property rights and ownership agreements to convince immigration authorities, who were usually extremely skeptical. The second option was to be smuggled across either the Mexican or the Canadian border and accepting what might always be illegal status. And the third and final option was entry through the "slot system," also called the "paper son" scheme.

Under U.S. law, all persons born on American soil are automatically citizens, as are the children of citizens even if they are born abroad. Few Chinese at the turn of the century were born here—but the San Francisco earthquake in 1906 destroyed most immigration and birth records. The result was that most Chinese in the country at that time claimed citizenship. As a citizen, a Chinese male, upon one or several of his returns from temporary visits to his ancestral village, could claim that he had married in China and that his wife was either pregnant or had given birth to a child or children in China. According to law, these children were automatically citizens of the United States. Specific names, sexes, and addresses were furnished to the immigration office. These then were the "slots" awaiting the children's eventual arrival.

The "paper son" or "slot" system soon evolved into a lucrative racket in which illegal immigrants paid fees to become "sons" of Chinese Americans, which in a way prefigured today's onerous debt payment system after arrival. The cost of a slot was calculated according to the age of the "paper son"—$100 per year of age. For a fifteen-year-old youth, it would be $1,500, approximately one year's salary. A purchaser would appear at a port of entry with fictitious name, based upon the earlier statements of the returning citizen, and would claim United States citizenship through purported relationship to the citizen. Stories of family histories, schooling, residences, deaths, births, and marriages were carefully rehearsed and painstakingly memorized.

No one really knows how many Chinese obtained entry into the United States in this way. There were extreme abuses. One eighty-seven-year-old Chinese from San Francisco's Chinatown sponsored the admission of fifty-seven "sons" from his village, immigration officials estimated.[1] During the McCarthy era, in fear of enemy infiltration, the INS instituted a "Confession Program" in 1956 that allowed all those Chinese who had entered the country illegally to come forward and be registered. From 1956 to 1965 (when the program was abolished), 13,895 Chinese came forward, thereby exposing 22,083 persons and closing out the possible use of an additional 11,294 "slots."[2]

The slot system (phased out in 1965 with the passage of the new immigration law, which permits large-scale Chinese immigration to the United States) never developed anything like the sophistication and international scale of the Fuzhounese illegal immigration network. The main reason was that the number of illegals introduced by the slot system was limited by the fact that it operated around individual citizens. Nor did the cost of illegal entry approach the levels charged by the Fuzhounese.

The patterns of the Cantonese and the Fuzhounese migrations seem to suggest that people do not migrate randomly. They employ a similar migration chain system based on close kinship ties formed within the confines of rural villages. Moreover, migration is a systematically organized enterprise whose networks only develop under specific favorable conditions. That in turn means that the enormous size of the floating population in China today does not automatically imply that they will all come over—though that is a specter some Americans have long feared as the "Yellow Peril."

A DEADLY EMBRACE

What the Fuzhounese are caught up in, however, is not a normal rural and kinship-based migration chain. Their migration has been helped by an organized human smuggling network, whose only concern is making a profit—not maintaining family ties and kinship unity. The network is interested in the Fuzhounese as potential clients only if two critical conditions exist: one, the client can pay; two, the client can be trusted to keep the operation secret from law enforcement.

Established by seamen who had jumped ship in the early 1970s, a "seed population" in New York has helped the Fuzhounese to fulfill the first condition. This seed population was expanded with the 1986 amnesty program and President Bush's 1989 executive order, which provided legal status for Chinese already in this country. The resulting relatively large, legal resident community of Fuzhounese had accumulated enough savings to pay smugglers for shipping their relatives over. The Fuzhounese fulfill the second condition of the smuggling networks by the virtue of their proven dedication to their family migration projects, for which they would be willing to keep quiet and even tolerate abuse by snakeheads.

In China, family members of Fuzhounese immigrants have a very different understanding of the smugglers and the conditions in America than might be expected of an exploited population. Those who are waiting to emigrate look to the smugglers as the providers of an essential service. When informed of the safe arrival of a family member in New York, the family in China invites the snakehead for a big community banquet, sets off firecrackers, and puts up big red wall posters in front of the family home to celebrate. If there is a debt payment dispute, the family in China as a rule sides with the smugglers, typically convinced that its own members in the United States are at fault. For the snakeheads have devised their own propaganda and misinformation campaign in order to attract as many innocent people as possible to the smuggling journey. When I confronted the relatives of illegals in China with accounts of torture, kidnapping, rape, and other abuses perpetrated by the snakeheads, they usually responded that the snakeheads have every right to punish those who are lazy and unwilling to pay off their debts. In a way, the snakeheads have already immunized the Fuzhounese from being critical of the human smuggling process.

After years of this type of indoctrination, the Fuzhounese in China have come to believe that America is a land of opportunity, where anyone can work for two years to pay off their smuggling debts and then, in a couple more years, buy a business. Those unable to do so are considered *mei-zu-shi,* useless and lacking in ambition. Even those family members not expecting to come to this country want to make sure the migration project succeeds so that their future in China will be assured by overseas remittances.

Of course, the Fuzhounese in America know that the snakeheads are far from perfect, but are too intimidated to challenge them. They cannot fight back lest they jeopardize the chances of other family members to make the trip. Besides, their relatives in China are vulnerable. The snakeheads could threaten family members there with violence or extortion. This kind of situation is taken seriously because local authorities are not likely to intervene.

More than anything, however, they keep quiet in order to maintain their "face" and family honor. One illegal immigrant who told me about being beaten and abused by the snakeheads during the sea voyage to the United States in 1994 explains, "I try not to think about it, treat it as if nothing has even happened. Most of all I work as hard as I can, and don't bother with whatever happens to others. I hear nothing and I know nothing."

The smugglers use the strong kinship ties of the Fuzhounese to keep their clients in line. If one member fails to pay, others will take over the responsibility. Because smugglers need new clients to generate more profits, the smugglers' interests coincide with those of the already established Fuzhounese immigrants, who need other villagers as cheap labor. The smugglers, therefore, need access to kinship networks to gain information on possible new recruits and the help of clan elders in advising them on the dependability of a particular client. They also need the kinship connection to gain the trust of their clients. In a way, the snakeheads, the illegals, the illegals' family members in China, and the established members of the Fuzhounese community in the United States are all locked in a deadly embrace.

REACHING THE LIMIT

The smugglers could have hardly found a more ideal population in China than the Fuzhounese. There are limits, however, to how far Fuzhounese resources can be exploited. The smuggling operations are increasingly limited by the U.S. Fuzhounese immigrant community's finances. As more Fuzhounese come, the debts are accumulating, and will eventually reach a point where the indigenous community will no longer be able to service their debt. Paul Smith of Pacific Forum estimates that between 1991 and 1994, there were 25,000 Fuzhounese illegals entering the United States yearly.[3] That means that at least

100,000 illegal Fuzhounese, not counting the thousands who came before and after that period, paid $30,000 each—a grand total of $3 billion. No new immigrant community can withstand this amount of debt.

By 1992 the influx of Fuzhounese illegals had reached a saturation point. Members in the community were having increasing difficulty raising the smuggling funds. To counter this trend, the snakeheads tried to squeeze more out of the illegals and their relatives by force. Kidnapping and torturing of illegals was the inevitable consequence. Knowing the importance of family structure to the Fuzhounese, the snakeheads used every means possible to exploit that weakness. They kidnapped and tortured those illegals with relatives to ensure speedy payment. They enlisted the support of debtors' families in China to exact maximum pressure on them. Most of all, they forced the illegals themselves to collect funds from their relatives. After all, who else would be in a better position to know exactly where the "hidden" family resources are?

Since 1992, hundreds of kidnapping cases perpetrated by Fuzhounese have been reported. This rash of activities has kept the New York police busy. The police department has sped up the recruitment and training of Fuzhounese-speaking officers.[4] But some of the kidnapping cases are fraudulent. FBI agents who work on this beat have complained that it is difficult to tell whether a kidnapping is for real. In one case, the bureau had worked long and hard to convince kidnappers to bring their victim to meet his uncle, who was delivering the ransom money at the drop site. Much to their surprise, when the FBI rushed in to arrest the kidnappers during the exchange, the victim tried to escape, refusing to embrace his uncle. As it turned out, the "victim," long unhappy with the uncle's familial authority, had staged his own kidnapping to extort money from the family.

These wayward indebted illegals are also recruited as enforcers. At times they simply go off on their own to prey on others as a way of paying off their own debts. They have been known to seize clients who have already paid and torture them in safe houses to force their relatives to pay again. The cost of ransom ranges from $1,000 to as high as $80,000, depending on the ability of the victims to pay. The head of the New York City FBI office, James Fox, believes that these crimes are usually the work of ad hoc freelancers on the fringe of the criminal community.[5] These marginal groups are also responsible for stealing other snakeheads' clients at Kennedy Airport by snatching arriving illegals before they are picked up by their own enforcers. They then demand money from the illegals' relatives.

A Fuzhounese gang nicknamed "Meihua" (Peach Blossom; also King of Spades in Chinese) specialized in kidnapping female garment workers returning home from work in the evening. They were known for their terrifying tactics in extracting ransom money from victims' relatives. Their methods included enslavement, torture, sodomy, and rape.[6] Guo Liqin, a thirty-eight-year-old illegal immigrant woman who worked in a Queens garment factory, was snatched off the street in August 1995 by three members of the gang and was locked up in a basement cellar of a Brooklyn house. Guo, the wife of an undocumented dishwasher and mother of two children, had borrowed $29,000 from her friends and relatives to come to the United States in 1994. Her family in China got a threatening phone call demanding $38,000 . . . or else. The family panicked. They still owed $30,000 for sending Guo's daughters to the United States and did not see how they could borrow more. After three days, the family could scrape up only $5,000.[7]

Enraged, the kidnappers chopped off one of Guo's fingers, raped her in front of the gang's two other victims, then wrapped a plastic bag around her head and tried to strangle her with a telephone wire. When that failed they smashed her skull with a television set. Before the kidnappers left the apartment, they picked out a King of Spades from a poker deck and placed it on the coffee table as a signature. Along with it they left a written warning: "Only death for anyone who refuses to pay ransom."

AS THE HARDSHIP OF DEBT BURDEN INCREASES, MORE FUZHOUNESE are being forced into crime. The civic order of Chinatown community is sliding into chaos. Rather than coercing just the illegal immigrants and their relatives, the unemployed snakeheads have turned up pressure on the entire Fuzhounese community for "easy money." Chinatown newspapers have received regular reports of kidnapping of the sons and daughters of established, well-to-do Fuzhounese who have nothing to do with anyone's debts.[8] They are often released for just a couple of thousand dollars.

Knowing the discreet nature of the Fuzhounese community and everyone's illegal background, the snakeheads are apparently not afraid to act brazenly. In the winter of 1996, one Fuzhounese restaurant owner in Wallingford, Connecticut, a suburb of Hartford, reported the kidnapping of his son Wei Yang. The FBI was alerted, and the whole suburban community was soon up in arms in fear and bewilderment. A week later the owner got his son back without the help of the FBI by paying $88,000—a lucky amount in Chinese folklore, for the character eight is pronounced "bar," which rhymes with the character "far," meaning prosperity. The restaurateur was evidently familiar with the customs of the smuggling trade—many of his employees, who live in his house near the restaurant, are from Fuzhou. In fact, according to one newspaper report, that kidnapping of Wei Yang was not the first time. He had been a victim of the same crime a few years earlier.[9]

The impact on the Fuzhounese community is clear: paying off debts and staying away from kidnappers are every newcomer's main concern. The debt-paying period is getting longer, the interest charged by the snakeheads higher. Some Fuzhounese have hoped to avoid these problems by moving to other states, but there is no escape—enforcers have simply followed. A municipal judge in Seattle sent a Fuzhounese youth, who had been kidnapped by enforcers, to an INS juvenile foster-care facility for protection, but he soon disappeared. He returned with a gang six months later to the same facility in Seattle and kidnapped other Fuzhounese youths there. After his arrest he pleaded not guilty, claiming that he had been threatened by his snakeheads, to whom he still owed money, into committing the crime.[10]

Finally, the snakeheads, in order to maintain the volume of their business, developed a modified form of "kinship sponsoring system." Rich Fuzhounese restaurant and garment factory owners and gambling and prostitution kingpins, who are legal and came to this country earlier, stepped in to sponsor new groups of "distant relatives." The snakeheads, knowing the reputation and reliability of the sponsors, smuggled the new recruits at a discount, some even entirely on credit. These new recruits have to work for the sponsors as unpaid labor for several years while the enforcers insure their complacency through control over their relatives in China. They are, therefore, trapped in a state of virtual indentured servitude. The Fuzhounese migration network rose on the strength of their strong family and ethnic ties; now they are reaping the negative effects, the flip side of the same coin.

WE ARE ALL NOTHING BUT SLAVES

With the flood of desperate, undocumented aliens willing to work under any circumstances, Chinese employers are in the position to depress labor conditions to the limits. Wages in the Chinatown garment industry, already low by American standards before the arrival of the Fuzhounese, have declined even further.

Testifying in 1995 at a Senate hearing for anti-sweatshop legislation, Mrs. Tang, once a schoolteacher in Guangdong Province who had emigrated ten years ago to Brooklyn, recalled that in the early eighties she worked eight hours a day and earned $40–50 a day. Today, with competition from the Fuzhounese, she slaves twelve hours a day to make a paltry $30[11]—she has to work almost twice as long to make the same amount of money.

Those who have worked in the industry for some time and are physically no longer able to keep up the pace are assigned to lesser jobs, such as cutting threads, and make even less. Immigrants from Fuzhou, who are usually younger, choose to work at nonunion shops in order to get more take-home pay, still averaging about $40 a day.

Competition from the illegals is forcing documented Chinese workers to settle for less if they want to maintain steady employment. Employers lay off workers as soon as their work orders are completed. In the slower months, from November to the end of the year, seamstresses make less than $200 a month. For immigrants paying off enormous debts, this sum is absurdly, desperately low. They line up outside the factory long before the doors open to be the first ones to begin work. At night, they refuse to quit even after ten, just to be able to get a few more pieces done for a few more dollars. Some of the seamstresses on sewing machines are known not to drink anything during the day lest they interrupt their work, calculated on piece rate, by going to the bathroom. One Cantonese garment worker has testified to a congressional committee that Fuzhounese illegals work until two in the morning, sleep in the factory, and start again right after sunrise. Sometimes, if they are not able to complete a given order, they ask their children to come in to help.[12] Now even Fuzhounese men work on the sewing machines, competing with the traditionally all-woman labor force.

However, Chinese workers of legal status blame the illegals rather than the employers for this situation. The complaints in the restaurant business are similar. "Dishwashing jobs used to pay $800 a month," a waiter explains. "Then the 'Amigos' [Mexicans] came, willing to work for $750. Now we have the Fuzhounese, who take it for $500."

Not surprisingly, the illegals have the best chances of getting and keeping a job. The employers like them for being young, committed, and willing to work long hours, and for their docility and uncomplaining nature. Some employers are only interested in undocumented workers. Longtime residents must either follow their example or lose their jobs. Thus employers have effectively erased the distinctions between legal and illegal immigrant workers. It is not surprising that the Chinese legal immigrants resent the undocumented interlopers, who they say have marginalized everybody's labor and worsened everybody's conditions. In every Chinatown discussion about workplace conditions, the Fuzhounese, the *wu-sun-fun* (people with no status), are the target of scorn.

UNCHECKED EXPLOITATION

The undocumented have given their employers the leverage to force workers to accept many obviously illegal labor practices. Home work, thought to have disappeared in America fifty years ago, is a common phenomenon in Chinatown, as is child labor, which has pushed down the already low wage scale in the garment industry. Employers are using every trick in the book to squeeze extra profits, including laying off workers to collect unemployment compensation while still asking them to work for less cash, or forcing them to work on contract-mandated legal holidays.

With the combined effects of low wages and bad working conditions, many Fuzhounese could no longer count on their relatives for adequate help. Some of them are forced to rely on public assistance, and the employers help them to "cook" their W-2 forms so their incomes appear to be below the poverty level, making them for food stamps and Medicare eligibility.

In another common scam, by now familiar to the Fire Department, gangs set up dungeons decorated to look like living spaces in Chinatown basements (with the cooperation of the local landlords) and then recruit dozens of Fuzhounese tenants, who pay a fee for the service. A day later, the gang starts a fire and alerts the fire department. When the fire department arrives and discovers the inhuman living conditions, it declares the residence in violation of fire regulations and evicts the tenants. Under New York City laws, those evicted under such unforeseen circumstances—even illegal immigrants—can get city public housing. In fact, they automatically jump to the head of the waiting line when they become homeless— the normal wait for public housing is five years. Undocumented workers who receive public assistance in this way are actually allowing the employers to pay them even less. The state has, in effect, been manipulated into subsidizing the sweatshop industry.

Seamstresses from Hong Kong—reputedly the most unregulated free-enterprise zone in the world—insist the working conditions in their homeland are better than those they witnessed in America. In Hong Kong, all work stops at six in the evening when building complexes shut down. Employers who intend to open the factories after hours have to obtain approval from the labor authorities. In Brooklyn, on the other hand, garment factories where mainly Fuzhounese are employed stay open until 4 A.M.

The most egregious practice at both unionized and nonunion Chinese garment factories in New York—and something far from common in Hong Kong—is withholding workers' legitimate wages. This problem has reached epidemic proportions. Previously, the normal withholding period was three weeks; now anything under five weeks is considered good. The length of wage withholding has become the single standard on which "garment ladies" choose a factory to work for. Of course, there is never a guarantee; after the employment starts, the employer can claim cash-flow problems or manufacturers' nonpayment to postpone his own wage payments. After a few weeks of unpaid wages, the workers are faced with the difficult decision of whether to hope against hope and work for another week or quit, and cut their losses. Street wisdom suggests quitting after six weeks of nonpayment.

Taking legal action against employers almost never succeeds. In the first place, the employers do not believe that illegals dare to file complaints against them. Even then, there are hundreds of complaints against Chinese employers for back wages filed with the New York State Labor Department, but so far there have been only two convictions. The first was brought in 1993, but the workers have yet to collect any back payment. More recently, in September 1996, workers won back wages totaling $59,000—for work done between August 1992 and November 1993. More typically, employers simply take advantage of legal loopholes and opt for bankruptcy proceedings whenever they face pressure for back wages. Workers arrive one morning to find the factory gates closed without a forwarding address or any other information. The same owners soon reopen nearby under a new corporate title with an altered partnership, refusing legal responsibility for the defunct factory.

The illegal Chinese workers were also used for union busting. In 1994, the owners of Silver Palace Restaurant—one of Chinatown's largest restaurants, which was unionized in 1980—locked out all their union workers, claiming that their wages were too high. The locked-out union workers picketed the restaurant for more than seven months. "If the owners win this one," the leader of the picketing workers stressed, "employers all over Chinatown could impose any kind of conditions they want on the working people, no matter whether they are legal or undocumented. We are then nothing but slaves." What was the outcome? The issue is no longer just the treatment of illegals. In Chinatown, where employers use illegals to depress wages for all legal workers, they have transformed the problem into a class struggle between labor and management.

DEBTS WILL BE THE DEATH OF US

After several years of working like machines, twelve hours a day and seven days a week, some Fuzhounese illegals begin to develop physical ailments. Restaurant workers complain of pinched nerves, back and shoulder pains, swollen feet, stomach cramps, and insomnia. Kitchen help can be temporarily blinded by the sudden rush of steam to the eyes from pots or dishwashers. Seamstresses complain of sore arms, headaches, dizzy spells, and heart palpitation. Bronchial asthma is common, caused by exposure to the chemicals used in treating fabrics. The worst problems develop from working with polyester, whose shredded fibers, if inhaled over a long period of time in the dry, unswept conditions of most workplaces, can cause nosebleeds and asthma. Some workers who handle the material develop loose skin and swollen fingers. The most dangerous job, however, is sewing on buttons. On old machines, a worker has to move the fabric around fast enough to allow the needle to go through all the but-tonholes, but if she is tired and unable to concentrate after long hours, the needle can easily injure her fingers. Other times, snapped-off needle fragments inflict wounds in the eyes of seamstresses.

Yet what Chinese workers fear most—next to having their wages withheld—is getting sick. Especially the illegal workers, for whom not being able to work is like death. If they get sick, they take herbal medicines, and only if that doesn't work do they consult an unli-censed doctor. It's hard not to notice the inordinate number of pharmacies and Chinese herbal doctors on East Broadway in Chi-natown.

Doctor Ling is a graduate of Guangdong Chinese Medical School who works frequently with this population, charging $10 per visit. After a diagnosis, established by feeling the pulse and looking into the patient's mouth and eyes, he prescribes an herbal medicine that costs around $15 for one week's dose. Dr. Ling confirms that his patients are mostly Fuzhounese with work-related illnesses. Some of his patients suffer from what he describes as working too hard, causing the body to *zuo-huai-le*—break down like a machine. The symptoms are dizziness, heart palpitation, generalized body aches, and finally numbness of the hands and inability to move them. Dr. Ling's advice is to rest. But none of his Fuzhounese patients listen, blaming him for his lack of medical acumen. A few have resorted to visiting shamans in the various Taoist temples around Chinatown.

Western doctors at several city hospital emergency rooms have also reported that the Fuzhounese come in complaining that their bodies have turned limp, lost all energy, and can no longer exert any force. Without legal status, insurance, or money, the only place illegal aliens can get professional help is in these emergency rooms. When the doctors at one emergency room tell them the same thing as Dr. Ling—that they need rest—they move on to another hospital, hop-ing to find a miracle cure.

The specialists I talked with said symptoms such as chronic head-aches, intense stomach cramps, fainting spells, menstrual irregularity, and the loss of energy cannot be proven to be directly related to work. The Workers' Compensation Board and the unions have generally accepted only claims related to repetitive stress injuries and work-related asthmatic problems.

Dr. George Friedman-Jimenez, a nationally recognized expert on occupational and environmental medicine, suggests that the symptoms I describe are nevertheless likely to be real. However, their causes are normally too complex to be attributed directly to a person's present job. Some of these illnesses may be related to previously existing health problems, exacerbated by working such long hours under primitive, nineteenth-century-like conditions. The fact of the matter is that, so far, there has not been any research done in the United States to determine the negative physical effects of working seventy to eighty hours a week for a long period of time.

Problems like repetitive stress syndrome can be avoided by taking regular breaks and by working shorter hours. As for back and shoulder aches, a change in the chair design and readjustment of one's seating position could minimize problems. Of course none of these changes, particularly working shorter hours, are an option for the Fuzhounese.

The consequences of physical collapse can be devastating. Mr. Lan, who left his wife and children behind in Fuzhou, came here illegally five years ago and worked hard to pay off his huge smuggling debt. Under heavy pressure and emotional stress, his health declined. His wife, realizing his predicament, came illegally to help him out. But this doubled his debt, and his health deteriorated to the point that he could no longer work. Thus the whole family started to depend solely on his wife's income as a seamstress—just to survive. The debts remained. One day, when his wife was out working, he hung himself.[13]

DYSFUNCTIONAL FAMILIES

The Fuzhounese work so hard that they barely have a family life to speak of. A husband and a wife who both work twelve to fourteen hours a day can hardly see each other. Having children is next to impossible. Yet many illegals want to have children in the United States as soon as they get married so that they will be protected from deportation as parents of American-born citizens. One major hospital in lower Manhattan established a Chinatown prenatal care clinic in 1994. Most of their patients turned out to be Fuzhounese who, even though undocumented, could legally receive full services. One of the counselors at the clinic was disturbed to find that most Fuzhounese women expressed little enthusiasm for having children. What they really wanted were the birth certificates to certify that their children were American-born. In the meantime, they took full advantage of the clinic's free services: free prenatal counseling, free checkups, free hospital delivery, and free supply of baby nutritional supplements.

What distressed the counselor the most was that, invariably, the parents sent their babies back to China as soon as they were old enough for air travel, for fear that caring for the babies would slow down the couples' earning power. Moreover, they knew their families in China, particularly the grandparents, would take good care of their children—after all, they are the family's ticket for legal immigration to America. A well-known travel agent in Chinatown estimates that there are 1,000 such births each year, based on the tickets sold to the parents. She also helps them find trustworthy individuals who are going back to China to carry the babies—at the cost of $1,000 a head. The children normally rejoin their parents in the United States when they are old enough to attend school.

However, such subversion of conventional family functions does not come without social cost. When the children return to America at the age of seven or eight, they are strangers to their parents. Having been spoiled in China by their grandparents, these children experience emotional trauma when thrust into the American environment. One of their most serious problems is their inability to catch up in the American school system.

Immigrant children normally have problems with English and cultural adjustment. In the past, Cantonese immigrants had to confront such problems, too. In the early 1970s, after the first wave of Cantonese immigrants from Hong Kong arrived, there were no Cantonese-speaking teachers and counselors in the public school system. The few Chinese with educational qualifications generally spoke Mandarin. It took another decade for the schools to recruit and train a pool of Cantonese-speaking staff. By the 1990s, however, most of the new immigrants turned out to be Fuzhounese speakers. In the whole public school system in New York in 1997, there are fewer than a handful of Fuzhounese-speaking teachers. Their services are in demand everywhere.

But the problem with Fuzhounese children is not simply language. Even more so, perhaps, it is the deficiency of rural Fuzhounese education. Children there, unlike those from Canton, generally don't start school until the age of eight, two years later than usual. Those with overseas connections are led to believe that they have it made, so they are not willing to study until they arrive in the United States anyway. Their problems are only compounded by the high illiteracy rate among the elders who raised them during their early childhood in China.

So when Fuzhounese children begin school here, they are proficient neither in English nor in Chinese. They need special attention, but the American school system is reluctant to place a child in a class that is below his or her age group. One Fuzhounese counselor fought for years to stop school authorities from sending ten-year-olds automatically to fourth grade. Such placement would quickly result in failure for most immigrant Fuzhounese students.

Fuzhounese are routinely shoved into ESL, bilingual, or special education programs. In a number of Chinatown area elementary schools, all the special education students are Fuzhounese. Unfortunately, they are not there transitionally—they are permanently stuck in these programs, and will never be able to integrate and compete with other students, even if they are bright and diligent.

Such children do not get enough supervision at home either, and the parents, complaining that they are unwilling to follow orders, say that they talk back, stay out late, even become youth gang members. Outside their traditional extended family environment, Fuzhounese parents are often unable to cope with the problems of childrearing in the United States. And again, many of these children were not, in fact, raised by them in early childhood.

So it is the social workers that have to deal with this serious situation. I went to a parents' workshop, organized by a group of concerned social workers in Chinatown. The Western-trained, bilingual experts tried to convince Fuzhounese parents to adopt a "liberal way" in dealing with their children: be patient, reason with them, listen to their problems, give them praise whenever possible instead of scolding them and, above all, never use physical punishment.

For the parents, the problems are complicated by the need to have the children work to contribute to debt payments. It is common to have Fuzhounese children as young as ten working full time in restaurants and garment factories alongside their parents. Some youngsters report to work seven days a week: on weekends they work eleven hours a day, and during the week they start right after classes, working from 3 P.M. in the afternoon until 10 at night.

Alexandra Jacobs, a former teacher at Seward Park High School, located on the outskirts of Chinatown, recalls that many of her students worked in factories and came to school exhausted, without having done their homework, only to fall asleep in class. It is usually difficult for a teacher who becomes aware of this problem to reach parents, either because the parents have difficulty understanding English or because they are out working all the time. Nor do the parents realize that their children need to devote extra time and effort to learning English and adapting to American society.[14]

School dropout rates among the Fuzhounese are high. Many of the frustrated dropouts are easily recruited into gangs to become enforcers and drug runners. Without the help of an extended family, without free time, without English, and without education of their own, the immigrant Fuzhounese illegals are incapable of fulfilling the responsibilities of being good parents. In fact, many of the

Fuzhounese families are dysfunctional—a bitter irony, since strong family ties are what brought the Fuzhounese to America to begin with.

Sometimes, the pressure of debts turn relative against relative. When Mr. Ling, a part owner of a take-out restaurant in Brooklyn who had come to the United States eleven years earlier, sponsored his nephew's emigration, the understanding was that the nephew would help out in the restaurant in exchange for room and board. Mr. Ling would in return pay the $30,000 smuggling fee. However, after working for his uncle for a year and half, the young man left to work for someone else. Mr. Ling was stuck with the debt. Considering his nephew's act a betrayal, Ling had a gangster threaten the impetuous young man to force him to come back.

The nephew, of course, gave a different story. He claimed that his uncle ordered him around, demanding all kinds of chores, as if he were a slave. The last straw was forcing him to ride a bicycle in one of the worst Brooklyn neighborhoods to deliver take-out orders. He was beaten, robbed, and had his bike stolen. Each time this happened, the uncle showed no sympathy, scolding him instead for the property loss and threatening him, saying, "At this rate, you will be working for me forever."

Family conflicts of this nature have become all too common within the Fuzhounese community, ironically, precisely because of the tightness of the Fuzhounese family ties that brought about the strength of this migration network. And it is precisely this celebrated "virtue" that has led the community into such serious jeopardy.

CHAPTER 5

Manufacturing Ethnicity

THE SHOCKING, INDENTURED SLAVE–LIKE CONDITIONS OF THE
Fuzhounese illegals are not a new and sudden development. They are
merely the next step down in a continuously deteriorating and already horrendous labor environment within the ethnic Chinese enclave. Unlike other immigrant workers, such as the Mexicans who
work for Korean green groceries, the Ecuadoreans who work for
Cuban garment factories, and the Polish illegals who work for Irish
construction companies, few Chinese are employed in an open and
competitive labor market. Although the other illegals generally have
to cope with low wages, long hours, undesirable and dangerous jobs,
and contend with employers who manipulate their productivity by
playing on their fear of deportation,[1] their predicament never reaches
the level of misery and degree of control perpetrated by Chinese
employers on Chinese workers within Chinese ethnic enclaves, beyond the scrutiny of American society.

THE ETHNIC ENCLAVE

Urban ethnic neighborhoods are not new. At the turn of the century,
they served as transitional orientation points where newly arrived
European immigrants adjusted to their new environment. Once they
learned English and found jobs in the general labor market, the
immigrants moved on to wherever those jobs were, eventually integrating into American society.

From the beginning, however, Chinatowns were different. After
the passage of the Chinese Labor Exclusion Act in 1882, which barred
Chinese immigration, those Chinese that were here were forced into
segregated neighborhoods by blatant discrimination and legislated
housing restrictions. The segregation was further maintained by the
exclusion of Chinese workers from jobs in the larger American labor
market, because for almost a century, whites refused to work alongside the Chinese.

[113]

When the new wave of immigrants from Asia and Latin America began to arrive after the passage of the new immigration law in 1965, new ethnic immigrant concentrations began to emerge again and old ones expanded. Because of the 1964 Civil Rights Act, these neighborhoods, such as Chinatowns across the nation, no longer owed their existence to legally sanctioned racial exclusion. One could therefore expect that they would finally play the role of transitional neighborhoods, like the old European ghettos.

But many of these new ethnic immigrant districts, like the Cuban community in Miami and Chinatowns across the country, have developed viable economic structures, providing new immigrants with jobs right in the midst of their ethnic immigrant communities without the need to ever learn English and move into the larger society in search of livelihood.

The rise of the garment industry in the immigrant Chinese community stimulated the growth of Chinese restaurants and other service trades, leading to a local economic boom and providing new job opportunities, which in turn attracted more Chinese immigrant workers and more Hong Kong investment. Chinatown's economy, with additional labor and capital, expanded both vertically and horizontally, adding more restaurants and service businesses while diversifying into wholesale food distribution, restaurant equipment, and the construction trades. This rapid growth also spawned new satellite Chinese communities in New York City's other boroughs, luring bilingual professionals to service the residents. By the early 1980s, Chinese ethnic enclaves had become thriving, predominantly working-class economic entities inhabited by non-English-speaking immigrants.

The original Chinatown in lower Manhattan and the newer enclave in Sunset Park in Brooklyn (established since the late 1980s) are very attractive to the arriving immigrants. They find plenty of jobs there as soon as they land in the United States without ever having to learn English. Chinese employers, on the other hand, can count on the service of this cheap labor supply, because these immigrant workers (without English and professional skills) have problems finding jobs in the open but competitive, low-wage labor markets outside of Chinatown. Studies have shown that Chinatown-type enclaves, like those in New York, San Francisco, and Los Angeles, have much lower unemployment rates than communities in the low-end, competitive, unskilled service type of work usually referred to as the "secondary labor market."[2] The new immigrant ethnic enclaves are different from present-day African American ghettos, which are characterized by their lack of capital resources and a high degree of unemployment. African American ghetto residents have no choice but to find jobs outside their communities in the mainstream American economy.

In contrast, new immigrant ethnic enclaves comprise both ethnic entrepreneurs and ethnic immigrant workers. Alejandro Portes and Robert Bach, authors of *Latin Journey: Cuban and Mexican Immigrants in the United States,* argue that the ethnic enclave economy established by Cuban refugees in Miami allows a significant portion of Cubans to escape the "dead end jobs" of the secondary labor market. Furthermore, the two authors assert that working in the enclave offers better pay, more promotional opportunities, and greater possibility of self-employment than working in the secondary labor market.[3]

In the same vein, UCLA sociologist Min Zhou came to believe that the Chinese ethnic networks within New York's Chinatown facilitate new immigrants' social mobility, eventually leading them into the American mainstream without losing their ethnic identity and solidarity.[4] To these scholars ethnic enclaves represent a real alternative to traditional American social mobility, which nearly always ends in complete assimilation.

Others disagree. Cornell sociologists Victor Nee and Jimmy Sanders have compared the wage levels of those working in the enclaves with those in the secondary labor market and concluded that, in fact, employment in the ethnic enclaves pays immigrant workers less than employment in the non-ethnic labor market.[5]

In his study of San Francisco, New York, and Los Angeles Chinatowns, Paul Ong of UCLA points out that focusing only on the lower unemployment rates in these enclaves, which many want to use as a symbol of the Chinese system of mutual help and ethnic solidarity, ignores the fact that the workers' chances of being laid off in Chinatown are much higher than for those working in the secondary labor market. Restaurant, garment, or construction jobs within the enclaves are susceptible to cyclical and seasonal fluctuations. Moreover, there is no indication that Chinese employers, because of ethnic sentiment, hold on to workers when there is a slowdown. And yet, according to Ong, despite the low wages, job instability, and limited returns, Chinese workers do not become "discouraged workers." To survive, they have no choice but to stay in the labor market until other jobs become available.[6] Staying in the labor market usually means having to accept ever lower wages.

Although it is easy for a new immigrant to settle within the Chinese enclave initially, it may not be the best option in the long run. Once settled there, new immigrants are not likely to learn English, since there is no such need for it in the daily activities and social interactions in the enclave. This is not to say that the immigrants lack desire to learn the language. Several different versions of "English Made Easy" audiocassette tapes and bilingual microcomputers are available in Chinese bookstores. Thousands of Chinese immigrants attend dozens of weekly English language classes offered by nonprofit groups such as unions, churches, and social service organizations. But spending two hours in a language class on Sunday, without a chance to converse and practice until a week later, produces meager results.

It is common to meet Chinatown residents who, having lived in the United States for more than twenty-five years, are not able to communicate in simple English. This, in addition to the fact that there are few jobs outside the enclave, closes out the option for Chinese immigrants to break out of the ethnic immigrant community, where they remain trapped and vulnerable to the power of Chinese employers. The very existence of ethnic enclaves like Chinatown inhibits new immigrants' attempts to look for other options. The options for Fuzhounese illegals outside of the Chinese environment are even more limited. This suits the Chinese employers just fine. In fact, they try to promote the ideology of ethnic solidarity to reinforce Chinese dependency on the ethnic enclaves.

WE ARE ALL CHINESE

From the moment of their arrival, Chinese immigrants rely on ethnic networks to survive. The newcomers rely on their relatives or friends to get them jobs and teach them how to do the work. With everyone working twelve hours a day for so little, no one except a close friend or a relative would take time to teach a newcomer how to sew, how to set tables, or how to drive nails.

The owners prefer not to get involved in the training process. They like the idea of their longtime employees recruiting others through their ethnic and kinship networks—it helps to screen out undesirable workers. Finding jobs through their friends' recommendations immediately forces newcomers into a system of social obligations. The friend performs a *ren-qing* (personal favor) by means of *guanxi* (connections) to get the newcomer a job. The newcomer then owes a *ren-qing* to the employer for giving him a job that could have gone to any one of a number of applicants. Moreover, the employer is credited for his good-heartedness in wanting to help a fellow Chinese and a fellow villager by taking the risk of hiring an illegal.

The newcomer is expected to return these favors when he is in the position to do so—to begin with, by being a compliant, hard worker. Respectful and loyal behavior ensures special consideration when it comes to individual job assignment, workload, wages, and benefits. Thus traditional Chinese regard for *ren-qing* transforms a typical labor–capital class relationship into an association based on personal favor and obligation.

The employers certainly play up the ethnic factor to inspire worker loyalty. They try to create a work environment that is culturally familiar by disregarding rigid American rules. Mothers, for instance, are allowed to leave work at four in the afternoon to pick up their children at school and bring them back to the factory. If the family is in financial distress, which all debt-paying illegals are, the owners "help out" by hiring their children or allowing them to bring consignments home, even though such practices violate U.S. labor laws. Lonely old ladies with nothing to do are allowed to work as thread cutters on completed garments, older men to wash dishes for a few dollars so they can feel useful and have others to gossip with during the day.

The rules on the shop floor are also casual. Working on piece rate, seamstresses are paid by the work completed. In order to make money, they turn out to be their own disciplinarians. If workers do not want to have the legally mandated half-hour lunch break, they can eat right at the machines. The owners usually set up a makeshift kitchen on the shop floor where the workers can heat their lunch boxes, and provide a pot of hot rice for everyone, free. Almost all workplaces, including restaurants, reserve a small corner for a shrine, regularly attended with fresh fruit and burning incense. On Chinese Lunar New Year workers get two days off, the longest holiday of the year. But even then they are expected to show up on the second day of the New Year at least for part of the day, to wish the employers happy New Year and to receive a red envelope with a small bonus— five dollars, usually. Then the firecrackers are set off and tangerines placed on the sewing machines and in all strategic locations to ward off bad spirits, so they would always have work and not get injured on the job. During the Moon Festival, every employee is given a couple of moon cakes to take home.

In addition, most employees see being paid in cash as a major benefit. It saves them from paying taxes and the impossible task of filing for returns if they are legal—illegals, of course, try to avoid all government scrutiny. The employers are quite flexible. They are willing to "cook the books" for those who work in union shops and need to show a minimum income of $7,000 a year to be eligible for union health insurance, or for those not in union shops but interested in receiving public assistance, such as food stamps, Medicaid, public housing, or even welfare, which requires them to have a total family income below the poverty line. The owners can even be accommodating enough to "sell" signed checks (at a percentage cost) for that purpose. Thus both labor and capital participate in Chinatown's underground economy by sharing a dirty secret.

Cash payment also demonstrates the leverage the employers have over the employees. If a legal immigrant wants to apply for a family member to come to this country, she has to show that a) employment is available upon the relative's arrival; b) the person applying has a certain annual income. In order to fulfill both requirements the applicant has to turn to her employer to notarize a document stating that her boss will provide the newcomer with a job and another stating that the applicant's annual income is above the minimum required, and then work out a tax arrangement with the employer to avoid problems with the INS. Illegals sponsoring relatives to come here are even more dependent on the good graces of the employers.

Why would an employer provide all this service? Because paying employees in cash results in a lower tax responsibility for him, and by reporting such low wages for his employees, the employer can claim that most of his workers are part-time, relieving him of his responsibility for making workers' compensation and other forms of insurance payments that are the normal obligations of American employers.

Most of all, employers paying workers in cash get a 5 percent "kick-back" ostensibly for the purpose of paying taxes, from the employees' total gross income. They deduct even more from illegals. Even though it is heartbreaking to see this money going to the bosses, they have to agree to it. If they don't like it, they can always look for another job—although wherever they might turn in Chinatown, they would most likely be confronted with the same practice. In a way, the Chinese employers have constructed the only "plantation" for unskilled Chinese new immigrants to work in.

To preempt hostile attitudes, employers appeal to the new immigrants' aspirations to ownership. They like to project themselves as new immigrants as well—they too were workers once, and had to work hard to come to where they are now. They like to stress that "we are all Chinese," desiring the same thing—ownership and prosperity. In the meantime, immigrant employees are lectured regularly that they should save every cent they make and avoid wasting money on smoking, drinking, gambling, and philandering.

Newcomers are made to think that working hard for someone else is just the starting point. Being a good worker teaches them the discipline and endurance that are necessary for entrepreneurship. They should focus solely on their work and not be distracted, for America is a very different country from China—there are a lot of bad people here. If one is *du-si* (nosy), one gets into trouble. The newcomers are warned not to trust anyone. Even when someone offers you a bundle of money, don't accept it, because it may be drug money being offered to get you arrested. If someone falls on the street, walk right on, for if you help and something happens, the Americans will turn around and sue you. Most of all, do not get involved in any form of politics—the consequences could be worse than in China.

YOU CAN'T TRUST THE "FOREIGNERS"
Even the immigrants who are unhappy working for Chinese employers in Chinatown have a difficult time imagining themselves working for "Americans," with whom they are not able to communicate even on the most basic matters. The language problem breeds an overwhelming sense of isolation and vulnerability. Garment ladies are resigned to work for a few dollars less per hour in Chinatown just so they do not have to contemplate the scary thought of traveling on

subways to "strange places" and working for "strange people." For this very reason, the Chinatown along Eighth Avenue in Sunset Park in Brooklyn boomed only after regular Chinese-run minibus services to and from Manhattan's Chinatown became available. For $1.75, one can be picked up anywhere between Fortieth and Seventieth Streets along Eighth Avenue in Brooklyn and be dropped off on any street corner in Manhattan's Chinatown. Consequently, many Chinese immigrants don't even have basic public spacial contact with "Americans"—let alone a clear understanding of American society. Ah Chong, an illegal alien from Fuzhou who had been here more than three years, confided that she had yet to befriend an "American," to visit a movie theater, or to travel anywhere outside of Brooklyn, where she lives and works—not even to the Empire State Building, Rockefeller Center, or the Statue of Liberty. Her isolation is such that in conversations she refers to native-born Americans as *lao wai*— "foreigners."

Because of this isolation, the Chinese employers are able to impart to their workers the image of a hostile and racist American society, which helps to construct a sense of "ethnic solidarity." The new immigrants are told that Americans are prejudiced and look down on the Chinese. This is not too difficult for the Chinese to accept, considering the long history of Western colonialism in China. Chinese employers explain that *Lao-fan* (barbarian) manufacturers offer the Chinese contractors such low prices for their contracts that nobody can make a living from them. Again, considering the way American manufacturers have been squeezing small suppliers, this putative discrimination is credible. Thus Chinese contractors blame "American" manufacturers as the source of all their problems, including why they cannot pay the workers decent wages, why they operate in dilapidated buildings, why they don't have the money to replace the old and dangerous machines, and why there is no proper ventilation and fire protection in the factories.

Chinese workers are instructed not to fight Chinese owners, but to appreciate that they are all victims of an unjust, racist system. But while they depict themselves as the victims, the contractors don't propose fighting the manufacturers. Their solution for the workers is to work harder to overcome all obstacles and show that Chinese immigrants can make it no matter what, consciously promoting the racial stereotype that Chinese, and particularly the Fuzhounese, are capable of unremitting toil, unlike the blacks or even the whites, who are soft and enjoy too much of the good life.

This sense of a hostile external environment is further strengthened by the employers' efforts to portray all outside intervening forces as harmful to Chinese interests. To depict trade unions as indifferent outside organizations interested only in collecting dues is an impression, again, not too difficult to convey. Almost 90 percent of the seamstresses working in the lower Manhattan Chinatown are members of Local 23–25 of UNITE, previously the International Ladies Garment Workers Union (ILGWU). And as union members their negotiated legal union minimum wage is supposed to be from $6 to $9.45 an hour (depending on the job title). Still, contractors take advantage of variations in clothing design to quote piece rates arbitrarily, so that they can vary even from one person to another working on the same consignment. The average hourly rates do not come near the federal minimum wage, let alone the union minimum.

In the early 1980s, Chinese workers regularly challenged and forced management to honor their piece rates according to the actual work involved. They would even stage sitdown strikes, until prices were adjusted. For the past ten years, however, in fear of driving the contractors to close their shops, the union has been reluctant to side with the workers in such disputes, and the workers have given up. As a result, a union contract is one thing, union wages another. Moreover, a 1992 internal survey conducted by the union's Sunset Park Garment Worker's Center revealed that non-union workers were better paid in some cases than ILGWU union members. The average gross non-union wage in 1992 was $4.97, while the average union wage was $3.73—at a time when the federal minimum was $4.25.[7] Both illegal and legal workers who are interested in making more money and are not afraid of health problems simply work in non-union shops.

Management plays the race card in dealing with government officials as well. They are able to convince the workers that Chinese, being a minority group, have great disadvantages in competing with American mainstream businesses. That's why they have to ignore American laws; otherwise, they will not survive. Chinese are told that American labor enforcement is nothing but a white racist plot to destroy Chinese small businesses and to take jobs away from Chinese workers.

In August 1996, soon after the intense media coverage of Kathie Lee Gifford's scandal on her sponsorship of a line of Wal-Mart clothing that was being made by children in abysmal sweatshops in Honduras and in the heart of Manhattan, Brooklyn District Attorney Charles Hynes conducted his own raids on Chinese sweatshops in Sunset Park in coordination with the New York State Labor Department, the New York State Department of Finance, and the New York City Fire Department. Dozens of officers, wearing bulletproof vests and armed with semi-automatic weapons, smashed into the sweatshops, ordering everyone to freeze, place their hands on the table, and keep silent.

In the meantime, government agents broke into employers' offices, turning over files and searching for incriminating documents. Several owners were arrested and handcuffed on charges of violating minimum wage laws, flouting the tax code, and breaking factory safety and fire regulations. The workers were permitted to leave the factories only after they were questioned, photographed, and their files reviewed.

The D.A.'s action was meant to enforce labor standards, but the high-handedness of the operation baffled and terrorized the workers. One illegal worker stated in written testimony that the police never explained that the raids were meant to protect the workers' interests by arresting employers who violate the law. None of the workers saw the raid in that light. The D.A.'s sudden interest in sweatshops, which had long existed in Brooklyn, gave credence to accusations that the raids were politically motivated.

The Chinese employers responded with defiance. While none contested government charges that they had violated the minimum wage and had operated their businesses under sweatshop conditions, they accused the D.A.'s office of racism for targeting only Chinese establishments. After the raids, several employers claimed that they were on the verge of closing down and could no longer pay their workers on time. They also spread the rumor that the real reason for the raids was to get information to arrest illegals.

The owners organized a counterattack a week later, in the form of a demonstration by 1,500 Chinese workers who were forced to march down Eighth Avenue, in the heart of Brooklyn's Chinatown, in order "to keep their jobs." The aim was to show the D.A.'s office that all Chinese, regardless of class, objected to police raids. The workers had banners at the rally that read "Garment Factory Is the Heart of Chinatown's Economy," "Closing of Factories Will Lead to Workers' Unemployment," "Against Arbitrary Arrest," and "We Need Our Jobs."

The owners, it seems, cleverly turned the clumsy handling of the raids to rally workers to their side. They closed the factories for a couple of hours that day and paid the workers three dollars each to show up at the rally. They orchestrated the whole event and even led the chants. The workers had no choice—they were afraid of being fired—and had to march. Unfortunately, the uninformed outsiders, unaware of such details, were led to believe that Chinese workers really did not mind working under sweatshop conditions and that the rally was a manifestation of Chinese ethnic solidarity.

THE EMPLOYERS' ORGANIZATIONAL POWER

In addition to drawing successfully an ethnic line that keeps their workers from all external contacts, Chinatown employers also dominate all social organizations within the Chinese community. When Chinese in the United States were forced into segregated communities in the 1880s, the political structure that emerged as the self-policing force of these communities was transplanted from the rural regions of China. In fact, it closely followed the pattern of local, unofficial civic organization that sprang up during the Q'ing Dynasty. Because Chinese communities in the United States remained in relative isolation until the 1960s, the imported structure had a long time to evolve and solidify. It is still operative today, despite the profound external changes of recent years.

The basic unit of this traditional rural structure was the clan. Early Chinese immigrants, the majority of whom were male, tended to live communally, sharing apartments to save money. This arrangement evolved into a formal collective called a *fong*, which literally means a "room." Members of a *fong* developed a close relationship and great loyalty to one another.

Several *fongs* made up of people from the same village formed a village association; several *fongs* composed of people of the same surname formed family or surname associations. A village association might raise funds for famine relief or for the building of schools and hospitals in the home village. But the associations also carried out joint functions and lent support to each other. They could accomplish more through collective action, they found, so then even larger organizations were created—a *huiguan* (a meeting hall) composed of several family and village associations grouped together. While the *huiguan* continued to carry out mutual aid and charity functions, they were more commercially oriented. They arbitrated disputes among members and served as credit and employment agencies. They ensured that members met their obligations in business transactions with others.

The associations were originally formed to defend their members against a hostile larger society and to provide order within the community. But an internal hierarchy soon developed: the members who owned shops and restaurants commanded the respect of other members, who depended on them for jobs. Those who received jobs and favors willingly became followers, forming patron–client relationships. The patrons thus became association leaders in addition to owning businesses. These association big shots, or *kiu ling*, were really the leaders of Chinese overseas communities, because as the most active and generous members of their associations, they pledged the most during community fund-raising drives. The resulting hierarchy that developed within the Chinese community was based entirely on wealth. Wealthy Chinatown shopowners and merchants used the associations to maintain social and political control of the community.

Each association was, in principle, independent, and serious disputes, particularly among the large associations, could result in continuous, unresolved fights. In order to avoid such conflicts, most Chinatowns in the United States established umbrella organizations like the Chinese Consolidated Benevolent Association (CCBA) in New York. The elite was also able to purchase the services of the *tongs*, secret fraternal organizations known for their criminal ties and violence, to enforce compliance.

Today, the class nature of Chinatown's political structure remains basically unchanged. Local power is still concentrated in the hands of factory owners, merchants, and landlords, who are able to impose their personal interests through their official positions in the associations. When association leaders gather in the CCBA, they comprise an informal government, representing the interests of the Chinatown elite. The community may be divided vertically along lines of kinship, village ties, trade, and fraternities, but the political structure does not cut across class lines.

Of the two hundred or so listed family, clan, surname, village, county, *tong*, and social welfare organizations in Chinatown, practically none represents the interests of the working people. Without an effective challenge from other forms of local association, the owners are able to set rules, define "acceptable behavior," and impose sanctions against violators, using tactics including blacklisting, public humiliation, ostracism, and the threat of physical violence.

Monopolizing the political, economic, and social structure of

Chinatown, the merchant elite are recognized as "community leaders" by outsiders as well. So whenever the mayor's office, federal officials, or law enforcement authorities want to reach out to the Chinese community, they address it through the Chinatown elite. The elite's hegemonic power is therefore complete.

THE FUZHOUNESE ELITE

The Fuzhounese are relatively new and marginal within the Chinatown power structure, but their local system operates the same way. Beyond family and kinship ties there are village and county organizations, as well as a number of province-wide Fujian associations. They are all dominated by the already established, successful early Fuzhounese immigrants. When wide public attention focused on the Fuzhounese community because of human smuggling, indentured servitude, kidnapping, and other crimes perpetrated by its members, its leaders accused the media of picking on the negative aspect of the community on account of "a few bad apples—people who do not like to work hard for a living." The leaders would prefer that the media focus on the community's success stories, be it in business or academia, where their children blaze a path of scholarship in Ivy League universities.

Actually, a number of Fujianese association leaders have been implicated in human smuggling. As early as 1990, federal authorities placed the Fukien-American Association under surveillance and detected that its members were using its office to collect smuggling debts. In one case a threatened relative was told to deliver a ransom of $50,000 to the association's headquarters at 125 East Broadway.[8] Yick Tak Cheung, an officer of the association, was convicted and imprisoned for nine months on charges of trying to smuggle four illegal Fuzhounese from Canada by raft across the Niagara River. The raft capsized, and three of his clients drowned. Cheung's wife is the famous Cheng Chui Ping, known as "Big Sister Ping" to her admirers and as the "Smuggling Queen" to law enforcement.[9] Ping, as a smuggler, over the years has emptied out the population of several villages around Fuzhion to the United States. and has made a fortune.

Still, Fukien-American Association officials deny their connections with human smuggling. At a 1993 news conference in Chinatown, the president of the association, Alan Lau, who was branded by the media as the "commander-in-chief of illegal smuggling," insisted that his is an open organization, that anyone can join, and it has no control over the activities of its members.[10]

It is true that Fujianese associations are voluntary organizations. American law enforcement and media have the tendency of casually classifying certain ethnic groups as "criminal" for easy identification, in part because of the American law enforcement's successful experience in dealing with the Italian Mafia. "In the past, whenever law enforcement thought organized crime, it thought Mafia," one FBI official admits. "That meant twenty-four families: each has a boss, and an underboss, etc., and among the families there's a commission. Now they look at the Chinese and they think of the triads . . . and if it's triads they think the Chinese too have an organizational chart . . . Chinese too have ten to twenty families. So let's identify them, bust them, and move on to the next case."[11]

But the Chinese human smuggling network is not based in any existing organizations, nor is it structured within Chinese triads. They are too sophisticated to operate from these highly visible organizations, thereby attracting unwanted attention and becoming an easy target for law enforcement. Their structure is much more operationally based. Individuals, who may be members of different organizations, come together only to work on an ad hoc basis.

It is, therefore, much more correct to say that the Fuzhounese associations in the United States are not directly sponsoring human smuggling, though individuals within these associations are involved. They are also using these associations as cover for their activities. Nevertheless, the smuggling business constitutes such an important part of the economy of the Fuzhounese community that leaders of Fuzhounese associations, who are the economic elite, cannot help but be drawn into that industry. They are working with the smugglers, knowingly or unknowingly, when they pay to sponsor their relatives to immigrate to the United States, when their travel agencies profit by assisting in the transport of illegals, when businesses acting as loan sharks provide credit to helpless victims so the snakeheads can collect, and particularly when they pay snakeheads to "sponsor" illegals to work in their businesses. Yet, they are very sensitive to public criticism of their roles. When a few within the community dared to criticize the Fuzhounese association leadership for not distancing itself from the smuggling business, they were threatened and silenced.[12]

The association leaders' public position is not at all critical of the human smuggling business. A senior member of one of the Fuzhounese associations once told me, "You should not look down on the snakeheads; they are, after all, providing a useful service. Many of them are helping their suffering countrymen to get out of China. Illegals appreciate their help. But it's like any businesses; some are good and some are bad." To describe an industry that reaps huge profits by forcing thousands of people into a hellish existence as a normal business is preposterous. Unless, of course, you are so compromised by your own dealing with the snakeheads that you no longer see clearly or care about what is happening to your own people.

The Fujianese associations' various annual banquets, such as the celebration of the Lunar New Year, are well attended by all the "important" Fuzhounese: the village elders, association officials, restaurant owners, store owners, travel agency operators, suspected snakeheads, and money launderers. On happy occasions like these, they project an image of ethnic unity and shared prosperity. The next day's Chinese newspaper will carry pictures of their smiling faces as they stand next to mainland Chinese consulate officials and American politicians who have accepted their contributions. This type of image sends a clear message about political power and dominance in the Chinese American community.

The Fuzhounese have a reputation among other Chinese for being fond of socializing, especially for inviting friends to expensive banquets at the slightest pretext: birthdays, anniversaries of all types, baby "coming out parties" (when the baby is one month old) and weddings. The host carefully plans where to hold the party, what price to pay for the banquet, how many tables to reserve, whom to invite, and where and next to whom each guest must sit—strictly conforming to the social and political hierarchy in the community. A community leader is expected to offer the expensive shark-fin soup as the main course at his banquet.

Such banquets, with brandy and soft drinks included in the price, run close to $500 per table. Normal banquets of this type should set at least ten tables—any fewer would be seen as cheap or "lacking of friends." "Honored guests" grace the head table, reflecting the host's ability to reach high. Other guests feel honored to be invited. Such occasions give them an opportunity to express their appreciation for the help they received from the host, by bringing along not only the standard $50 cash per person in a red envelope—the customary "share" for the cost of the banquet—but also expensive gifts, such as custom-made glass-encased gold-plated plaques bearing the host's name and auguries appropriate for the occasion. The gifts are displayed during the party. Their quantity and quality reveals the host's standing in the community.

A typical worker is not likely ever to have to endure such expenses, but there are always a few ambitious ones, interested in upward mobility, who borrow money to throw expensive parties for their peers, and much more importantly, for the "honored guests" to repay the *ren-qing* debts they owe. The public display of deference for the "honored guests"—usually employers, supervisors, and sponsors—shows the host's submission to their authority. The honored will not forget to take good care of the host in the future.

These rituals, called *li* in Chinese, are a public manifestation of the ties and mutual dependency of community members, but they also reinforce unequal individual status within the community. The proper observance of *li* in the Confucian tradition is believed to ensure an orderly and harmonious community. The practice of *li* in Chinatown obliterates the concept of a class society. The bosses see to it that gift- and banquet-givers get preferential treatment in the workplace. Even the chief of the dim sum pushcart ladies crew at a major Chinatown restaurant has seen to it that those who attended her daughter's wedding banquet and presented gifts were rewarded with better dim sum delivery routes and lighter workloads.

Despite their claims, Fuzhounese associations hardly deal with problems that affect the average Fuzhounese. Several Fuzhounese take-out restaurant owners claim they had no mediating organization to turn to in their disputes with fellow Fuzhounese who opened competing copycat restaurants right cross the street from their locations. One might expect organizations living by the motto of ethnic solidarity to intervene. But they don't. In the meantime, the original owner turned to Chinatown youth gangs for help. The copycat hired another gang to retaliate. The result was total anarchy.

When Fuzhounese businesses are attacked in African American ghettos, they have no idea whom to turn to for representation in the dominant community. A Chinatown church activist wishes that the Fuzhounese were more united. "We need to learn from the Koreans. They have strong organizations to represent them and fight for them," he says, unabashed in his admiration. "Koreans, instead of complaining that they have been treated unfairly, reach out to the black community by doing things like awarding ghetto children with scholarships. We Fuzhounese need to learn from the Koreans to know how to be part of the American society." Most people would not think of using Koreans as a model for inter-racial relations, but this comment points to the extent of Fuzhounese marginalization.

The final indicator of the Fuzhounese associations' failure to represent their community is the close relationship between the Fuzhounese associations and the mainland Chinese government. Ever since the founding of the People's Republic of China in 1949, New York's Chinatown community had been under the political dominance of those who supported the Republic of China in Taiwan. For forty-five years, the CCBA, the unofficial Chinatown "City Hall," blocked any public expression of support for the PRC. Double Ten (October Ten), the national day in Taiwan, was the only national holiday allowed to be celebrated. Very few organizations were able to challenge this political orientation.

In mid-1980s, a pro-mainland United Chinese Association of New York was formed, first by several small assorted associations. By the 1990s, it had a membership of fifty-seven organizations but over forty of them are Fuzhounese family, county, village, and even high school associations. The Federation has strong ties with PRC Consulate General's office in New York. Fuzhounese leaders are regularly invited to China during important national celebrations and are received as honored *kiu ling*—"overseas Chinese leaders"—by the Chinese government. In the meantime, the Federation is forever arranging banquets for visiting PRC dignitaries and receptions for incoming or outgoing consulate officials.

In 1995, a public celebration of the PRC national day, which falls on October 1, was held for the first time in New York's Chinatown. And around July 1, 1997, the date of Hong Kong's reversion to mainland China, the Federation has planned a major demonstration to celebrate the event in midtown Manhattan. These activities by the Fuzhounese elite are quite ironic, since thousands of Fuzhounese risk their lives and pay smugglers $30,000 just to leave mainland China. One wouldn't think them likely to venerate the government they fled. Certainly, many illegals hold no affection for Chinese officials, considering how the Chinese Consulate General's Office in New York had gouged them $2,000 each for a phony "replacement" passport (as mentioned earlier in chapter 2).

This overt pro-mainland fever represents the interests of the Fuzhounese elite, which wants to use its close relationship with PRC to gain "legitimacy" within the larger Chinese community. It is equally interested in maintaining an excellent relationship with the Chinese government for trade and business purposes. The smugglers, too, need a good relationship with Chinese officials to protect their activities and assets back home.

CONTROL OVER FREEDOM OF EXPRESSION

The power of the Chinatown elite is further enhanced by their domination of the Chinese-language press. Chinese immigrants are dependent on Chinese-language newspapers to inform them about the world around them. But four out of five local papers are extensions of large Chinese news operations originating from Hong Kong, Taiwan, or mainland China. The main coverage of these papers is simply reproduction of news already in their Asian editions. None of them expend much cost on local news reporting, nor do they need to in order to attract more readership. On the whole, none of them is interested in becoming involved in community controversies that would risk their relationship with the Chinese local establishment. After all, these papers still need advertising revenue from local businesses. Their pro-business and pro-establishment slant is, therefore, not surprising.

Chinese reporters are regularly warned not to cover "unfavorable information regarding the Chinese community." When a Chinese-newspaper reporter translated a court indictment against a *tong* leader that had been printed in *The New York Times,* the *tong* leader himself called the Chinese-language paper two days later to complain and threaten retaliation. The editor of the paper ordered the reporter to apologize to the *tong* leader in person or be fired. I once wrote an article for the *Village Voice* about organized crime in Chinatown. Many Chinese-language reporters called to compliment me on it, but a reporter of a pro-mainland Chinese-language paper explained that she could not translate the article because, "If I put that in, my editor would simply take it out, and if not, someone will come to complain. Then I'll be the one losing my job."

The community elite is able to regularly influence local news coverage, blacking out major opposition developments. On January 23, 1997, New York State Attorney General Dennis Vacco announced that, after months of investigation, his office had filed a lawsuit against Jing Fong's management for allegedly cheating fifty-eight employees of over $1.5 million in tips and wages and firing the waiter who blew the whistle on the scam. Mr. Vacco stated in a news conference, "We are dealing with immigrants who have come to this great country for a chance to live the American dream, but instead are exploited by individuals who want to line their own pockets."[12] Of course, the accusations against Jing Fong can be applied to a lot of businesses in the community, so for damage control the business community quickly rallied to work on Chinese reporters. Even after Attorney General Vacco provided the press with hundreds of pages of written testimony taken from workers at Jing Fong Restaurant against the employers, the Chinese press still carried only management's side of the story, accusing the attorney general of pandering to "racial politics" by attacking the Chinese community in order to gain voter appeal during an election year.[14]

Ying Chan, a respected *New York Daily News* reporter who had worked as editor for several major Chinese-language papers, is one of the very few journalists to cover the Fuzhounese smuggling problem consistently, exposing the operations in great detail and naming the chief Chinatown offenders involved with the smuggling networks. Her daring coverage has earned her the prestigious national George Polk Award for investigative reporting.

At the time of the award, Ying Chan's friends decided to organize a banquet in her honor, but she was warned by a "reliable" informant from the Fuzhounese community that she should not have the party in Chinatown because Big Sister Ping was angry with her, and someone had put out a $50,000 contract on her head. Chan reported the threat to the police. The *New York Daily News* provided her with a twenty-four-hour bodyguard for two weeks. The fact that the smuggling network did not shy from intimidating a national English-language newspaper reporter is a measure of its power and arrogance.

With the silencing of labor, outsiders have no idea what is going on nor does it really matter. For instance, even with the labor vio-

lations at the Jing Fong Restaurant, in 1995, Governor Pataki gave
Mr. Chung Ko Cheng, one of the Jing Fong Restaurant owners, the
Asian-American Heritage Award.

NEW AMERICAN VALUES

The indifference of American society to problems within the Chinese
community is not all due to ignorance, but rather a result of the
dominant neoconservative ideology making us not interested in seeing these conditions as problems. Faced with the economic and social
problems of the country today, many Americans have identified the
lack of a work ethic and the failure of family values as the central
causes of the national malaise. They have turned with envy to the
immigrants' attitude toward hard work, disciplined reliance on their
own family and ethnic resources, and nondependency on public
assistance. The dynamic growth of ethnic Chinese immigrant enclaves seems an ideal alternative to the poverty and deprivation of
African American ghettos.

Inevitably, the issue of immigrants and ethnic enclaves has turned
ideological. Hardworking Chinese entrepreneurship is now being
praised not just as an immigrant phenomenon but as a Chinese
cultural phenomenon. As American corporations have spread glo-
bally, they have encountered Chinese overseas capital playing a dominant role in many of the Pacific Rim countries. Their success is
studied and marveled at. Herman Kahn, the futurologist and founder
of the Hudson Institute, observed as early as 1979 that neo-
Confucian societies create "dedicated, motivated, responsible, and
educated individuals and the enhanced sense of commitment, organizational identity, and loyalty to various institutions," and that "societies based upon the Confucian ethic may in many ways be superior
to the west in the pursuit of industrialization, affluence, and modernization." Joel Kotkin, author of *Tribes: How Race, Religion and
Identity Determine Success in the New Global Economy,* builds up
traditional Chinese family, clan, and kinship networks into the idea
of "networks based on Confucian principles," which he calls "global

tribes held together by group feelings"—a superior form of economic entity when it comes to modern global competition.

Ironically, only twenty-five years ago the American business community looked to the Chinese Confucian heritage as the very cause for its economic "backwardness." Every modern Chinese leader of this century, including Dr. Sun Yat-sen and Chairman Mao, saw Confucian ideology as the obstacle to China's modernization. Now all of a sudden Confucianism, which stresses discipline and order, is given as the very reason for Asia's economic success.

One of Confucianism's top new advocates is Singapore's statesman Lee Kuan Yew—a self-proclaimed citizen of the world. While he is proud of his gentleman's education at Oxford, he practices authoritarianism at home, claiming that "democracy is not conducive to rapid growth." He likes to point out that the Philippines is democratic but its economy never got off the ground simply "because democracy is too chaotic." Even China's communist leaders have turned neo-Confucian. During a 1989 conference on Confucianism, China's President Jiang Zemin pleaded with the overseas Chinese to show support for China's precious cultural heritage and public interest in the name of "Confucianism's far-reaching influence upon the common culture and psychology of the Chinese nation," which stipulates that "loyalty is superior to profit."

While marveling at the new economic successes of East Asian countries, we have ignored the social and political cost borne by their citizens in the name of development. The well-publicized Chinese government's market reforms have practically eliminated all labor laws, labor benefits, and protections. In the "free enterprise zones" workers live virtually on the factory floor, laboring fourteen hours a day for a mere two dollars—that is, about 20 cents an hour.

It is one thing to want to find ways to reform the American economy. It is another to subscribe to an "ethnic ethics myth" as a miracle cure. Most of all, this form of ethnic chauvinism ignores the conditions of class exploitation suffered by the Chinese immigrants at the hands of their co-ethnic employers. Certainly, lowering our labor standards and compromising our democratic principles in exchange for discipline and productivity—as we are today in our nation's ethnic enclaves—is not a responsible solution to our national crisis, and his inevitable diabolic consequences.

CHAPTER 6

The Exclusion of Chinese Labor

THE CURRENT PREDICAMENT OF CHINESE IMMIGRANTS WORKING FOR ethnic employers in the isolated ethnic labor market is not solely a product of the present economic restructuring that favors small, decentralized subcontractors. It is a condition born of a long history. For over a century, one of the dominant forces that kept the Chinese out of the open American labor market was racial hostility.

It is true that all new immigrant groups have confronted hostile responses from the groups that arrived earlier, because the newcomers are always seen as competitors for jobs. However, given time and particularly during periods of economic expansion, opposition to the new groups wanes. They will integrate into the American labor force, become part of the American working class, and eventually even benefit from the common struggles as part of the American labor movement. This, however, is a scenario applicable mainly to ethnic whites.

It was the powerful American labor movement in the first half of this century that brought about steady improvement in American workers' economic conditions, though many of them were new immigrants from Europe. The gains they won were eventually institutionalized in the New Deal laws of the 1930s: the right to form a union, the right of collective bargaining (in the National Labor Relations Act and the Wagner Act), and the right to enjoy the benefits of a social safety net in times of unemployment and retirement (in the Social Security Act).

After World War II a number of federal government programs were instituted that were designed to assist demobilized GIs and young American families. Almost eight million GIs took advantage of their educational benefits under the GI Bill to attain college educations. The Federal Housing Administration funded the massive construction of low-income housing. And the Veterans Administration provided young GIs with low-interest mortgage loans to purchase homes.[1] By the 1960s, with the American workers' collective bargaining power at its peak just as America's post–World War II economic prosperity was at an all-time high, a significant portion of American workers achieved middle-class status. But these advances largely benefited the white working class. Those working in the primary labor sector, mainly European immigrants and their offspring, benefited the most.

Colored minorities were at first not even allowed employment in the open labor market. Blacks, for example, were enslaved on plantations. Only half a century after the Civil War were blacks recruited into America's industrial labor force and even then they were relegated to the low end of the secondary labor market suffering from lower wages, high unemployment, limited mobility, and exclusion from organized labor. While the post–World War II federal government instituted programs to help ethnic whites, it did its best to shut and double-seal the postwar window of opportunity in African Americans' faces.[2] To this day, they have not experienced the general upward mobility of ethnic white workers.

The Chinese did not fare much better, despite being one of the earliest immigrant groups to arrive in the United States. The first wave arrived on the West Coast as early as the late 1840s, and they were recruited to work as laborers in the mines during the gold rush. Their arrival coincided with the so-called "Old Immigration" from Europe (as contrast to the "New Immigrants" who were primarily Italians, Poles, Greeks, Jews, and others from Eastern and Southern Europe who began to arrive around the 1890s), consisting of mainly Irish fleeing starvation induced by British colonialism, the commercialization of agriculture, and the Potato Famine, as well as German democrats fleeing the failed Revolution of 1848, who faced a bleak future in the period of repression that followed the collapse of the constitutional and nationalist movements in Europe.

The Irish immigrants, arriving poor and Catholic, brought the wrath of many native-born Americans in the form of the mid-nineteenth-century "Know-Nothings." They were mistreated and scorned as "white Negroes." The Irish were not only exploited as laborers, they were also left to compete for jobs and pitted against workers of other races, including African Americans and Chinese.

But, unlike the Chinese, the Irish were in fact "white," eligible to become naturalized citizens; unlike African Americans, they were never slaves or ex-slaves. They had learned to distinguish themselves in racial struggles and to establish their claim as "whites." They did this by taking up arms for the white Republic against the blacks in the Philadelphia race riots and the New York draft riots of 1863. They also took part in the anti-Chinese movement in California. In the 1870s, Irish demagogue Dennis Kearney mobilized his California Workingmen's Party to rid the country of "cheap Chinese labor" with the rallying cry, "The Chinese Must Go!" An Irish weekly declared in 1870 that the Chinese subverted Christianity, committed crimes and were immoral, and such "degraded races" as "Niggers and Chinamen" were "incapable" of understanding the democratic principles for which the Irish had continually fought.[3]

The Irish, in the meantime, were able to integrate themselves into the American political process through their participation in the Democratic Party. Before the Civil War, the party courted them to support its pro-slavery cause. In exchange, the party adopted a strong anti-nativist position. The hope was that it could counterbalance the numerical advantage of the Northern free states and maintain slavery by the assimilation of the Irish into the white race. In the end, many of the Irish fought in the Union Army, but the tactic worked out very well nonetheless for the Irish themselves: they have since developed solid ties with the Democratic Party that continue to this day. As voters, they consciously cultivated and promoted Irish "Green Power." Through their ethnic voting blocs they were able to establish networks of patronage and build a Democratic Party machine in major Northern cities that was responsive to their needs. By 1890, the Democratic Party organizations in New York, Boston, Chicago, and San Francisco functioned like Irish "Robin Hoods," taking taxes from the Yankee middle class and giving revenues to the Irish through public payrolls. By 1900, the Irish accounted for 30 percent of the municipal employees in these cities.[4]

Far from achieving similar gains in the same course of time, the Chinese could not even become U.S. citizens according to the Nationality Act of 1790 because they were not "free white persons." And when the 1882 Chinese Exclusion Act was passed, it specifically barred Chinese from becoming naturalized. This climate of exclusion shaped the political and economic makeup of the Chinese American community ever since.

EARLY CHINESE IMMIGRANT LABOR

When the Chinese came to America in the late 1840s to work in California's gold mines, they were seen as cheap replacements for black laborers, unavailable at the time because of the heated national debate over slavery. The Chinese worked in groups segregated from white American workers, under the control of co-ethnic labor contractors. It was the Chinese contractors who negotiated with white railroad company managers to determine the workers' pay, labor terms, and provisions. In fact, most Chinese laborers were recruited by Chinese contractors in China to begin with. This isolation of the Chinese often made them appear to other workers as the willing partners of the employers, "timid and docile, deficient in active courage."

The Central Pacific Railroad began hiring Chinese by the thousands in the mid-1860s. They drove a rail line from San Francisco to Promontory Point in Utah, through the most difficult stretch of the Sierra Nevada Mountains. Central Pacific Railroad manager E. B. Crocker boasted that "they [the Chinese] prove nearly equal to white men in the amount of labor they perform, and are far more reliable. No danger of strikes among them." The Chinese carved a path out of the perpendicular cliffs above the American River by lowering one another in wicker baskets by a pulley system to drill holes, inserting gunpowder in the rocks, and then lighting the fuses, quickly hoisting themselves up the line before the explosion. Because of management's interest in completing the project—two rival railroad magnates had laid a wager on which would lay the most track until they met—the Chinese had to work in the dead of winter, drilling a tunnel through the Donner Summit while their camps lay buried under snow. Many who were killed in snowslides were not found until the following summer.[5] It is estimated that more than 1,200 Chinese perished before the two railroad lines were united with a solid gold spike.[6]

Throughout the construction period, the Chinese worked consistently from sunrise to sunset, several hours longer than the white workers. On average, a white laborer was paid $35 per month plus room and board; a Chinese laborer received between $26 and $35 per month, but had to provide his own food and lodging.

Despite their reputation as docile workers, the Chinese fought for their rights when given the opportunity. In June 1867, Chinese workers in the high Sierras went on strike. They demanded a raise in pay to equal that of white workers, the reduction of the workday in the open to ten hours and in the tunnels to eight hours. "Eight hours a day good for white men, all the same good for Chinamen," a spokesman for the Chinese was reported to have said. They also called for the abolition of whipping and freedom for any worker to quit, if and when he chose.[7]

For a week, 5,000 Chinese laborers walked out as "one man." They all stayed in their camps; they would walk around, but not a word was said and nothing was done. The management of the Central Pacific Railroad moved to break the strike. First, it wired its New York office to inquire about the feasibility of transporting 10,000 blacks to replace the striking Chinese. Then it cut off the food trains from entering the camps to starve out the strikers. Virtually imprisoned in their Sierra camps and forced into starvation, the strikers surrendered within a week.

THE CHINESE CLASS STRUGGLE AND BATTLES
AGAINST CHINESE CONTRACTORS

The strike was widely reported in the San Francisco papers, if only briefly, but there were no reactions from white workers nor any public interest in the incident.[8] What's more, the problems confronting the Chinese were not limited to struggling against white employers. Because they were under the control of contractors, any demand pressed on the employers inevitably lead to conflict with their Chinese overseers as well, which often ended up in bloody intra-ethnic disputes that were regularly referred to by the outsiders as "*tong* wars" or "gangland warfare." In reality, they were class conflicts.

In June 1875, approximately 150 Chinese workers at the large Booth Company salmon cannery in Astoria, Oregon, refused to work when their Chinese contractor failed to pay their wages on time. Only after assurances by the owner that their pay was forthcoming did they return. The following year, when the workers' demand for higher wages from the employers failed, they turned their anger against Chinese foremen for pushing the crew too hard and failing to pay wages promptly.[9]

In 1876, Chinese laborers at the shoe factories owned by the Einstein Brothers and of Buckingham, Hecht, and Company in San Francisco felt that management and their Chinese contractors had defrauded them. They struck, without results. The laborers finally armed themselves and attacked the contractors in a bloody war that roiled San Francisco's Chinatown for weeks. In March that year, the Chinatown police detail had to send for reinforcements to restore calm to the neighborhood; the wounded were carried away in an express wagon.[10]

Just as Chinese garment contractors in Chinatown today point at white manufacturers as the real cause of low wages, Chinese contractors during the last century blamed the stinginess of white employers for their labor problems. But because of the racial bigotry of their fellow American laborers, who made sure they were excluded, Chinese workers were left with no choice but to submit to their co-ethnic contractors. "The greater the pressure from outside," historian Alexander Saxton comments, "the more cohesive became the vertical structure of the Chinese establishment, and the more unlikely any horizontal cleavage within [the Chinese community]."[11]

After the railroads were completed the Chinese began to compete in the open labor market in a number of trades, including tobacco rolling, textile processing, fishing, and agriculture. For a while it seemed the Chinese could become an integral part of the American labor force. As the organized labor movement grew in the state of California, the Chinese too came under its influence. Labor historian Ira Cross observed, "Another source of irritation for the white employers was that the Chinese learned to use the strike as a means of exacting higher wages and improved conditions of employment."[12] In 1884, Chinese tobacco workers in San Francisco conducted a successful strike for an increased rate. They had formed a union called Tang Dak Tong, or Hall of Common Virtue. In the fall of the same year the Chinese tobacco workers struck again, this time demanding the dismissal of two Chinese workers who were not members of the union. The Hall of Common Virtue was probably the first Chinese union formed in North America, and the first to make demands for fair wages and an all-union shop.

But the sad reality was that these actions by Chinese labor did not receive the least bit of support from white trade unions; rather, they elicited their scorn for beginning "to feel overbearing in their strength."[13] The San Francisco Merchants and Manufacturers' Association stepped in to stiffen the white proprietors against further concessions, and the strike failed.

CHINAMEN MUST GO!

The economic depression of the early 1880s and the drastic wage cuts accompanying it gave the American labor movement its greatest impetus for growth. The Knights of Labor, the largest craft union at the time, boasted 15,000 local assemblies representing between 700,000 to one million members.[14] But the racial prejudice of the white workers was too strong to allow cooperation with the Chinese. The whites claimed that the Chinese were "inassimilable elements" that should be barred from immigration, and demanded that those already in the country be put out of the labor force and prevented from "competing" with whites. From 1870 on, virtually every labor newspaper and organization in the United States supported the exclusion of Chinese immigration. The International Workingman's Association passed an anti-Chinese resolution only one year after it had called for "complete political and social equality for all, without distinction of sex, creed, color or condition."[15]

Some white workers understood the employers' attempt to use ethnic and racist elements to undermine working-class solidarity. A letter from a trade unionist in the *Labor Standard,* published in Paterson, New Jersey, proclaimed, "the cry that 'the Chinese Must Go' is both narrow and unjust. . . . It is merely a repetition of the cry that was raised years ago by native Americans against the immigration of Irishmen, Englishmen, Germans, and others from European nations." The article went on to say that, "the workingmen have distinctly stated that they welcome workingmen from all nations, and that their warfare is only against the system of low wages and all those who support it . . . that no action but international labor action, and no cry but that of high wages and short hours will lead us into the promised land of peace, plenty and happiness."[16]

In 1870, the largest trade union at the time, the Secret Order of Saint Crispin, organized a strike at Sampson's Shoe Factory in North Adams, Massachusetts, to demand higher wages and an eight-hour workday. The management decided to fight the union by introducing a "wedge" into the conflict—a contingent of Chinese workers from San Francisco. At first the Secret Order of Saint Crispin tried to promote working-class solidarity by organizing the Chinese into the union, but not much later, at a meeting in Boston, white workers quickly turned against the Chinese and condemned management for attempting to reduce American labor to the Chinese standard diet of "rice and rats."

Throughout this period white organized labor refused to make common cause with the Chinese, a position best expressed by contemporary labor reformer George McNeill: "From his cradle, the Chinese serf is disciplined in the doctrine of nonentity . . . an element trained in such school cannot possibly sympathize with our plan of co-operation."[17]

Although the Chinese were often used as strikebreakers, the employers' favor was fickle and short-lived; in fact, they saw Chinese labor as little more than a convenient stopgap, to be shunted aside when it had fulfilled its purpose. When pressure against hiring Chinese workers became too great, employers were quite willing to move on to other immigrant groups, especially because by the 1880s, the Chinese who had arrived ten or fifteen years earlier were becoming "old."

After getting rid of the Chinese, employers began to encourage Japanese workers to immigrate. Later, white workers rallied to exclude the Japanese, pressuring the U.S. government into signing the infamous "Gentlemen's Agreement" of 1907 with the Japanese government, which barred Japanese laborers from leaving Japan for America. The exclusion of the Chinese and Japanese did not, of course, stop the employers' demand for a continued supply of more cheap labor from Asia, nor white labor's insistent demand for the exclusion of all Asians. Waves of Koreans, Filipinos, and East Indians came one after another to replace those previously excluded. In fact, this cycle of recruitment, harassment, and exclusion goes on in California even to this day, its latest manifestation being the passage of Proposition 187 in 1992, which called for the denial of health care, education, and other public services to undocumented immigrants and their offspring—this time mainly directed against immigrants from Mexico.

According to labor historian Herbert Hill, from the middle of the last decade of the nineteenth century to well into the twentieth, hardly an issue of the *United Mine Workers of America Journal*, the official publication of the union, left the presses without some warning of the "yellow peril." The miners' union joined the American Federation of Labor in arguing that it was the role of labor unions, above all, to uphold the "Caucasian ideals of civilization." They argued that unions were the white man's best hope in the contest for "domination," and the union conducted a campaign urging its members to purchase products "made by white men."[18]

AN INDISPENSABLE ENEMY

The anti-Chinese issue in the 1870s, argues Alexander Saxton, provided the focus to rally white workers, who otherwise had little to unify them. The white workers in California during that time had been driven west by a variety of factors. Some were European immigrants fleeing political persecution or economic dislocation, others were skilled Eastern and Midwestern American workers whose jobs had been usurped by mechanization and the use of unskilled labor, or small farmers pushed westward by the constant encroachment of a more complex and commercialized agricultural system. Politically, too, this was a diverse population, including Republicans with abolitionist or Free Soil sympathies, Democrats whose belief in the work ethic was coupled with notions of racial superiority, and socialists coming from a strong European working-class tradition. The leadership of the California labor movement was correspondingly fragmented. The only strategy able to promote working-class unity, ironically, was the use of Chinese immigrants as scapegoats.

The most sustained effort toward racial exclusion came from members of the craft unions—perhaps the most powerful force in the anti-Chinese crusade. There is a certain logic to this, since occupational exclusion was a key principle of craft unionism. Before the industrialization of the twentieth century, only workers with skills had enough collective bargaining power over the employers to form effective unions. They were able to restrict their numbers by controlling the transfer of skills through tight apprenticeship programs. According to Alexander Saxton, the craft unionists were "economically rather than politically oriented" and "their leaders sought to maximize bargaining power through union-controlled competition for skilled jobs. To this purpose they strove to define the limits of each craft, to restrict entry by means of rigorous apprenticeship and hiring."[19]

When immigrants such as the Irish first arrived in America from Europe they were willing to do the lowly menial work originally performed by African Americans. Once taken on, they raised racial barriers to exclude and force the blacks out of their jobs. One of the tactics by which white skilled workers controlled the labor market was by withholding apprenticeships and training from blacks.[20]

The 1870s was a period of rapid growth for the craft unions. However minimal the actual threat, the specter of Chinese encroachment on such skilled trades as cigar and shoe manufacture enabled craft unions to forge coalitions with the Democratic Party and other groups that controlled California politics; hence, their influence came to extend far beyond a few members in particular trades. Moreover, craft union discrimination against Chinese deflected competition in the skilled trades in two different ways. If the Chinese were forced into menial and unskilled occupations, the unskilled white job-seekers were less likely to come to California. At the same time, the craft unionists blamed the Chinese as the reason the unskilled whites in California could not get jobs, thus warding off their demand to enter the skilled trades. The anti-Chinese movement, therefore, enabled the craft unions to influence the unskilled white workers without having to assume any responsibility for getting them jobs. The Chinese truly became the craft unions' "indispensable enemy."[21]

American unions did not stop at lobbying for legal prohibition of Chinese immigration and the passage of the Chinese Labor Exclusion Act of 1882. After the act took effect, anti-Chinese forces turned their attention to those Chinese still in the country by unleashing an "abatement" campaign to drive them from the mines, ships, and lumber camps by force. Already in the 1870s, miners had been rioting and striking, ostensibly for higher wages and for shorter hours, but more importantly for the discharge of the Chinese, even though white workers were generally receiving twice the pay of the Chinese. Ironically, the white workers were often themselves not yet American citizens. It was, Mary Coolidge wrote, an uprising of European foreigners, generally led by Irishmen, against the Chinese.[22]

Later, the League of Deliverance attempted to compel all San Francisco employers to replace Chinese workers with white union members. In February 1880, under labor pressure, the California State Legislature passed a sweeping bill against the employment of Chinese. It stipulated that no "Chinese or Mongolian" could be employed as "officer, director, manager, member, stockholder, clerk, agent, servant, attorney, employee, assignee, or contractor to any corporation now existing or hereafter formed under the law of this state."[23]

Despite the opposition of employers, labor's exclusion strategy was warmly supported by two powerful political parties: the Working-men's Party of California and San Francisco's governing Union Labor Party. The law was later ruled unconstitutional by a circuit court, but needed to "maintain California for us and our kind of people," boasted Paul Scharrenberg, state secretary of the AFL.

In protecting jobs for "our kind of people," the Irish building contractors in 1870s were able to expand to constitute a fifth of all contractors in the United States. An "Irish ethic" led the contractors to give preferential treatment to compatriot subcontractors and workers. Irish workers eventually monopolized many of the skilled construction trades and shared job opportunities only with their sons and compatriots. Heavily concentrated in the building trades, Irish workers later became highly unionized. Many of the prominent leaders in the labor movement were Irish. Through their leadership of the unions, Irish immigrants were able to "rise from rags to riches," according to Yale University historian David Montgomery[24]—to move upward as a group into the higher-paid, skilled, and unionized trades.

The Chinese, forced out of the American labor market because white workers objected to working alongside them, could not get working-class jobs and were forced into self-employment, mainly in restaurant and laundry trades. They were driven into isolated ghettos, where they fell under the control of Chinese contractors and the merchant elite. They were not part of the American working class, not part of the American workers' struggle—and therefore in no position to benefit from the gains made by the American labor movement in the 1930s.

INDUSTRIAL UNIONS AND CHINESE LABORERS

By the end of World War I, the United States had become the most industrialized nation in the world, yet only 14 percent of its workforce was unionized, primarily in craft unions. But by the 1930s these craft unions were in decline. Technological advances had increased the scale of U.S. industry while simplifying production processes; what the new industrial giants required were large numbers of unskilled laborers who could be hired directly by management, not skilled workers selected through the craft union apprenticeship system. If this new labor force was to bargain effectively with management, its unions could not be limited to particular trade or craft but had to be industry-wide. The largest union at the time, the AFL , was unwilling to abandon the exclusive craft union concept; as a result, in 1935, a group split off from the AFL to form the Congress of Industrial Organization (CIO), which became the foremost organ of the new "industrial" unions.

Industrial unions, if only for self-protection, had to be more egalitarian in their membership policies, or those not included would scab, which would depress the wage level and working conditions for all workers. The CIO broke with the craft unions not only in organizing the unskilled, but in adopting a less discriminatory racial policy as well. Although the organization of minorities progressed at a slow and sometimes uneven rate, the 1930s did witness the inclusion of unskilled African Americans in a number of unions, among them the United Mine Workers, the National Maritime Union, and the United Auto Workers.

The broadening of mobilization targets could also have included the Chinese. But by the 1930s, most Chinese were trapped in their "chosen" self-employed professions. There were a number of Chinese workers in small Chinese-owned enterprises experiencing exploitation, especially in restaurants, but American unions made very little effort to reach out and incorporate them into the union movement.[25] Most unions were not interested in organizing Chinese workers because they were employed in small-scale, labor-intensive, relatively unprofitable and ethnic-centered businesses.

Even with the transition of the American labor movement to industrial organizing, the racist attitude of white organized labor toward blacks did not change completely. The CIO in many situations had to accept black workers as members in order to organize their industries. If they were excluded, blacks recruited by employers as replacement workers would constitute a serious threat to these emerging labor organizations. However, once they became part of the union, white workers established controls in the shops to institutionalize racial inequality by denying blacks equal promotion and seniority rights, and limiting them to unskilled jobs in segregated labor classifications.[26]

On the other hand, progressive labor organizers believed that racial conflict among the workers was a consequence of class relations manipulated by the capitalist class to divide and conquer. Many unions resented dealing with the race issue because it was considered to be disruptive to internal unity and an obstacle to the formation of labor unions. This attitude ignored the deeply entrenched and enduring racism of the white working class. Organized labor's deplorable record on racial issues became evident in its attempt to counter the NAACP's lobbying effort to include agricultural and domestic workers in the collective bargaining provisions of the Wagners Act. Without this inclusion, a large segment of black labor would be left out.

Even at the time of the passage of the 1964 Civil Rights Act, the AFL-CIO and affiliated unions insisted on modification of the act's power to apply only to *future* discrimination practices, and to insulate the act from changing the established seniority system—thus preserving the racial status quo in employment for at least a generation.[27] Even to this day, unions, such as those in the construction trades in New York City, still fail to incorporate any significant minority membership.[28] In fact, they have even tried to stall minority demands for entering the trades through the federally funded apprenticeship programs. Once a minority worker completes the program, there is no guarantee that he will be accepted in the union, and once in the union, no guarantee that he will ever get a job assignment.

AMERICAN UNIONS AND CHINESE SEAMEN

The Chinese, whose numbers were much smaller than those of African Americans and who were employed mostly outside of the mainstream labor market, had almost no success in establishing union membership. One rare exception were Chinese seamen and their involvement with the National Maritime Union of the 1930s. Their experience is of great relevance to the Chinese illegal immigrants of today.

During the Great Depression, with thousands of American seamen unemployed, shipping companies still preferred to hire foreign crews, including many from the Caribbean and from China, because of the conditions they could impose on them. The Chinese seamen, among whom a large number came from Fuzhou, were forced to sign contracts that allowed the shipping company to withhold 50 percent of their wages until their discharge. Each Chinese seaman had to post a $500 bond to guarantee compliance and promise not to join associations of any kind or else be returned to Hong Kong at his own expense.

American seamen resented the Chinese for the way shipowners used them to depress wages. When the SS *Lincoln,* a Dollar Shipping Company vessel, reached New York in 1933 with a crew of mostly Chinese sailors, the Seamen's International Union (SIU) protested the use of the Chinese crew and demanded their immediate discharge. The union also arranged for the immigration office to arrest the Chinese at the docks for illegal entry and to confine them to Ellis Island. The SIU then pressured Congress to pass a bill barring all foreigners from working on U.S. ships, claiming that "Chinese seamen charge low wages, thus taking away jobs from Americans."

The effort was unsuccessful. Its criticism of the Chinese notwithstanding, the SIU was in fact a corrupt and ineffective "company" union, which had done little about its members' low wages and could not even establish a limit on working hours. Some of the SIU officials might actually have been paid by the owners *not* to organize. The seamen gradually realized that the SIU did not represent their interests and founded a new organization, the National Maritime Union (NMU), which within a few years became the largest maritime union in the United States.

The most unusual feature of the new union's constitution was a clause providing that there be "no discrimination against any union member because of his race, color, political affiliation, creed, religion, or national origin." By promising equal participation, the union hoped to encourage potential scabs to join the union rather than work for the companies. With this understanding some 20,000 black seamen, primarily stationed in southern Gulf ports, joined the 1936–37 seamen's strike, insuring its success.

At the time of the strike many Chinese nationals were employed on U.S. vessels, but they occupied the most menial positions— usually as cooks and stewards—and were paid an average of $45 per month, compared to $60 for U.S.-born seamen. When the NMU called the strike, thousands of Chinese seamen were stranded in New York harbor. Without any contact with the American union they had no idea how to deal with the situation.

However, some of the Chinese seamen were members of the Lien Yi Seamen Society, which was a seamen's organization popular in China at the time. The NMU's New York strike committee promptly approached Lien Yi and urged its members to join the strike. Lien Yi members were cautious at first, pointing out that the shipping companies still held the $500 bonds on the Chinese seamen. Moreover, as "aliens," many of them did not even have the legal right to land in New York. After some discussion, Lien Yi made an offer: the Chinese would join the strike in return for NMU's support in presenting the companies with the following demands: 1) equal treatment of Chinese seamen; 2) their right to shore leave in U.S. ports; and 3) an equal wage scale. The NMU readily agreed.

The NMU asked for officials from the Chinese Consulate to negotiate with the Immigration Office so that Chinese seamen could claim the right to shore leave. It also promised that if any Chinese lost their jobs because of participation in the strike, they would have an equal opportunity for employment after the strike was over. During negotiations with management, the union demanded equal pay for Chinese seamen. As a result, 3,000 Chinese seamen participated in the strike. This opened a rare opportunity for Chinese workers to become part of the U.S. labor movement, gaining fair wages and job protections.

The start of World War II in Europe in 1937 provided a different type of opportunity. Though it had not formally taken sides, within a few months after the start of the European conflict, the United States provided supplies to the besieged nations of Great Britain and the Soviet Union, principally on U.S. and British vessels called "Liberty Ships." So many of these ships were sunk by German U-boats patrolling the North Atlantic that the casualties suffered by the merchant marine on the supply convoys crossing the Atlantic surpassed even the U.S. Navy losses in the first year of active American engagement in World War II. The high casualty rates created a sudden need for sailors. By the early 1940s 15,000 Chinese seamen, again many from Fuzhou, were hired in Hong Kong for duty on Western convoys.

The major problem for the newly recruited Chinese seamen was an old one: U.S. authorities' refusal to grant them shore leave because they were not U.S. citizens. Some Chinese sailors remained on the

Atlantic Ocean for months without setting foot on land, although they were taking as great a risk as any for the Allied cause. In one instance, a Chinese seaman drifted in the ocean for forty days before being rescued—and then had to be treated on board a ship tied to the docks because he was "foreign."

The NMU helped the Chinese seamen with public statements in support of their right to shore leave and ran articles in the union's organ, *The Pilot*, urging equal treatment for all seamen. In 1942, six New York Chinatown community groups held a public forum urging U.S. authorities to change the rules. The Justice Department finally gave in, marking a significant advance in the Chinese battle against racial discrimination, in which the NMU played a big role. Chinese membership in the NMU increased from 1,000 in 1942 to 3,000 in 1946. A Chinese section was set up and played an active role in the union.

The NMU continued to speak out on issues concerning its Chinese members. In 1942 it officially supported the repeal of the Chinese Exclusion Act of 1882. In 1944 it asked the Congress to pass legislation giving the right of naturalization to all foreign seamen who had worked on U.S. vessels for more than three years during the war. Though this proposal was never approved, the U.S. Department of Transportation did allow non-citizen seamen to continue working on U.S. ships if they had been hired before July 30, 1945. Thousands benefited from the ruling. And with the union's support more Chinese seamen, both U.S. citizens and non-citizens, were hired during the postwar years.

The NMU's enlightened view on labor organizing, which stressed equality and international solidarity, strengthened its power and influence. The inclusion of the Chinese benefited them greatly, and in turn insured their loyalty to the union. The NMU's experience shows the folly of a narrowly nationalistic approach to labor organizing. It also shows that, given the opportunity, the Chinese are as ready as any other ethnic group to be part of the working-class struggle—even if they are not American citizens. The number of unionized Chinese seamen may have been small, but it was symbolically significant both for the American labor movement and for the U.S. Chinese community.

THE POSTWAR CHINESE LABOR MOVEMENT

During and after World War II, there were other encouraging signs that the Chinese were slowly breaking out of their ethnic isolation. For one thing, the United States joined the war on the same side as China, fighting the Axis powers. As historian Harold Isaac points out, because China's anti-fascist policy coincided with U.S. objectives at the time, the attitude towards China and the Chinese underwent a dramatic change from "contempt" to "admiration." Chinese President Chiang Kai-shek made the cover of *Time* magazine as "Man of the Year" in 1942.

The new image of China affected the status of the Chinese in the United States. In 1943 public pressure was placed on the U.S. Congress to revoke the Chinese Exclusion Act of 1882. American literature on Chinese Americans began praising the "upstanding character" and "orderly behavior" of Chinese youth, although only a decade earlier they had been depicted almost exclusively as sinister, opium-smoking hatchet men.

The World War II effort demanded a massive mobilization in all U.S. industries related to national defense, and minority groups, including the Chinese, began to enter new fields of employment. President Roosevelt issued an executive order calling for an end to racial discrimination, declaring that it is "only through the unity of all people that we can successfully win the war, regardless of race, color, and creed." The Chinese, formerly denied access to the industrial labor force as well as to most white-collar jobs, were suddenly released from the low-paying "service ghettos" to which they had been restricted. Jobs in factories, shipyards, offices, and laboratories gave them the opportunity to learn new skills, and enabled employers to learn how capable Chinese workers could be. In the long run, this experience helped dispel prejudice among some employers, who continued to hire Chinese after the war.

During the war itself, a great number of Chinese served in the U.S. Army. Some 3,000 from New York's Chinatown alone were drafted at the very beginning of American participation in the war. The reason was ironic: because of the Exclusion Act, most Chinese males could not bring their wives to this country, and as a result few had dependents; according to the law, they were the first to be called. Many welcomed military service however, anticipating that the special skills they would learn in the army could be useful in civilian life and that, as veterans, they would enjoy many benefits denied them in the past.

These small inroads into the American mainstream came too late for most of the Chinese locked in the Chinese ethnic labor market, mostly those in the laundry and restaurant trades. Besides, when American politics abruptly turned to the right during the McCarthy era after the Korean War, the more liberal and progressive wing of American organized labor, including the NMU, began experiencing serious political difficulties.

The 1960s again brought radical changes. First there was the civil rights movement's ultimately successful drive to outlaw overt racial discrimination, which was hugely significant for the Chinese in America. Then the 1965 Immigration Act set equal legal immigration quotas for colored minorities and opened the floodgates for Asian immigration. After its passage, many relatives of Chinese Americans arrived to join their families in the United States. The population of Chinatowns across the nation surged, and more concentrations of Chinese developed.

Before the 1960s the Chinese were trapped in Chinatowns because they could not get industrial jobs outside in the larger American labor market. Now, due to the decentralization of American industries, the situation was reversed—manufacturing jobs and service jobs came to the ethnic communities to tap their special labor potentials. The majority of the Chinese in Chinatown today are no longer self-employed operators of businesses. They are truly working class, employed by others. Chinatowns have, in effect, been transformed from small-business ghettos into working-class neighborhoods and manufacturing centers. Although most residents now hold manufacturing and service jobs, they are working under an ethnic subcontracting system. They are still isolated in their own ethnic community, exploited by their own ethnic elite, and continue to work in conditions below American labor standards.

CHAPTER 7

Ineffectual Enforcement of Immigration and Labor Law

THE CONTINUED INFLUX OF UNDOCUMENTED ALIENS SATISFIES
this country's need for cheap, docile, and unskilled labor. In the past,
this need had long been met by waves of European immigration. As
European wars and the ethnic quotas established by the 1924 National Origins Act slowed down immigration from Eastern and
Southern Europe, America's labor needs were fulfilled by blacks (and
whites) moving from the rural South to the urban North, and by
Mexicans flooding across the border into Texas and California.

The 1965 Immigration Act made no provisions for the continued
inflow of unskilled labor, unless the would-be immigrants could
claim a close blood relation to an American citizen. The new act
ended the bracero program, which had found temporary jobs for
some 4 million Mexicans between 1942 and 1960, reaching a peak in
the late 1950s.[1] The termination of the program, however, had little
impact on the demand for such labor—wages, in fact, rose because
of domestic demand. Workers who in the past came legally under the
bracero program now infiltrated the border illegally. The need for
cheap labor has remained the same but the legal definition has
changed—as the number of Mexican immigrants shot up in the late
1970s, it became a national preoccupation symbolizing America's
inability to control its borders and enforce the rule of law.

Considering this economy's unending thirst for docile low-wage
labor, America really could not come up with a comprehensive approach to dealing with illegal immigration. The 1986 Immigration
Reform and Control Accountability Act (IRCA) was its first real
attempt. Before IRCA, federal policy was based mainly on intercept-
ing illegals at the border and (to a much lesser extent) on appre-
hending them at their job sites, bus stops, in immigrant
communities, or anywhere they could be located. The rate of apprehension fluctuated according to the domestic labor needs of the

country. The employers, on the other hand, could not be held accountable for employing an undocumented immigrant.

The 1986 IRCA attempted to stop the illegal immigration flow by first granting amnesty to the undocumented aliens already in the country and then penalizing businesses who "knowingly" hired illegals in the future. The second part, known as "employer sanctions," imposes fines and even criminal penalties on guilty employers based on the assumption that it is their action that attracts illegals to come to this country to begin with. Cutting off the job supply would eliminate the "magnet" that attracts undocumented aliens. The two provisions of the act are somewhat contradictory, because the first acknowledges the contribution of undocumented labor to the American economy by allowing it to remain in the country, while the second tries to stop more of this useful labor from coming in.[2]

The act initially had a slightly dampening effect on the flow of illegals, but the number of immigrants quickly escalated, surpassing levels prior to its passage.[3] The "employer sanctions" are fraught with loopholes and impossible to enforce. America's underground economy has in fact grown in scope, and reports of employer violations—not paying the minimum wage, violating home work regulations, withholding back wages, and employing child labor—have dramatically increased.

Although the IRCA was passed mainly in response to illegal immigration from Mexico, it has greatly affected illegal Chinese workers. Prior to its passage there was very little public awareness of Chinese illegal aliens. The amnesty provision legalized a significant number of Fuzhounese illegals already in the United States, providing the healthy "seed population" that would sponsor thousands of other illegal Chinese immigrants. But the conditions for workers in Chinese communities have become worse since the passage of employer sanctions.

Therefore, the massive influx of illegal Chinese immigrants has created a set of problems for the United States that spread like ripples from the overcrowded ghettoes where the illegals settle. The large and persistent influx of undocumented aliens has led to the emergence of involuntary servitude, as a result of exorbitant fees charged by the sophisticated human smuggling networks, which has in turn led to the brutal exploitation of the illegals by employers violating American labor laws.

The use of Chinese illegals has already devalued the labor of legal Chinese workers in Chinatown. Their continued influx through a back-door subcontracting system into the mainstream labor markets—from the garment and restaurant trades to the electronic, construction, trucking, and farm industries—threatens to erode the wages of all other American laborers as well. Such practices are already setting low working standards for other third world immigrants.

Worse is the virtual indentured slavery of the illegal aliens, which has generated little public outrage even as it has spread among immigrants of many ethnic backgrounds. Thai women were discovered in Elmonte, California, working and living in a locked and fenced-in factory because they could not repay their transportation fee. They were routinely abused, and told that if they escaped their captors would "go to their homes in Thailand to burn their houses down."[4] A similar situation is emerging within the Asian Indian community where human smugglers are charging aliens as high as $28,000 for their passage to this country.[5]

This type of involuntary servitude is even more common in the sex industry. Young Korean, Thai, and Cambodian girls are promised jobs as "hostesses" in America, but frequently find themselves in massage parlors performing sex for money. With no legal status, they are held as virtual prisoners by the international sex trade.[6] One such operation in Chinatown was located right across the street from a junior high school for several years without provoking any official action.

WHY THE POLICE CAN'T STOP IT

Attacking the Chinese immigration problem has proved difficult for American law enforcement. For one thing, the coordinating heart of the smuggling network is located outside the United States. Second, the network's higher-ups do not handle the undocumented aliens once they cross U.S. borders—that's left to bottom-rank "enforcers." In addition, it should also be said that law enforcement officials are not particularly enthusiastic about cracking down on the undocumented aliens. A federal-level law enforcement official once confided to me privately, "Most of the top brass are Italians or Irish, who have an immigrant tradition of their own. Stopping people who want to come to this country for better opportunities is not their cup of tea."

In any event, even if the local police were to discover a human smuggling operation, they have no direct jurisdiction unless the operation involves murder, torture, kidnapping, forced prostitution or drug trafficking. Human smuggling has to be dealt with at the federal level, most specifically by the Immigration and Naturalization Service. But the INS claims that it is short of resources and too overwhelmed with other concerns to crack down on human smuggling, which requires elaborate RICO-type investigations and prosecution. According to officials in New York, the INS is much more interested in the interdiction of illegals at the borders. And why not? Border arrests get media attention and also placate complaints by American citizens residing in border states, who have long been the loudest and most organized opposition to immigration. Whereas, cracking down on the human smuggling network takes years of law enforcement effort just to solve one single case, and in the end gains limited public relations impact.

Also, American politics often interfere with immigration law enforcement efforts. First, there was the 1986 amnesty program. Then, in 1989, after the Tienanmen Massacre, President George Bush issued an executive order providing legal shelter to thousands of Chinese students and Chinese nationals in the United States. Finally, appealing to the conservative pro-life interests, he extended the right of "political asylum" to those Chinese who claimed to be opposing China's "one-child policy." His action greatly increased the expectations of would-be Chinese immigrants. "It's like giving a green light to the smugglers," a frustrated immigration officer commented privately on Bush's executive order, which gave 80,000 Chinese the right to apply for legal status. "It's like telling them, 'It's okay, bring people here, we'll let them stay.'"[7] In fact, many undocumented Fuzhounese whom I have talked to are betting their future on the next amnesty coming sometime soon.

Even the new 1996 Immigration Reform and Immigration Responsibility Act passed by the U.S. Congress, which tightens eligibility and legal recourse for individuals applying for political asylum, nevertheless allows a "1,000-person slot" for Chinese who seek protection based on their opposition to China's "forced abortion" policy. It was clearly a move from some members of U.S. Congress to express their displeasure over the Chinese record on "human rights." But how is a Chinese in Fuzhou to know whether she is eligible for political asylum, unless she arrives in the United States to appeal for it? This new regulation is likely further to confuse potential Chinese illegal immigrants and encourage the expansion of the human smuggling trade.

Any illegal alien arrested in the United States can still appeal for political asylum. Of the 1,500 boat people arrested in 1993, not one has been returned to China; most requested political asylum. Kenneth Yates, a detective with the Metropolitan Toronto Police Service, who has dealt with Chinese smuggling in the past under a similar Canadian policy of giving political asylum, calls it insane. "We are encouraging more smuggling because it delivers huge profits! And the risk of getting caught is virtually nil."[8] He insists that this open-door policy must be changed if we are to deter the number of people arriving at our doorstep.

The United States only began to deal with the problem of Chinese human smuggling seriously after the *Golden Venture* incident. By then, the transportation fee had escalated from $1,800 in 1980 to $18,000 in 1986 to $33,000 in 1989. The network was shipping 25,000 to 50,000 immigrants into the country per year.

Very soon after the ill-fated ship went aground off Queens on June

18, 1993, President Clinton declared that "We will go after smugglers and their operations at the source," and he said, "We will take measures to interdict and redirect smuggling ships when they are in transit. We will expedite procedures for processing entry claims and for returning economic migrants smuggled into the United States and will ask Congress to pass legislation to expedite this process further."[9]

The National Security Council has since taken over the coordination of the anti-smuggling effort from the INS. At the same time, the CIA, the FBI, the Department of Defense, and the Coast Guard have all been mobilized. With increased resources and high-tech information-gathering, the effort against Chinese smuggling has dramatically improved. The interdiction effort by the Coast Guard on the Pacific Coast has led to a dramatic decline in the number of smuggling vessels in U.S. territorial waters. Ships suspected of carrying illegal Chinese aliens are now routinely boarded by U.S. Coast Guard officers for inspection on the high seas. If aliens are found on board, the ships are confiscated and their passengers returned to the host country. Boarding foreign vessels on high seas is a highly irregular and problematic practice in view of international law, but it helps to prevent illegal aliens from landing on U.S. soil and thus acquiring the right to seek political asylum, which usually means a complement of exclusion and deportation hearings before immigration judges and endless legal appeals. The U.S. Coast Guard interdictions of Chinese migrants at sea reached a high of 2,464 in 1993—and a dramatic low of 442 in 1995.[10]

Another supposed victory was the arrest of a prominent snakehead, the leader of the Fuching gang, Guo Liang Chi, also known as Ah Kay. The FBI has called him "the kingpin of Chinese trafficking in alien smuggling." Ah Kay is now acting as a "deep throat" and the Bureau hopes that, through his information, alien smuggling will be effectively smashed by a single bold stroke.[11]

Claims of victory, however, may be premature. While interdictions are down, it could simply mean that the trans-Pacific routes are being used less in favor of the sea route via the Caribbean and air routes via Eastern Europe. Even INS Commissioner Doris Meissner admitted in an interview in Mexico City, "We've stopped that illegal boat traffic, but there are still a lot of people coming from Asia, many through Central America and Mexico."[12] More accurately, the decline in boat traffic Meissner mentioned was only true in so far as Pacific crossings were concerned.

The vast, sophisticated and tremendously profitable smuggling network is surely aware of the difficulties U.S. officials have in patrolling U.S. borders. The cost of interdiction on the high seas is certainly prohibitive, according to a report by the Coast Guard. Catching the smuggling vessel *Jung Sheng No. 8,* for example, which was initially spotted 800 miles southeast of Hawaii by a Coast Guard aircraft, took the chasing Coast Guard cutter Jarvis several days, steaming hundreds of miles to stop and board the suspected vessel. After discovering appalling conditions on board, the Coast Guard had to supply food and water to the near-starving captive illegals, then provide fuel for the vessel and accompany it another 2,000 miles to Wake Island. There the Coast Guard had to negotiate for the repatriation of the illegal passengers and their enforcers with the Taiwan and Beijing governments. Finally, it had to dispose of the empty *Jung Sheng No. 8* by towing it back to Hawaii for auction. The Coast Guard spent $4 million and covered 6,000 sea miles in this single operation. At this cost, the defense of the expansive Pacific boundary is hardly sustainable.[13]

Besides, unending reports of new illegal arrivals, especially from Wenzhou, keep coming from the streets of Chinatown all the same. In the meantime, the smuggling fee has recently increased to $40,000—hardly a sign that demand is down.

Many experts dispute the FBI claim about the importance of Ah Kay's arrest. After all, insiders say, Ah Kay, while familiar with some operations and personalities, was only in the outer circle of the smuggling syndicate. Certainly, the international human smuggling network is far from quiescent.

One way to bypass the declining level of Fuzhounese savings in America is to develop alternative financial resources for illegal smuggling in mainland China. Big Sister Ping, the "Smuggling Queen of New York," one of the most notorious smugglers, who has practically emptied out several villages around Fuzhou, has amassed $40 million from her apparatus. Nonetheless, she was convicted only once on a "first offense" charge in 1991, receiving a mere four-month jail term.[14] American authorities have recently claimed that Big Sister Ping got out of human smuggling to devote herself full time to a money-laundering scheme that "helps" Fuzhounese immigrants send money home to their relatives.[15] Ping and a number of other smugglers who have accumulated a significant amount of money from the smuggling trade and have access to mainland Chinese local officials are in a position to set up financial institutions that can grant loans to would-be illegal immigrants who have no relatives to sponsor them financially.

Their rationale is that, as long as the illegals come to the United States, get jobs, and generate income, they will be able to pay their transportation fees. In other words, the Fuzhounese who have already made money from the human smuggling trade now act as "bankers," extending loans to the illegals with which to pay their snakeheads and thus maintain the cash flow and profitability of the human smuggling trade. The traders' enforcers in the United States have recently been insisting on receiving their smuggling and kidnapping payments in China, pointing to the existence of a secret banking system capable of processing large sums of money.

Another strategy of the network is to shop around for potential new clients. Wenzhou has become their latest target area.[16] Like Fuzhou, Wenzhou is a historic seaport with early exposure to the outside world. There are presently large populations of Wenzhounese in France, Holland, and Spain. But the immigration laws in Europe are tightening. France's new anti-immigrant Alien Law has placed all those recently arrived, including immigrants from Wenzhou, North Africa, Turkey, and Kurdistan, on the expulsion list. These Wenzhounese are seeking new locations for resettlement. Those with legal status in Europe who are already established are capable of paying for their relatives' smuggling fees to come to America.

On the other hand, large Chinese settlements in Eastern Europe, in Hungary for instance, have immigrants from Fuzhou, Wenzhou, and also from the northern city of Tianjin and the province of Shandong. Some of those settlers, who have successful import and export businesses, are also capable of sustaining a migration chain to North America.

Human smugglers, in the meantime, are exploring the central and coastal provinces of Zhejiang, Sichuan, Shandong, and Anhui–and wherever there are villages with significant past overseas emigration and wherever there are large enough "seed populations" that have accumulated sufficient capital to support migrant trafficking.

INEFFECTIVE BORDER INTERDICTION

Cracking the human smuggling network requires a lot more time, money, and human resources than American law enforcement can afford to spare. Border interdiction is still easier and is assured of public attention and support. Yet U.S. law enforcement has never successfully used interdiction as a means to check illegal immigration. The experience along the Mexico–U.S. border is the best example. The INS started in early 1990s a number of highly publicized efforts with fancy names like "Operation Gatekeeper" and "Hold the Line" to show the effectiveness of the Border Patrol in the San Diego and El Paso areas, which encompass a 70-mile stretch of the border. They claimed to have apprehended 565,581 illegal migrants—an average of over 1,500 a night. Yet the overall number of illegals entering the country has not slowed down. They have simply shifted their entry points to other areas along the 2,000-mile border, away from the border control concentration.

The current INS preoccupation with using apprehension numbers to show the effectiveness of its border control is reminiscent of the futile "body-count" mentality of the Vietnam War era. Additional border control agents would only mean increased inconvenience and higher cost of illegal entry. According to some sources, "Operation Gatekeeper" merely compelled an increased number of would-be migrants to seek out professional smugglers.[17] Almost all who attempt to cross the border are now said to use the aid of professional smugglers and trafficking fees have greatly increased. The "coyote" fees across the Mexican border have gone up from about $300 in the pre-Gatekeeper era to about $900 today. Nothing short of a full "militarization" or the building of a "Great Wall" along the 2,000-mile border—as suggested by Pat Buchanan—is likely to prevent determined illegals from entering the United States.

Still, according to some immigration experts, only 33 percent of all undocumented aliens entered this country along the Mexican borders. Smugglers are increasingly sending their clients through the less-enforced U.S. border with Canada. But then there are also those coming in through the air and sea routes, not to mention those entering legally and becoming illegal by overstaying their visas. Even the INS's own officials believe, "You could give the national defense budget to the INS and it would not dramatically change the character of the problem."[18] As one reporter working on a border control story wrote: "The truth about illegal immigration is that until such time as U.S. laws barring the employment of illegal aliens are enforced—or U.S. wages drop below those of the third world—poor foreigners will continue to come here."[19]

ATTACKING THE DEMAND SIDE

The American version of attacking illegal immigration from the demand side is contained in the "employer sanctions" provision of the Immigration Reform and Control Act of 1986. The act focuses on employers "knowingly" hiring illegals as a violation of the immigration law, rather than dealing with the abuse of a cheap and docile illegal labor force as a violation of the U.S. labor law.

Employer sanctions were the best compromise Congress could come up with after long years of debate and controversy. From the very beginning a coalition of groups, including the Chamber of Commerce of the United States, Western and Southern agricultural interests, and Mexican American leaders opposed it. Growers of perishable fruits and vegetables have very good reason to be concerned. An article in the *Wall Street Journal* remarks: "California's $14 billion agriculture industry owed its harvest to illegal labor almost as much as to the sun and rain."[20] During the congressional debate of the employer sanctions proposal, an officer of the National Council of Agricultural Employers testified to the Select Commission on Immigration and Refugee Policy that "We're very concerned . . . that there may be legislation which would prohibit the employment of undocumented workers. And if such legislation is passed, then we feel with great alarm the problem of where we will get enough U.S. workers to do the jobs that have to be done."[21] The growers believed that American workers would not be attracted to "stoop labor" jobs.[22]

In the end, the opponents of employer sanctions from the business community succeeded in forcing Congress to make implementation easy for employers; by doing so, they also make violations easy. Moreover, the opponents were able to weaken the law by establishing a number of complicated exceptions. First, employers are not subject to sanctions for employees hired before November 6, 1986. Such employees retain "grandfathered" status even if they have been absent from work, demoted, transferred, or laid off for lack of work. Second, the sanction does not apply to "casual domestic employment," meaning employment by individuals who provide domestic service in a private home that is "sporadic, irregular or intermittent." Third, the sanction does not apply to independent contractors or persons who are self-employed.[23] In addition, employers are given a number of opportunities to correct their "mistakes" with warnings before fines are imposed. Finally, the sanction prohibits the INS from making raids in open fields without a warrant.

Even before IRCA was enacted, doubts were voiced about whether the law could be effectively enforced, for in 1971 California had already passed legislation that prohibited employers from consciously hiring workers who lacked legal right to reside in the United States. Ten years later, not one employer had been prosecuted.[24] In addition, minority groups, including Latino and Asian civil rights organizations, had lobbied heavily against the passage of IRCA, believing that the act would accelerate ethnic-based job discrimination. Their fear was confirmed by a General Accounting Office (GAO) follow-up report which found that 16 percent of employers—more than 500,000 of them—admitted that after the enactment of IRCA they either started or increased discriminatory practices, such as hiring only U.S. citizens or checking only the papers of workers who "looked foreign."[25]

The way in which the employer sanctions provision was written allowed for easy evasion of accountability. It operates on the principle that the employers have the responsibility to determine the "eligibility" of applicants. On the other hand, they are supposed to apply this judgment equally to all applicants, and not just to those racial groups who may appear to be foreign. But it is very difficult to charge employers for "knowingly" hiring illegals without a reliable, computer-based identification system. Introduction of such a "fraud-proof" system would call for the implementation of a national ID, which would be sure to encounter stiff resistance on civil libertarian grounds.

After the 1986 law had been passed, it was estimated that by 1990 there were still 4 million illegal immigrants in the country. Since then, the number of illegals has steadily increased (in 1996, the INS reported that the illegal population has reached 5 million[26]) and sweatshop conditions across the nation have worsened. A 1990 GAO report pointed to three factors that limit the effectiveness of the law: insufficient staff resources, inadequate penalties for violations of federal wage and hour statutes, and limited coordination among enforcement agencies.[27] The report concluded, for instance, that in New York City alone there were 4,500 businesses with 50,000 workers who were working under sweatshop conditions. Yet the INS has only about 36 agents to inspect some 300,000 businesses in southern New York.

There are few provisions of the 1986 IRCA that have failed as saliently as those in agriculture, which employs more undocumented workers than any other industry in the country. The growers continue to employ illegals with little fear of fines or prosecution. By some counts, half of the estimated 700,000 farm workers in California are undocumented. While the INS pours millions of dollars into trying to stop illegal immigrants at U.S. borders, it has been conspicuous in its failure to enforce "employer sanctions" violations: from 1989 to 1991, its agents visited only 32 of the 82,000 farms in the state of California.[28] And between 1989 and 1994 only forty-six farm operators, packers, and shippers in California were fined for immigration violations.

"Employer sanctions" were supposed to improve working conditions in the United States by driving a particularly exploitable group of workers—the undocumented immigrants—out of the country. The act was not enacted to inflict suffering upon the illegals, but to benefit the U.S. workforce overall by controlling undocumented immigration. However, the intended results failed to materialize. There is no indication that the numbers of the undocumented have decreased, nor have the conditions of U.S. workers improved; instead, the exploitation of both legal and illegal workers has increased.

How could a law produce such confounding results? Before the passage of the IRCA, it was not against the law for an employer to hire illegals; most instead followed their own "don't ask, don't tell" policy. However, after the IRCA, employers have to inquire about the legal status of their workers in order to protect themselves. After checking, if an employer still hires an illegal worker, he has leverage over him. He can now offer less pay, because the illegal alien is not likely to complain, lest he risk a firing or even a report to the INS. Now the employer is in a position to get away with all types of abuses: paying below the minimum wage, imposing long hours, or forcing the workers to accept cash payment, which means that when a wage dispute occurs, there are no records to prove the wrongdoing of the employer. Moreover, the illegals are reluctant to change jobs and risk new problems with new employers, and are thus tied down to narrow options. Employer sanctions have only increased the vulnerability and potential for exploitation of the undocumented, forcing them further down into a subclass of American society.

Wing Lam, the executive director of the Chinese Staff and Workers' Association, a major immigrant rights group in New York refers to the "employer sanctions" legislation as "the slave law." According to him, if workers have papers, many bosses will tell them that there is no work available. From the bosses' perspective, the illegals are better; they are usually young, compliant, and willing to work long hours. But if a worker cannot produce documentation, the boss says he will do him a favor and hire him. Because the boss is doing the worker such a big favor, the worker is expected not to mind being paid less—say, 20–30 percent less.[29] Wing believes that in the end employer sanctions hurt all Chinese workers, legal or illegal, in that "before the law, few people worked a seven-day week, but now it's very common. They have nowhere to go. It's like they're working on [a] plantation."[30]

The employer sanctions have helped employers to create a larger army of surplus labor and forced the immigrants to work for whatever rates they can find to keep bread on the table. The employers can keep *all workers'* wages down by hiring illegals—which is exactly the opposite of what the IRCA had intended, and exactly what employers had hoped for.

ECONOMIC RESTRUCTURING AND THE CAPSULIZATION OF AMERICAN LABOR

It is not particularly surprising that enforcement of the IRCA has been ineffective. Abuses of the illegal immigrant labor force are only a part of the larger strategy for restructuring the American economy, which has as its ultimate goal the destruction of American labor standards.

The use of illegal immigrants is a common practice in today's small, competitive, and labor-intensive "peripheral firms," which do the work of corporate "outsourcing." Workers in this segment of the economy, classified in the scholarly literature as the "secondary labor market," contend with low wages and unsafe working conditions, are rarely unionized, and live with job instability and chronic unemployment. Their experience is in direct contrast to that of the workers employed in the "primary labor market." Their jobs are in "core firms"—large, capital-intensive monopolies that earn large profits, employ advanced technology, and maintain a steady demand for their products. These workers make good wages, work in a clean and safe environment, and enjoy union membership, benefits, and stable employment.[31]

American corporations have responded to global competition through a strategy of restructuring that calls for production decentralization but maintains control by farming out work to smaller suppliers. The corporations can still control prices and product quality through competition among the many small suppliers, whose survival depends on the security of such subcontracts. The labor practices of small subcontractor suppliers are the same as those of the previously identified "peripheral firms." As a result, America's secondary labor market has expanded. The competition among the small suppliers is so intense that they have to accept a low rate of profitability, which forces them to abandon the capital investment needed to maintain modernized production as well as the desire to train and upgrade their workforce.[32] While they bear the brunt of the ups and downs of market fluctuation, the small suppliers have the additional responsibility of managing the workforce, minimizing labor costs by adopting tactics of union busting, and freezing or cutting wages. Typically they will hire less-educated and less-skilled workers—often immigrant labor. Illegal immigrants are best of all, because they are not organized or legally protected.

In short, to win competitively, small firms employ what is called a "low road" strategy. The losers are the employers who do precisely what common sense says they should do: invest, train, innovate, and hire well-educated, legal workers. The recent efflorescence of sweatshops in the apparel industry in New York and Los Angeles should not be a surprise. New York has an impressive history of labor struggle against sweatshop conditions, particularly by immigrant women garment workers in the early part of this century. But since the 1970s, sweatshops have reappeared. They are most prevalent in New York because employers there know that they can break the law with impunity.

Some of the most important elected officials in the state are susceptible to political influence from employers. They lack concern for labor issues and have no qualms about taking contributions from sweatshop operators. Governor Mario Cuomo, for example, appointed former Chinatown Planning Council Executive Director Charles Wang as the Deputy Commissioner of Social Services. Charles Wang had been charged by the National Labor Relations Board with violating labor laws when, as part of a program that was financed with federal government funds earmarked to train Chinese immigrants to be construction workers, he hired a group of workers to do unskilled renovation jobs and paid them less than the agreed upon wages.[33] Then the governor crossed the picket line at the Silver Palace Restaurant, where union workers had been locked out by the management, to attend a fund-raiser.

Governor George Pataki also crossed a picket line and attended a banquet at Jing Fong Restaurant in New York's Chinatown in November 1995 to award the "Outstanding Asian American Award" to Cheng Chung-ko, the owner/manager of the restaurant, who was accused by his workers of labor violation. In fact, the governor gave the award right after the New York State Attorney's Office had issued a complaint against Cheng's restaurant. And, in 1997, the attorney general's office formally filed suit against Jing Fong management, charging it with cheating fifty-eight workers of more than $1.5 million in tips and wages.[34]

The New York State Apparel Industry Task Force, regarded as the watchdog of the industry, has just five inspectors to monitor more than 4,000 clothing factories. Once they cite a factory for a violation, the task force rarely reinspects it to ensure compliance. Besides, the majority of the cases cited for violations involve failure of registration for firms doing business in the apparel industry—the absolute minimum level of compliance. The task force has not devoted much effort to dealing with registered firms that violate labor laws right and left. It usually complains of "workload problems" to justify its inefficiency.

Unionized shops do not offer much help in prosecuting the violations, either. Even the International Ladies' Garment Workers' Union (now UNITE), which has organized nearly 90 percent of the shops in New York's Chinatown, has proved a surprisingly ineffective foe of unscrupulous sweatshop operators.[35] In 1995, of all the thousands of sweatshop violations, only eleven cases were referred to attorney general's office for criminal prosecution; eight cases were disposed of, and no one got a jail term.

The judicial process always seems to run in the employers' favor. Despite all the serious violations, the state has given employers a way to avoid monetary penalties by agreeing to send their management to "educational seminars" to learn about labor laws. A cynical state-level staff worker doubts there is much Chinese employers don't already know about abusing the system. "Their accountants work to a science. They know exactly how many weeks to withhold wages, avoiding taxes before they close the operation and reopen under another corporate title to get the maximum out of the system. They need no educational seminars."[36]

On the other hand, labor laws are so complicated and labor law enforcement so cumbersome that very few individuals except labor lawyers know how to wade through the obstacles to make a complaint. Certainly no one bothers to teach the workers how to do it.

There are many stories that illustrate this truth. Three owners of the Empress Fashion garment factory in Manhattan started with-holding workers' wages in late 1993. When the sum they owed work-ers grew to $60,000, after almost twenty weeks of nonpayment, the workers first approached the ILGWU but got no response. Then they informed the State Department of Labor about the situation. After weeks of investigation, the department turned the case over to the state attorney general's office for prosecution. The owners then ap-proached the workers for an out-of-court settlement, offering half of the amount they owed. The workers refused.

Two of the owners admitted guilt in court, but refused to pay anything to the workers. In the meantime, all of their personal assets had disappeared. The court convicted one of the two to six months in prison and the other fifty hours of community service. But the state attorney's office declined to pursue the case any further. Three years later, the workers still have not received a cent. They were told to collect through a civil case instead of in criminal court. Weak labor laws and the lack of will to enforce them obviously favor the em-ployers who continue with abuses. Any observer of the Empress Fashion case would most certainly be deterred from court action. Workers' voices are silent almost everywhere.

STOP, IN THE NAME OF THE LABOR DEPARTMENT!

The principal federal agency responsible for enforcing the "em-ployer sanctions act" is the Department of Labor. Employers must complete an Immigration and Naturalization Service form (I–9) for each person hired, regardless of their citizenship status. The Depart-ment's agents have the responsibility to investigate employees' work permits and legal status during workplace inspection in order to determine whether employers have violated the employer sanctions provisions.

On June 2, 1992, the Labor Department and the INS, in order to ensure "more efficient use of resources, reduce duplication of effort, and delineate respective responsibilities," signed a "Memorandum of Understanding" that commits the two agencies to share and exchange information in their respective investigations.[37] Thus, if during a labor inspection, the Labor Department finds irregularities in a company's I–9 forms, the agency is required to report this to the INS. Such reporting will often result in the deportation of the undocumented workers found in the inspected workplace.

The INS generally refuses to acknowledge the labor-law implications of its actions, insisting on pursuing deportation proceedings against workers involved in labor disputes. So if an employer is found guilty of withholding back wages by the Labor Department or the National Labor Relations Board, the victimized employee, if an illegal, is not able to collect on the judgment—instead, she risks being deported.

The National Immigration Project of the National Lawyers Guild in 1995 conducted a survey of community organizations, immigration and labor lawyers, legal services providers, and union organizers in areas with large immigrant populations. They almost unanimously agreed that the convergence of immigration and labor laws was deterring immigrant workers from asserting their rights to the minimum wage, overtime pay, safe working conditions, and union representation.[38] The failure of federal agencies to protect undocumented workers' rights on the job means that illegals will not complain of violations and that they will be left at the mercy of the employers. Legitimate businesses employing legitimate workers are finding it difficult to compete in marginal industries like apparel, where labor law violations are rampant. In short, the government is enforcing employer sanctions in ways that undermine U.S. labor standards.

Any report of substandard conditions by the Department of Labor ultimately triggers the termination of undocumented employees or an INS raid—or both. On the other hand, INS agents also target businesses "traditionally associated with illegal employments." And it also investigates these employers to assess whether they knowingly violated the law, which could result in "substantial fines, possible criminal prosecution or other penalties."[39] The INS and DOL, in effect, are indistinguishable in their roles in dealing with immigration and labor enforcement issues.

Extensive reporting in local media on raids against the illegals has a "freezing effect" on workers' willingness to complain about labor abuses. Chinese employers even use the situation to their advantage. After the Brooklyn district attorney's office raided the garment sweatshops in the Sunset Park area for labor violations, Chinese employers told their workers not to side with the D.A.'s office, for its real aim was arresting illegals. Sure enough, several weeks after the sweatshop operation, the INS raided garment factories all across the city.

But the employer sanctions have not only undermined labor laws by increasing the vulnerability of undocumented workers, they have also made the traditional remedies inapplicable. Even without employer sanctions, protecting undocumented workers against exploitation is complicated and difficult. The employer sanctions only increase the difficulties. Federal agencies cannot enforce reinstatement—one of the traditional means of redress for labor violations along with the returning of back pay—if employers can ask the reinstated employee for documentation.[40] With the threat of deportation, undocumented workers have no incentive to come forward and report labor violations. Without informants, labor enforcers have to investigate and search out violations on their own, which they claim they cannot do because of the "work load problem."

Probably the most devastating consequence of the employer sanctions is that it enables the employers to hire illegals, while making unionization at the workplace almost impossible. All of this has contributed to the further weakening of the power of labor.

If the objective is to prevent employers from hiring illegal workers so American working conditions will not deteriorate, we need a different logic and a different approach. This is essentially a labor and not an immigration issue.

STRICT, ACROSS-THE-BOARD LABOR ENFORCEMENT

The only way to immunize American workers from the damage caused by the presence of illegal alien laborers is by across-the-board enforcement of all U.S. labor laws, affecting all employers in the U.S.—whether foreign or U.S. citizens, employing foreign documented, undocumented, or domestic labor. Strict enforcement means adherence to American labor standards, particularly in regards to the minimum wage, the forty-hour workweek, and OSHA health and safety regulations.

Strict enforcement also means uncompromising prosecution of reported violations without regard to whether the information was provided by an American-born worker, a legal, or an illegal immigrant. Only then will all the victims speak out and the labor abuses stop. At the same time, the extension of American labor standards to all workers will eliminate employers' incentive to recruit and exploit illegals.

Immigration policy, then, deals with stopping aliens from entering the country illegally and should be limited to that. The punitive response of hunting down illegals once they are already in the country only forces them to retreat further underground, where they are even more vulnerable to unscrupulous employers and subjected to even stronger control by the organized crime. The end result is the further degrading of the value of American labor.

Linking immigration with labor enforcement, as with the present employer sanctions provision, does not work. The "Memorandum of Understanding" between the Immigration and Naturalization Service and the Department of Labor should be abolished; thereby the two agencies would no longer exchange information regarding their separate immigrant and labor enforcement responsibilities. When illegal workers seek compensation from employers for violations of labor laws, the INS should not interfere or subvert that process because of the illegality of the claimants.

The above proposals are not new. In 1978 the Labor Department's Employment Standards Administration (ESA) established a task force to investigate firms suspected of hiring undocumented persons and of violating of labor laws. ESA targeted employers for prosecution only. The idea was to take away the incentive to exploit illegal workers by paying them substandard wages under unlawful conditions. As one ESA official put it, "We are committed to eradication of illegal working conditions affecting persons regardless of their citizenship status."[41] This approach protected the undocumented but also made it less profitable to employ them rather than lawful residents. Unfortunately, this experiment was limited and was later discontinued with the enactment of the IRCA.

In enforcing labor law across the board, the most serious labor violations affecting immigrant workers occur in the subcontracting system. Utilizing the ambiguity of liability laws, employers and subcontractors both deny culpability, leaving the suffering employees dangling. The California legislature, with the support of organized labor, passed laws holding employers and subcontractors responsible for the working conditions of employees.[42] However, Governor Wilson twice vetoed such bills, claiming their passage would lead to the exodus of industries from the state of California. Despite his action, the direction of reform taken by the legislature is correct. Passage of such laws should be pursued on the national level.

The practice of withholding wages affects the undocumented workers the most, as in the case of the Chinese. Again, organized labor and labor rights activists have worked to pass legislation to eliminate such abuses. Several bills have been introduced in the New York state legislature. Some of their most important provisions should be adopted on the national level. These include making nonpayment of wages a felony, rather than a misdemeanor; deterring nonpayment of wages by increasing penalties for wilful or repeated nonpayment of wages to double the total wages due; strengthening bankruptcy laws, requiring owners to disclose assets at the time of registration and to provide timely notice to the employees before closure of businesses.

LABOR PROTECTION SHOULD BE EXTENDED TO UNDOCUMENTED workers, if for no other reason, for our self-interest. Most Americans would not want to risk the spread of infectious disease by vaccinating only selected individuals. Even diseases as deadly as smallpox have been eradicated successfully on the global scale—because everybody in critical areas got the vaccine. Not treating illegal workers as part of the American labor force and not protecting them against the employers' abuses only helps to casualize all American labor.

Unless big capital's strategy of using illegal immigrants to divide American labor is confronted directly, the decline in labor conditions will go unchallenged. Our indifference to the silencing of undocumented Chinese workers hurts native-born American interests: not only are the employers able to continue violating labor laws and degrading American labor standards, their continued employment of illegal aliens provides criminal snakeheads with more business opportunities and higher profits.

How realistic are these above proposals? Although none of them is radical or original, passage of effective labor enforcement bills can only come about through a committed campaign on the part of labor. Presently, organized labor is fighting to reverse years of decline. Politically it is still relatively weak and fragmented. Protection of the rights of immigrants is not its leaders' top priority. But this is the ultimate challenge for labor: if it can rally to achieve these minimum reforms to protect the most vulnerable segment of the working class, the foundation of a broadly based new labor movement will have been laid.

CHAPTER 8

Waiting for Organized Labor

EMPLOYER SANCTIONS, ORIGINALLY PASSED TO PROTECT AMERICAN labor, have ultimately provided unscrupulous employers with better cover in exploiting illegal workers, and little fear of censure. Illegals, such as the Fuzhounese, Poles, and El Savadorans, continue to come and work under subhuman conditions. As long as employer sanctions are in effect, new federal laws against illegal immigration (including the Immigration Reform and Responsibility Act passed in 1996) will not be effective because they only drive the illegals further underground, making detection more difficult, while enhancing the employers' control over them. Employer sanctions are actually useless and counterproductive; they only function as a "symbolic law," a pretense of state action to check illegal immigration with which to placate the American public.

The fact that the U.S. Congress can pass laws that are detrimental to the interest of American workers shows the absence of powerful organized labor to oppose them. Only an organized labor movement with an active membership and a strong national political presence could pressure the Congress to pass laws that would effectively protect American workers. Only a mobilized union rank-and-file could monitor the enforcement of labor laws at their workplaces. Unfortunately, no such national labor movement exists in the United States at present.

THE DECLINE OF THE AMERICAN LABOR MOVEMENT

Despite the Teamsters' widely publicized August 1997 victory over UPS, which to many signalled a revival of U.S. organized labor, the American labor movement is still much weaker than it was three decades ago. Union membership among American workers dropped from 35 percent in 1955 to 11 percent in 1995.[1] Unions are losing membership even though the American workforce continues to expand, especially in the service industries. Contrary to the often-heard assertion that the American working class is shrinking in this highly technological "information age," the labor force has in fact *grown* from 82.3 million in 1970 to 131 million in 1994.

The American economy seems to be in good shape. The growth rate in 1994 was a brisk 4.1 percent. Around the time of Bill Clinton's reelection in 1996, the unemployment rate was lower than 5.5 percent, inflation was nowhere to be found, and the stock market soared to historical highs, boosted by a moderate increase in American productivity.

Conventional wisdom has it that labor gains in times of economic prosperity, yet the living standards of a broad spectrum of American families remain in continuous decline despite the good performance of the national economy. Family incomes have been stagnating since the 1980s. Only the increasingly common stopgap of combining the incomes of two wage earners prevented a significant drop in family income. Poverty grew at the bottom end of the social spectrum, while the incomes of the wealthy soared. Trends have been even worse in the 1990s. Median family income fell in every year from 1989 to 1993—the only time in the postwar era that income fell four years in a row. This has also been the first time that income continued to fall two years after an economic recovery.[2]

The most common explanation for these confounding results is the "skill mismatch" theory—the deficiency of education in the new "knowledge economy." Robert Kuttner, however, shows us that the skill gap is largely a mirage. It is true that there are people at the bottom of the labor market who are effectively not hireable, but they constitute only a very narrow segment of the workforce. Millions of people are literate, numerate, and have good work habits but still receive dismal wages.[3] Katherine Newman's research shows that there is enormous competition in Harlem among qualified workers who can read, write, show up on time, and efficiently service customers for a very small supply of entry-level jobs. Besides, variation in wage levels reflects not only skills and education but a range of other factors, such as gender, race, union coverage, firm size and industry of employment. For instance, the salaries of women with higher education do not match those of their male peers.[4]

The wage expectations of Americans have collapsed because workers—union and nonunion, college educated and non-college educated, white collar and blue collar—have lost bargaining power with their employers during this period of economic restructuring. Paul Samuelson, Nobel Laureate in Economics, remarked in a television interview that during the uncertainty of certain economic restructuring, American workers have been "cowed" into accepting lower wages.[5]

Large, high-wage firms are taking the "low road" by downsizing and relying more heavily on low-wage suppliers. Through the subcontracting system, capital is moving more and more high-wage jobs into the "secondary sector" crowded with workers competing for lower wages. The disappearance of high-wage jobs in the "primary sector," which were the targets of union organizing efforts in the past, can alone explain the decline in union membership.

Organized labor has had trouble in developing an adequate response to capital's aggressive tactics of outsourcing, leveraged buyouts, relocations, and contingent employment.[6] The white ethnic labor leadership inherited from the past is getting old and is out of touch with the rank-and-file membership. Many unions, no longer engaged in the militant crusades against large corporations like those that had dominated the 1930s, have themselves become well-paid and powerful bureaucracies. They shunned organizing in the secondary labor market in the past for a simple cost-benefit reason: to unionize low-income workers in small, separate workplaces costs more and requires more organizing effort than to unionize large, centralized plants. The bureaucratized union leaders have lost the fire in their bellies to do the tough work that is necessary in "organizing the unorganized" to rebuild union membership.

Besides, union bureaucrats are often interested in maintaining themselves in power within the union hierarchy. They are fearful that if low-ranking organizers become too successful and too close to the rank and file, the bureaucrats' hard-won positions might be threatened. The problem is worsened by the lack of union democracy. Most unions keep their members at a distance from real decision-making. As Thomas Geoghgan points out in *Which Side Are You On?—Trying to Be for Labor When Labor Is Flat on Its Back,* only a handful of unions give their membership the opportunity to vote for their representatives. Rank-and-file members, in most instances, are treated as "clients" of the unions, not as active participants in their own struggles.[7]

Chinese immigrants entered the American labor market in significant numbers just at the point of American organized labor's decline. Their experience with the ineffectual unions reflects the present crisis of the American labor movement.

LABOR'S FAILURE TO ORGANIZE CHINESE GARMENT WORKERS

The first Chinese immigrant workers to be organized by American unions inside their ethnic enclaves were those who worked in the garment industry. They were brought into the fold of the International Ladies Garment Workers Union (ILGWU). Most of the Chinatown garment shops were organized in the mid-1970s, when Chinese contractors agreed to unionization by the ILGWU in their shops in exchange for a promise that the union would help commit large clothing manufacturers to providing Chinese contractors with a steady supply of job orders. From the beginning, Chinatown factories were thus unionized from the top down, without the ILGWU ever having to mobilize Chinese workers to organize in the factories (today, almost 90 percent of Chinatown's garment workers in Manhattan's Chinatown, both legal and illegal, belong to the ILGWU, now UNITE).

The ILGWU has since made very little effort to involve the workers on individual shop floors, even though most of them are new arrivals, unfamiliar with the laws of this country. In fact, many factories have no shop representative to whom workers can report their grievances (despite a provision in the union contract that makes the union responsible for appointing one in every shop). Without a shop representative, the business agents—the union's overseers of individual shops—become the only union presence in the factories. The most commonly voiced complaint among the Chinese seamstresses is expressed in a labor newsletter: "The business agent rarely visits our shops, and when he/she does come, he/she never talks to the workers."[8]

In some factories the ILGWU business agents get along better with the owners than with their own members. This is not surprising, since the success of the union is based on its ability to maintain a dues-paying membership, and that depends heavily on the cooperation of Chinese business owners.[9]

The union's strategy of "organizing from the top" worked as long as the manufacturers wanted a steady, stable supply of labor. After the manufacturers adopted flexible production, the ILGWU continued to tie its survival to the cooperative relationship with the manufacturers. It watched as production moved south, to third world countries, and to nonunionized immigrant communities, powerless to stop the process. Moreover, the union leadership no longer knows how to mobilize, being too old and ethnically different from the rank and file, yet it is unwilling to give away institutionalized power to a new ethnic group.

Unable to fight back, the union has blamed cheap foreign imports and high rents in Manhattan for its inaction. It implicitly justifies its weak enforcement of contracts with the fear that a strict reading would put Chinese owners out of business, although there is no indication that the threat is real. The Chinese contractors certainly do make this complaint, almost constantly in fact, but plenty of help wanted ads for workers appear in front of factory gates and in Chinese-language papers every day.

Beginning in the mid-1980s, Mr. K. L. Lin, a Hong Kong–born American citizen and a onetime 1960s radical, got involved in the profitable business of importing garments manufactured in China to the United States. By the mid-1990s, he decided to move his operations back to America, because contractors in New York who ten years ago asked $3.75 for one piece of sewing now offer to do the same job *plus* cutting the garment before sewing for just $1.75. "It's actually cheaper to do it in New York," he says, "because labor cost in New York has come down, if you add the cost of transportation, purchasing of the U.S. import quota [restricted licenses, which limit imports to the United States, have created a lively market in quota transfers among garment importers], insurance and all sorts of taxes imposed by the Chinese government, it's not worth doing it in China anymore." Besides, he adds, "you get a much faster turnover rate in New York." In fact, a number of factories like Mr. Lin's have moved from Hong Kong to New York in recent years.

The ILGWU's sole interest in the 1990s has been fighting for its own survival by holding on to its dues-paying membership. Its focus has been in shifting all the blame onto foreign competition. One of the ILGWU campaigns has consisted of asking members to attend "Buy American" rallies in order to induce Congress to pass restrictive import legislation. But foreign competition is hardly the issue of most concern to American workers: rather, it is that the conditions in the United States have already declined to third world standards. It is ironic for the union's Chinese members to be picketing against their fellow workers in China and Hong Kong. The prevailing wage in Hong Kong stands at around $3.50 an hour—almost comparable to sweatshop rates in America.

After a number of embarrassing exposés of sweatshop conditions in some of the unionized shops, the union has currently embarked on "A Partnership for Responsibility" campaign to stop sweatshops. Its literature proposes a program to urge American consumers not to purchase sweatshop-made goods, charging manufacturers and multinational corporations with responsibility for the working conditions under which their products are made, and demanding that the government enforce labor laws.[10]

Calling for corporate responsibility and consumer boycotts is fine. It isn't clear, however, what the union proposes to do itself. It has shown neither the ability nor the willingness to organize the unorganized. Even those it has organized are not protected from working under substandard conditions. In any event, counting on public vigilance is never going to be as effective as mobilizing union membership. And a corporate campaign would be more effective if the union rank and file were behind it.

THE ILGWU'S RISE AND FALL

The union's passivity in defending the interests of its Chinese membership stands in sharp contrast to the union's history. The ILGWU, one of the largest and most powerful unions in America, was built by young Jewish immigrant women from Eastern Europe. They came to America almost a century ago to work in primitive sweatshops under a piece-rate subcontracting system that often employed child labor.

In 1909, these women fought back and staged one of the most dramatic strikes in American history, when twenty thousand seamstresses walked off their jobs. Their cause was just. The horrible work conditions they had to endure won them broad public sympathy. Yet because of their limited organizing experience, their continued sporadic revolts and strikes at workplaces brought them very few concessions from management. It took the tragic Triangle Shirtwaist Fire of 1911, which took the lives of 146 workers—mostly young Jewish women—to escalate the organizing effort. Meanwhile, the workers' leaders braved police arrests, court injunctions, and imprisonment.[11] Between 1909 and 1920, a wave of strikes and mass organizing campaigns swept through the garment trades, changing a largely unorganized industry into a union stronghold.

By the end of World War I, clothing workers were among the best-organized members of the American labor force. The ILGWU had 100,000 dues-paying members in 1920.[12] By 1934 the union claimed a membership of more than 200,000, and by the end of World War II its members were among the highest-paid workers in the country. The union had developed one of the most extensive social service programs for its members, providing union clinics, low-rent housing, and generous retirement plans. Unfortunately, having achieved these important gains, the ILGWU became institutionalized. Workers' rights were now protected by labor bureaucrats and union officials, without the workers' participation.

The union's record on racial matters is less than stellar. Although African Americans and Puerto Ricans were incorporated into the union in the 1930s, union members who belonged to these groups continuously accused the union of tolerating employers' paying them lower wages than the whites. Whenever African American and Puerto Rican workers were unjustly fined and threatened with dismissal, the union was passive. For example, the ILGWU took no action when Puerto Rican women complained of being sexually harassed by their employers and foremen.[13]

Resentment against the union's conservative leadership was so intense that in 1957 Puerto Rican and African American workers petitioned the National Labor Relations Board to decertify the ILGWU as their representative. They even demonstrated in front of the union headquarters, accusing it of failing to negotiate fair contracts for them. In 1958, Puerto Rican workers at Q-T Knitwear Company in Brooklyn charged the union with negotiating a "sweetheart contract" with their management. They marched around the factory carrying signs that read: "We're Tired of Industrial Peace. We Want Industrial Justice!"[14]

Before the Chinese entered into the garment industry in large numbers in the 1970s, both African American and Latino workers had protested vociferously about their subordinate position in the union and about their lack of adequate representation in the top union leadership. Jews, and to a lesser extent Italian Americans, continued to hold these positions even after the rank-and-file membership had largely shifted to African Americans and Puerto Ricans. It was Puerto Rican seamstresses who played the crucial role in the survival of the garment industry and of the union in New York City during the 1950s, 1960s, and early 1970s,[15] before the Chinese entered into the trade.

The Chinese entered New York's garment industry just at the time of its decline because of competition from Southern states and third world countries. Between 1969 and 1982, the number of jobs in New York's garment industry fell by almost 40 percent. This decline, however, has been reversed since the influx of the Chinese. A study commissioned by the International Ladies Garment Workers Union and the New York Skirt and Sportswear Association showed that "central to the revival of the industry's fortunes in New York City has been the emergence and growth of the garment industry in China-town."[16] During this period, the number of Chinese women working in New York's Chinatown garment factories increased from 8,000 to 20,000. Yet, even with their importance to the industry and the fact that they are unionized, their wages and conditions are deplorable.

THE RANK-AND-FILE GARMENT WORKERS' MOVEMENT

The ILGWU had long considered Chinese women to be docile and tied to Chinatown's political and social structure. In the summer of 1982, during negotiations for a new contract, this stereotype was shattered. The negotiations involved the renewal of a three-year contract and called for the standard wage increase. The manufacturers signed the contract; in fact, the same contract had already been signed to cover 120,000 non-Chinese garment workers on the East Coast. But the Chinese subcontractors balked. They were angry because even though 85 percent of the firms affected by the contract in the Local 23–25 were Chinese-owned, there were no Chinese on the negotiating team. As their business constituted the backbone of New York's garment industry and the most vital segment of Chinatown's economy, the subcontractors expected the community to rally behind them, particularly in this clear case of "racial discrimination." The contractors said to the workers: "We are all Chinese and should be able to settle this in our own house; there is no need to go to the white man's union."[17]

The union had hardly expected a roadblock in Chinatown, but it had to head off the confrontation. The union called for a demonstration by its membership in Columbus Park, on the edge of Chinatown. According to reliable accounts from within the union, the union officials had no idea how the Chinatown women would react, since their staff had not been close to the membership. Some even doubted that the Chinese would turn out at all. But they did. Just days before the demonstration, grass-roots organizations like the Chinese Staff and Workers Association spoke out publicly against the Chinese contractors. The rank-and-file ILGWU union members quickly mobilized. Hundreds of women volunteered to operate phone banks to contact individual members, urging them to turn out. Others wrote bilingual leaflets, banners, and propaganda material. On the day of the demonstration 20,000 workers turned out, making it one of the largest union demonstrations in the city's history. After the mass demonstration, the Chinese contractors backed off, and the workers won a new contract.

This militant demonstration showed that the Chinese workers were more class- than race-conscious on issues relating to their work, when given a chance to participate and take a stand in the American labor movement. Unfortunately, the ILGWU did not take advantage of the workers' activism to build a strong rank-and-file powerbase. The union coopted the most active members into manager positions. It treats the rest of its membership as "clients," not as an organizable spearhead of its power and continues to operate as a social agency for the workers.

The union leadership still pretends to be fighting for its members. In the spring of 1997, a presidential task force that included representatives of human rights groups, labor unions, and apparel industry giants like Nike, Liz Claiborne and L. L. Bean, reached an agreement to end sweatshop conditions by creating a code of conduct on wages and working conditions for apparel factories that are to be used by American companies around the world. According to the task force's co-chair, Robert Karp of Liz Claiborne, "the industry, human rights, labor and the Clinton Administration shared a commitment to improve the working conditions around the world."[18] One of the most active participants in the task force was Jay Mazur, the president of UNITE. His participation, one assumes, was to aim at elevating the labor standards of third world countries in order to slow down the U.S. industry job losses to the third world factories—a complicated task, fraught with contradictions.

One stipulation of the agreement was a maximum sixty-hour workweek—the maximum standard workweek would be forty-eight hours in countries that do not already have a standard of fewer hours, with the maximum number of overtime hours set at twelve. Of course, the task force assumes that the American labor market is quite different, because the U.S. standard workweek is forty hours, so it modifies the American law by not imposing a limit on how many overtime hours can be worked. Under the new code, the industry agrees not to force employees in its American factories to work more than twelve overtime hours beyond the forty-hour workweek.

All of this is quite ironic. While the UNITE president busies himself helping to impose "humane" working standards in the third world factories, members of his own union in America are not protected. During the new three-year contract negotiation in 1997 between Local 23–25 of UNITE and Chinese contractors, the union, trying to put pressure on the contractors, revealed the results of its own membership survey, which asked union members to list their greatest grievances on their jobs. The number-one complaint, according to the survey, was working extremely long hours, including Sundays, without overtime pay.[19] UNITE members in the United States, under union contracts, have been working over sixty-hour weeks without overtime pay. American employers, under contract with UNITE, headed by Jay Mazur, are violating the task force's new code aimed at introducing humane conditions for third world factories—in the midst of New York City.

Did the union need a membership survey to come up with this information? Where has it been all this time and why has it not imposed union standards at its Chinatown shops? And, if the conditions in its own shops are so deplorable, why go around the world—in the name of human rights—drafting standards for others to follow?

The institutionalization of the labor movement has robbed the workers of their strength to fight back. They have become alienated and isolated, and they are not expected to be competent enough to do anything for themselves. Wing Lam, the executive director of the Chinese Staff and Workers Association, describes this as a profoundly "dehumanizing process." No wonder most Chinese members know the union only as their health-care provider—not by any means an insignificant role, since most of the seamstresses' husbands work in restaurants without health-care coverage. But most importantly, the union has not been able to stem the decline in labor conditions in the Chinese community, which have worsened after the influx of illegal immigrant workers.

ORGANIZING CHINESE RESTAURANT WORKERS

The second largest segment of the workforce in the Chinese community is employed in the restaurant trade. The restaurant workers' experience with organized labor is even more disappointing. American organized labor is simply not interested in organizing the Chinese in this field.

In the late 1970s, there were a number of expensive and well-known Chinese-operated restaurants on Manhattan's Upper East Side whose owners never worried about unions and routinely treated their Chinese workers badly. Waiters were paid low wages and worked long hours; they had neither job security nor benefits. It was common for management to order them to do chores, such as dumping garbage, mopping floors, cleaning bathrooms, or buying cigarettes and running errands for the owners' wives. Some establishments provided poor-quality, fatty leftover meats for the workers' meals and charged them for it. A few of the more political Chinese waiters, frustrated by their working conditions, asked the Hotel and Restaurant Employees and Bartenders Union Local 69 for help. The union had no plans to organize the Chinese but agreed to help as long as the workers themselves assumed the mobilizing responsibility.

In May 1978 Uncle Tai's, a profitable Upper East Side establishment serving Sichuanese food, became the first Chinese restaurant in the city in almost forty years to become organized. Others soon followed. By 1979 workers in at least four other non-Chinatown restaurants had joined Local 69. Each restaurant was organized with overwhelming worker support, because the workers, having accumulated grievances over a long period, had finally found a vehicle for dealing with their problems.

The waiters who joined the union, however, were soon disappointed. Local 69 regularly refused to enforce contracts and allowed management to get away with labor violations. Union members at one restaurant accused the union representative from their local of sitting by while they were replaced by nonunion workers.[20]

In response to these complaints, Chinese labor activists formed the Chinese Staff and Workers Association (CSWA). Its main objective was to encourage unionization in the Chinese community and to establish a strong voice to pressure the restaurant union to be responsive to the needs of Chinese workers.

The response from Local 69 was not encouraging. In 1981, waiters and kitchen staff at Peng's Restaurant on the Upper East Side expressed their desire to be unionized. Despite dismissal warnings and threats by the owner, the workers voted 14-to-2 to join the union. The owner closed the restaurant and reopened three months later under a new name. The "new" owner allowed the workers to be organized by Local 69, but refused to rehire those who had voted for unionization under the "old" management. The union went along with this arrangement. The old workers smelled foul play and brought a suit against the new management with the National Labor Relations Board. They won after five long years of court proceedings, but during the trial the union testified for the management.

Similar bitter experiences with Local 69 have been repeated at other Chinese restaurants. Its irresponsibility turned the Chinese against organized labor altogether, suffocating their growing movement in its infancy.

In February 1980, a dispute broke out at the largest Chinatown restaurant of the time, the Silver Palace. The dispute was triggered when management asked the waiters to kick in an additional share of their tips for the business managers. In Chinatown restaurants, a waiter's tip is customarily divided into equal shares, two of which go into the managers' pool. In the Silver Palace case, management argued, business was so good that the waiters ought to contribute two additional shares. The waiters were paid less than $150 a month in wages, which was already a violation of labor law, and relied on tips as the major part of their income; naturally, they protested. The management fired fifteen of them and immediately hired others to replace them.

The fired waiters approached the CSWA. After discussions, they decided to picket the restaurant in order to force the management to negotiate. The CSWA mobilized other waiters from uptown unionized restaurants, and called on its membership and contacts in Chinatown to lend support. They also organized mass meetings and formed a support committee. The fired waiters, their supporters and waiters from uptown restaurants, took turns on the picket lines.

Such open defiance in Chinatown was a shock to the community. Most people did not think union organizing was possible in Chinatown. It was all the more surprising because the workers dared to take on the politically well-connected management of the Silver Palace— one of the partners was the president of the Chinatown Restaurant Association, and several others were well-known leaders of the notorious Hip Sing *tong*.[21]

Nevertheless, the picketing was successful, severely reducing business at the Silver Palace. The community honored the picket line because countless residents were working, had worked, or had close family members who worked in restaurants. Even some of the owners believed the management at the Silver Palace had gone too far. The

Silver Palace owners finally withdrew the demand for additional shares of tips and rehired the strikers. When the workers realized that they had won, they understood that simply getting their jobs back would not ensure job security. They decided, by an overwhelming vote of 27 to 7, to form an independent union. Silver Palace thus became the first restaurant in Chinatown to be organized. The "3–18 Independent Union" (March 18, 1980, was the date they were fired) signed a contract with management that included all the basic terms and benefits routinely guaranteed outside of Chinatown: a forty-hour workweek, overtime pay, paid holidays, health benefits, collective bargaining, and job security. The terms were revolutionary—no other Chinatown workers had ever enjoyed anything comparable.

Within two years, several other Chinatown restaurants were unionized, but soon thereafter the momentum slackened. Because of the successful organizing at Silver Palace, owners quickly improved labor conditions at other restaurants to avoid similar "labor problems." Some shrewdly co-opted a few "leaders" among the workers into managerial positions, offering them, in several cases, company shares. Most of all, Chinese workers had shown militancy but lacked the organizational strength to maintain their gains. Since the workers in each restaurant formed an independent union, the organizational base was weak. CSWA served as a coordinator for the different independent unions, but without funds for full-time organizers and a large strike fund, the unionization movement could not grow.

THE ORGANIZING STYLE OF THE CHINESE STAFF AND WORKERS ASSOCIATION

To organize the rank and file in the Chinese community—without resources, without political power, without the help of larger American society—is close to impossible. But when unionized workers have a problem with an employer and the existing American union refuses to intervene, they have nowhere to turn—certainly not to the traditional Chinese associations nor the social welfare agencies, which usually avoid antagonizing Chinatown's business community so as not to threaten their funding sources. They can file a complaint on their own with state or federal labor authorities or with the National Labor Relations Board but, many being recent immigrants, they usually lack the knowledge and confidence to take on the issue by themselves.

The Chinese Staff and Workers Association has become, by default, the only hope for Chinese immigrant workers. Whenever workers come to the CSWA for help, its staff has to explain that the association is not a social service agency—that it would help them and fight *with* them, but not fight *for* them. The initial help, for instance, consists of advising them to file the case with the New York State Labor Department rather than at the federal level because, based on the association's experience, the former is tougher on employers who withhold wages, and it will prosecute cases without investigating the plaintiff's legal status. The association also helps in filing the case, but the effort that really makes the difference has to come from the workers. The workers that come to the CSWA office are told that they need to get the rest of the employees in the factory or restaurant involved, and that they should elect from among themselves several delegates to coordinate the campaign. They are told to act as a group when approaching the labor department; otherwise, the department will not take them seriously and will simply play a delaying game. To add pressure on the labor department and the employers, and to encourage hundreds of others who face the same problem to come out as well, the workers are advised to speak out publicly in the community.

CSWA's approach to organizing—"from the bottom up"—is not new. It is based on the belief that real power comes from the participation of the rank and file, not from organizers, so the number of paid employees at the CSWA is kept intentionally small. Staffer Wah Lee explains, "The workers do not come to think that the CSWA will do everything for them. If that were the case, we would have robbed them of their power and energy."

This kind of approach is easier said than done. It is difficult for the workers to learn to do things for themselves. It is especially difficult to mobilize female Chinese workers. Rodha, a women's labor organizer, explains that "the first and most difficult task in working with Chinese women is to raise their level of self-confidence. They tend not to believe that they can accomplish things by themselves nor that what they do will make a difference." Growing up in a male-dominated culture, most immigrant Chinese women tend to be reticent and to subordinate themselves to men. Once in the United States, they feel even more vulnerable—ill at ease in the English-speaking environment, burdened with child care, housework, and the stressful, tedious jobs they must take on at garment factories to "supplement" their family income. They feel physically and psychologically tied down and unable to do anything for themselves.

All of this contributes to their low self-esteem, so the first task for the CSWA is to try to alter that self-perception by exposing the larger external factors that determine the women's condition. The Association's Women's Committee holds regular Sunday afternoon discussions attended by women from different factories. They use this opportunity to air their concerns, giving participants a chance to see that others have the same problems—that their problems are not the result of their own faults or incompetence. But their experience shows that Chinese workers come out only when suffering extreme hardship and abuses.

CHINESE WORKERS NEVER FALTER

To be certain, without legal and organized labor protection, most Chinese workers do experience extreme abuses, but the will of Chinatown's workers has never faltered. As the number of Chinese immigrants steadily increased during the 1980s, many began to look beyond the garment and restaurant trades for other opportunities. In 1988 the Chinatown Planning Council (CPC) received a federal grant to institute a training program for workers in the construction industry. The program promised job placement after graduation. Some forty Chinese immigrants enrolled, but it soon became clear that the CPC had no program; instead, it used the trainees as menial laborers in renovating CPC's own office space, and paid them five dollars an hour, half the amount stipulated by the government contract. CPC administrators expelled those who complained.

As a way of protecting themselves against the CPC's arbitrary policies, the remaining trainees formed a union. They were also promptly dismissed from the program, but they decided to sue. After considerable deliberation, the federal court ruled in the trainees' favor. The CPC was found guilty and was told to pay back full wages plus underpayment based on the market rate for construction work, which was then approximately $17 an hour. The total amount the CPC owed the workers came close to $2 million. The CPC appealed but lost. It then pleaded poverty as a nonprofit service organization, and tried to shift responsibility to the City of New York, which had contracted the CPC to run the program. The city, too, resisted, and the case dragged on.

Publicly funded training programs, such as the one advertized by the CPC, are greatly needed and much appreciated by Chinese immigrants who have long been trapped in ethnic ghettos and limited to employment in the restaurant and garment trades. The opportunity to break into a new trade, such as construction, is rare for Chinese Americans. A number of Chinese immigrants from Hong Kong in the CPC training program had jobs as construction workers in Hong Kong, but they were unable to find such jobs in America because of the restrictive nature of the construction unions, particularly when it comes to hiring minorities. The way the CPC case was handled clearly demonstrated that neither the federal nor the city government had any intention of integrating the construction trade.

But the CPC trainees did not give up. They decided to make a two-pronged attack on the construction industry. First, they sought to expose the CPC by picketing its annual fund-raising events, dropping leaflets and demonstrating at the homes of members of its board of directors. They met with some success—after six years, the city and the CPC finally came up with the funds to settle the case. In 1991, the trainees along with other Chinese construction workers formed the Chinese Construction Workers Association (CCWA) in alliance with the city-wide Coalition to End Racism in the Construction Trade. Chinese workers began to fight for jobs at construction sites alongside African American and Latino workers. In the early 1990s, Chinatown experienced a construction boom, with a number of large buildings coming up, including several banks and a Chinese senior citizen home. But none of the builders wanted to hire Chinese workers, who had to picket to get a few odd jobs. Chinese construction workers' first serious confrontation with the building industry came in 1992, when major construction for an annex to the Federal Plaza and an extension of the Federal Court House began at Foley Square, right on the edge of Chinatown.

The CCWA first approached the General Service Administration in charge of all federal construction. The GSA refused to discuss the matter. The CSWA and CCWA then mobilized the Chinatown community in two major demonstrations, drawing close to one thousand residents into the streets. Demonstrators held banners that read "Stop Exclusion" and "Equal Access to Jobs," and hundreds of garment seamstresses took time off from work to show their support for Chinatown's construction workers. One seamstress explained: "I don't know any English nor do I have any skills, that's why I am slaving away in a garment factory. But it is wrong for the Americans to exclude Chinese who have construction skills from getting jobs." After negotiating with the Chinese Construction Workers Association, the contractors at Foley Square finally agreed to hire one hundred Asians. Their victory represents an important example of Chinese immigrants' attempt to integrate American labor.

ORGANIZING THE UNORGANIZED

Chinese immigrants are not the only workers who need and want to be organized. Millions of Americans in the secondary labor market are not organized, among them women, service laborers, and white-

[203]

collar office workers. But the fastest-growing segment of the unorganized work force by far is immigrant workers. The size of the Hispanic labor force alone has grown four times as fast as the non-Hispanic workforce since 1980—to over 10 million workers. Among them Mexican Americans account for the largest group (6.3 million), followed by Central and South Americans (1.6 million), and Puerto Ricans (900,000).[22] Now that the big national unions are fighting for survival, the comfort of organizing the well-off part of the working class is no longer an option. The union's "old guard" have to move into this new territory to organize workers whom they had kept at arm's length in the past. John Sweeney, the new president of the AFL-CIO, is talking seriously about organizing them for the first time. An Irish Catholic native of the Bronx, Sweeney has not been identified with union reform movements in the past, and had headed the Service Employees International Union (SEIU). The president of SEIU's New York City local and Sweeney's handpicked successor, Gus Bevona, pays himself more than $400,000 a year and runs such a secret operation that members can't get into the local offices without an appointment.[23] In fact, while Bevona's union has waged numerous campaigns to persuade corporations in New York to employ only union members to clean their offices, it itself employs nonunion workers to clean its own headquarters in Manhattan. The seventy workers it hired had to sign an agreement denying them union protection in grievance disputes over dismissal, wages and working conditions.[24]

Sweeney did campaign against the AFL-CIO's old guard, promising to organize more workers. He has also replaced many cobwebbed "organizers" who for many years seemed to be organizing only the file cabinets in their offices.[25] In the last year or so, he has focused on raising wages—he has even written a book, *America Needs a Raise*—while his union lobbied hard and successfully in Congress for a hike in the minimum wage. But this is hardly an issue that affects most immigrant workers, for their wages have not yet reached the *old* minimum.

Since becoming president of the AFL-CIO, Sweeney has been criticized by a number of union activists and labor historians such as Peter Rachleff for not pushing for union democracy and failing to take a particularly strong stand against labor–management cooperation.[26] The AFL-CIO has also been attacked for counting on the Democratic Party to save the union by spending $35 million on congressional races in the 1996 general election, with debatable results, considering that the Republican Party maintains control of the House and the Senate and that the reelection of a center-to-the-right president takes labor's support for granted and has appointed a pro-business executive as labor secretary. Sweeney is also talking about spending $20 million on organizing, which will buy some 200 organizers nationwide—a paltry amount compared to the $100 million the union is investing in a real estate project in San Francisco or the $6 billion it collects from its memberships' dues every year.[27]

Reformers in the Teamsters for a Democratic Union (TDU), which has been struggling to clean up union corruption, are also challenging the AFL-CIO model of organizing based on professional organizers, the only model officially endorsed by John Sweeney. Ken Paff of TDU explains that "to pay all the organizers we need would cost billions. We've tried instead to create a culture in the union based on rank-and-file organizing—to create 10,000 volunteer organizers that will work through volunteer committees."[28]

The only way American unions can survive is by organizing the unorganized; the only way unprotected working people can look to a better future is by being part of the larger American labor movement—a revitalized one.

CHAPTER 9

The Undocumented Immigrant as Part of American Labor

THE MOST EFFECTIVE WEAPON USED BY AMERICAN CAPITAL IN WEAK-
ening the power of organized labor has been to hire immigrant
workers. As we have seen, immigrants are cheap and controllable.
The conditions they toil under make a mockery of the already low
American labor standards—the most regressive among the advanced
industrial nations. The United States, unlike other nations, does not
even ban the permanent replacement of striking workers.

Most Americans think of America as an "immigrant nation" and
they accept as an article of faith the notion that new foreign workers
create a net plus for the U.S. economy—they do the unpleasant
work at low wages which native-born Americans are not willing to
perform. An increasing number of economists, however, argue that
the influx of low-skilled (both legal and illegal) foreign workers into
the United States has substantial negative effects on the earnings of
the native-born workers. An official report commissioned by the
National Academy of Science concluded that while immigration benefits the U.S. economy, the newcomers do hurt the job prospects as
well as the income of low-skilled native-born workers. The report
states that the immigrants were a factor in "about 44 percent of the
total decline in wages of high-school dropouts from 1980 to 1994."[1]
George Borjas of Harvard University maintains that immigrants help
the owners of businesses that employ them, and that their employment has a particularly negative impact on African Americans in
large urban centers. Again and again, surveys confirm that white
employers prefer new immigrants of virtually any nationality or ethnicity to U.S.-born African Americans.[2]

One does not have to be a racist or a nativist to appreciate the
downward pressure the low-skilled immigrants exert on American
wage levels. Legal Chinatown residents are the first to point out how
the illegal Fuzhounese are hurting their incomes. In this light, it is
not surprising that 55 percent of Asian American voters in California

[207]

supported Proposition 187, the measure to restrict benefits to illegal aliens (about the same percentage as in the African American voting pool).

Illegal immigrants, however, are not at the root of the problem of depressed wages, although the employers, who recruit them, intentionally attempt to create precisely this impression. It is not that the illegals are doing the jobs that no Americans want to do—it is American employers who do not want to hire American workers, preferring the immigrants and the illegals. Richard M. Estrada, a commissioner of the U.S. Commission on Immigration Reform, testified at a U.S. House of Representatives hearing that whenever employers claim that "they are not able to find workers, they fail to complete the sentence. What they really mean is that they can't find workers at the extremely low wages and working conditions they offer."[3] In the same testimony Mr. Estrada used the example of California's agribusiness to show that employers "do not want so much a stable supply of labor, but rather a dependable system of constantly disposable and replenishable labor. Foreign labor is best for their needs precisely because . . . such labor . . . illegal or legally admitted . . . 'work hard and scared.' "[4]

Illegal immigrants can increasingly be found as the critical labor force in a number of industries. In addition to the garment, domestic service, and agricultural industries, the most vulnerable of foreign workers, including Mexicans and Central American illegals and Southeast Asian refugees, have now been aggressively recruited as beef, pork, and poultry packers in the Midwest, to perform some of the most dangerous jobs in the country. Journalist Marc Cooper reports a staggering illness or injury rate of 36 out of every 100 workers annually in the meat industry. "The entire debate over whether or not immigrants are of economic benefit is disingenuous," Cooper quotes Mark Grey, an expert on the packing industry, as saying. "No one wants the truth—that food processing in America today would collapse were it not for immigrant labor."[5]

By recruiting illegals, capital is attacking the weakest link in the

American labor chain, because illegal immigrants are the most difficult workers to organize. American labor has always been reluctant to
deal with the illegals. A typical view is expressed by an AFL-CIO
official: "Illegals seldom join unions and they almost never go on
strike or otherwise complain about their wages or working conditions, because they fear deportation and the return to the poverty in
their homeland."[6]

But the importation of legal and illegal immigrant workers, such
as the Fuzhounese, is an integral part of the global strategy employed
by U.S. capital. Leaving them outside of the labor movement plays
right into the hands of capital—dividing the working class and thereby thwarting its attempt to build a powerful labor movement.

Immigrants are bearing the brunt of the restructuring process in
the American economy. They fill the "bad" jobs offering low wages,
high turnover, and poor working conditions. In the meantime, immigrants have become scapegoats for the unemployment of native
American workers, for depressed wages, and for other social problems. Most of all, argues Berkeley sociologist Manuel Castels, "the
utility of immigrant labour to capital derives primarily from the fact
that it can act towards it as though the labor movement does not
exist."[7]

It is high time for immigrant labor to become organized, not just
for simple humanitarian reasons but because, by default, they have
become the last line of defense against the further decline of American labor standards.

AGAINST THE SUBCONTRACTING SYSTEM

According to data furnished by the Bureau of Labor Statistics, Hispanic Americans have the lowest average income among all major
racial groups. The median weekly income of an Hispanic worker is
only $329, versus $383 for blacks and $494 for whites. Hispanic
Americans also have the lowest level of educational attainment and
the highest percentage of individuals living in poverty,[8] and yet this

is not because they are not working—in fact, their labor participation rate, at 80.2 percent, is higher than both that of whites at 73.9 percent and blacks at 64.2 percent.[9] If Hispanic illegal immigrants were added to the calculation, the rates would be even worse than these statistics indicate. But precisely because of this situation, the militancy of Hispanic labor has been rising dramatically in the 1990s, just as the American labor movement is in decline everywhere else.

Of course, labor organizing of the Hispanic community is not new. Chicano workers attracted nationwide attention during the 1960s and early 1970s when trade unionist Cesar Chavez and his United Farm Worker Organizing Committee brought new life, imagination, and bold tactics—like the historic grape boycott—to an otherwise quiescent labor movement.[10] Today, Hispanic immigrant workers are not waiting for reforms in the existing unions; they are forcing the unions to deal with their problems. Hispanics now constitute about 10 percent of the U.S. population, 10 percent of the labor force and roughly 8 percent of unionized workers. This last number represents the result of a rapid increase in the last ten years, having started from almost nothing. These newly organized Hispanic workers are this country's most marginal and lowest-paid workers; they are new immigrants and many of them are undocumented. Their rank-and-file movement has rebuilt garment industrial unions in Texas, Florida, and Chicago. Elsewhere, thousands of Hispanic farm workers, drywallers, janitors, hotel workers, and other low-wage workers have engaged in massive strikes, militant action, and civil disobedience to bring public attention to their struggle and demands.[11] Their militancy has galvanized the American trade unions and has catapulted Hispanics to the forefront of today's labor movement.

In Los Angeles, for instance, Hispanic immigrant workers have led the way in one of the most successful new organizing efforts, the "Janitors for Justice" campaign. At the beginning of the 1980s, the Service Employers International Union (SEIU) organized janitors who worked for large corporations. The jobs were secure and relatively well paid. Then the corporations began to replace their in-house cleaning contracts with nonunion subcontractors, often employing immigrant laborers. SEIU first tried concessionary bargaining in an attempt to stop the outflow of jobs. Cooperation with corporate management was the order of the day, but the result was a continuing, massive loss of union jobs. Forced by their rank and file, the union leadership developed the concept of "Janitors for Justice," directly challenging the subcontracting system in the cleaning service industry. This subcontracting system had, they discerned, led to the emergence of a pyramidal structure, with building owners and corporations at the top, the cleaning firms that bid for contracts in the middle, and janitors who do the work at the bottom.

Cleaning contractors and building owners conveniently created a vacuum of responsibility, benefiting from exploiting the workers while pointing fingers at each other. "Janitors for Justice" circumvented the pyramid's middle section with a "corporate campaign" strategy that was successful because workers adopted old-time militant tactics—blocking freeways and bridges, staging guerrilla theater in front of corporate offices, disrupting shareholder and city hall meetings, picketing the homes of corporate executives, and taking over their offices.[12] These tactics gained them better contracts and new members. The membership of SEIU Local 399 in Los Angeles has swollen to 8,000—at least 70 percent of all janitors in the city's commercial office buildings.

In 1991 SEIU Local 1877 in California's Silicon Valley led immigrant janitors, many of whom were illegal and spoke little English, on strike against Shine Building Maintenance, Inc., for low wages and mistreatment of workers. Rather than picket Shine headquarters, the union organized demonstrations to bring pressure on Shine's high-profile client, Apple Computer, Inc. The workers specifically demanded that the contractor stop threatening and laying off illegal workers. The organizers of the strike argued that regardless of whether the janitors were in the United States legally or not, they were entitled to their dignity and decent benefits once employed.

"So what [if they are illegal]?" one of the leaders said at a news conference. "If they are so horrible, how come they're hired? We had the same battle with growers; we thought we had risen above such insensitivity." In March 1991, the National Labor Relations Board issued a complaint against Shine alleging violations of federal laws, including threatening employees and arbitrarily laying off workers. The abrupt layoffs had followed an audit of the firm by the U.S. Immigration and Naturalization Service. A union organizer claims that the INS appeared just as the workers were trying to organize. "It has been our experience up and down the country that companies will use the INS as a union buster."[13]

With the success of SEIU Local 399 in L.A., the wave of grassroots worker organizing has led to conflicts between the entrenched union officials and the rank and file. In the summer of 1995, a group of rank-and-file janitors calling itself the Multiracial Alliance charged their local's leadership with obstructing democracy within the union. "Most of the labor movement are old white men, while an increasing number of rank-and-file members are people of color," a spokesperson for the group said. "This creates tensions between leaders and the rank and file."[14] The militant workers forced the union to act, exposing the inherent contradictions within the trade union structure.

The task facing minority and immigrant workers is not only to join unions, but to challenge American organized labor's racial hierarchy and its elitist from-the-top-down organizing approach. Yet, as the Chicano organizing experience shows, even in the context of global economy, even when the organized labor has lost its way, and even when the workers are immigrants and many of them undocumented, the workers' struggle goes on.

WE WILL FIGHT EVEN IF IT MEANS DEPORTATION

The Mexican immigrants' spirit of struggle prevails among the Chinese immigrant workers and the Chinese illegals as well. Few people would expect Chinese illegal aliens to be labor activists. But, like any other human beings, pushed beyond the limits, the Fuzhounese illegal workers will fight back. As the old Chinese saying goes: "Forced into the corner to face death, everybody fights back and takes you down with him."

In the late 1980s, Wai Chee Tong and Stanley Chang operated a garment factory in Manhattan's Chinatown where they withheld thousands of dollars in workers' back wages. When workers demanded payment, the partners closed the factory, but they opened a new one under the name Wai Chang in October 1989 in Brooklyn's Sunset Park district. None of the workers from the old shop pursued the case any further, and the new employees in Brooklyn knew nothing about the partners' past. This time, the two entrepreneurs decided to hire mainly illegal workers—Fuzhounese, Malaysians, and Hispanics—approximately seventy in all.

Mrs. Lee, a middle-aged Chinese woman from Malaysia, was one of the employees. She was at first thankful that the owners hired her despite her illegal status; they even gave jobs to her three daughters and a son, ranging in age from twelve to fifteen. The oldest daughter worked as a seamstress, while the younger ones cut threads. The four of them together worked 200 hours a week for a paltry $100. Yet Mrs. Lee, whose husband was a low-paid restaurant waiter, appreciated the owners' gesture for, as she put it, "every bit of extra money helped." The owners even "promised" at one time to sponsor her application for legal immigration.

Evidently, the owners were "nice" to a number of other Chinese illegals as well. Several diligent workers, whose services were particularly helpful during rush periods, were given rented spaces in the factory to live in. The partners were also attentive to details. In mid-summer, the wife of one of the partners organized a barbecue cookout of Polish sausage, spare ribs, and hot dogs in the factory's backyard. Around Christmas, the workers were invited to an "American" drinking club somewhere in Manhattan, where one of the owner's sons worked, to celebrate. When the employees had to work overtime—beyond the regular twelve-hour shift—the partners ordered take-out food for everyone after nine in the evening. The courting paid off. The partners gained the loyalty of their workers, who did not complain about working eighty-four hours a week. In fact, the workers often worked even longer, when the owners needed them to complete a particular order.

But around September 1990, just at a time when the shop was particularly busy, the owners stopped paying wages. They blamed their cash-flow problem on a break-in through the fire escape door—a story everyone in the factory knew was bogus. The workers demanded payment and threatened action. But the owners treated them all to a banquet dinner at a Chinese restaurant in Flushing, Queens, instead, and pleaded for more time to resolve their financial difficulties. Weeks after that banquet there was still no payment, even though the factory was turning out an average of 15,000 garments per week. By then, the owners of Wai Chang owed one female worker $3,000; another $6,000, one year's back pay; a couple a total of $10,000; and a seventy-year-old male worker $1,900.

The situation was becoming critical, and a number of workers could no longer hold on. Angela Liang, a twenty-eight-year-old immigrant from Guangdong, had received her last check in August. She was earning as little as $3 an hour for making hems, yet was owed $2,000 in back wages and was getting by with her three-year-old son on the $250 her husband earned each week as a cook. "I'm at work in the morning even before my eyes are open," said another worker, "for thirteen to fourteen hours. It's midnight before I return home, but all the money I get is not enough for my subway fare." Yet another claims that his wife and kids left him because he was not able to bring money home.

When the partners began claiming that the money they owed had gone to the other shareholders of the company, whom they could not touch, the workers finally met and voted for a one-day strike on December 22.[15]

Nothing happened as a result of the strike. Then they organized a second stoppage on January 2, and the partners brought a nasty-looking gangster onto the factory floor to threaten them. "If you want to fool around with the management, step outside to talk with me, face to face," he snarled. The owners also threatened to report the workers to the Immigration and Naturalization Service. "They took advantage of the fears of undocumented and elderly aliens," remembers Angela Liang.

By the beginning of 1991, the owners owed seventy workers a total of $170,000. The workers met as a group repeatedly, and decided to ask for help, first from the Chinatown Planning Council. They then approached the Chinese Staff and Workers Association for assistance. The association helped them file a complaint with the New York State Labor Department, whose investigation quickly halted when department officials "could not locate the owners." By then, the partners had already closed the factory, transferred their accounts out of the corporation, liquidated their properties, and disappeared. The department also refused workers' requests to contact manufacturers who subcontracted to Wai Chang and ask them to withhold their payments to the partners until the back wages were paid.

But the workers did not give up. At a news conference open to the Chinese- and English-language press, two undocumented workers contended that because the partners knew that they had no green cards and were afraid of having their status exposed, the factory owners thought they could get away with not paying wages. The two workers vowed to pursue the case to get back their hard-earned pay, *even if it meant deportation,* and offered to testify in court against the owners to achieve that objective. The workers then filed criminal charges with the New York State Attorney General's Office.

After four months of investigation the owners, Wai Chee Tong and Stanley Chang, were charged with forty-one misdemeanor counts for failing to pay wages and keep accurate payroll records. The judgment stipulated that Tong and Chang pay over $80,000 in unpaid wages to forty workers who sued, making it the largest suit ever won in New York's garment industry.

The prosecution, however, could not move forward because the two owners "disappeared" again. Wai Chang workers applied for a warrant for their arrest, and organized a rally in the Chinese community seeking help in locating the owners and encouraging others in the community who had suffered from the same type of mistreatment to come forward. During the rally, which was attended by a meager number of sympathetic politicians, the workers urged the state legislature to change the legal classification of withholding wages from a misdemeanor to a felony. At the same time, the workers spent weeks assisting the attorney general's office in their search for Tong and Chang. They stayed up for nights on end to monitor a number of residences where the two were expected. Finally, at seven-thirty on the morning of December 13, 1991, they spotted Stanley Chang walking out of his hiding place and had him arrested. He was convicted and imprisoned for nine months. Again, the imprisonment of an employer for holding back wages was the first in New York State history.

Unfortunately, after he got out of prison Chang claimed bankruptcy and refused to pay the workers. When the workers again brought the case to court, the prosecutor from the attorney general's office refused to press the case any further, saying "What more do you want? It's not as if he has killed somebody."

But most of the workers did not care whether the owners went to prison; they just wanted their hard-earned wages. Six years later, they are still pursuing the case in civil courts. In the latest development, lawyers at the Asian American Legal Defense and Education Fund were trying to obtain a judgment against the owner's real estate property—a building—which the owners had conveniently sold to their relatives for one dollar.

Having risked retaliation from gangs and employers, the additional legal tangles the Wai Chang workers have had to contend with are discouraging. Yet making a stand has given them a measure of human dignity. All they are asking for is one of the most basic rights of every working individual—the right to be paid after the work has been done.

THE POWER OF THE RANK AND FILE

The Wai Chang workers' action has served as an inspiration to many others, showing them that they can fight even if they are undocumented aliens. Thousands of workers employed in hundreds of Chinatown factories and restaurants have experienced similar problems with unpaid back wages. The employers count on the fact that labor laws on this issue are lenient and never enforced, and on the assumption that Chinese workers, particularly the undocumented, would not fight back. One Chinese community organizer describes the issue of back wages sprouting like "green grass after a spring rain." The militant action of the Wai Chang workers has shown the others that they should not be afraid of their bosses.

Soon after hearing of Stanley Chang's arrest, workers at Judy's Place Fashion, a unionized shop in Chinatown, went to the CSWA for help. The owner of Judy's Place Fashion owed them over $20,000, and the CSWA urged the New York State Labor Department and ILGWU Local 23-25 to investigate the case. Both started their investigations slowly, and failed to follow through when they "could not find the owner." Workers quickly realized that they had to rely on their own efforts. Several took time off from their jobs to follow Jimmy Tse, the owner, from his home to another garment factory he managed in Queens. There they confronted him, but Tse fled. The workers called a news conference to alert the press, the ILGWU, and the Department of Labor of the need to take immediate action. They then increased pressure on Tse by holding public rallies and setting up tables in Chinatown to solicit residents' signatures demanding official action. After a few weeks, Jimmy Tse finally paid back his workers at Judy's Fashion.

Even workers in the restaurant industry have been affected by the movement started by Wai Chang workers. Employees of a number of uptown Manhattan Chinese restaurants went on strike to demand back wages as well. Chinese workers, the undocumented included, are clearly ready to fight for minimal rights despite having to confront the co-ethnic business owners, the threat of gang violence, pro-business labor laws, indifferent labor officials, and even the possibility of deportation.

Their grass-roots mobilization has surprised the employers, just as their militancy has surprised the unions and the labor authorities. The Department of Labor finally saw fit to set up a federal task force to investigate labor conditions in New York's Chinatown restaurant and garment industries. Local 23–25 of UNITE has now set up a special task force to handle back-wage complaints, and it has been getting results—though those familiar with this new service complain that workers are usually able to reclaim only 50 to 75 percent of the full amount owed. The union is also criticized for not publicizing the names of the violators, to warn the other workers. Naturally, it is not very helpful to those not in the union, nor is it effective in dealing with unionized shops that shut down after owing back wages.

The grass-roots action of the workers has brought a flurry of political activity. New York Governor George Pataki is pushing for a "Hot Goods Law," which will hold the manufacturers responsible, ensuring that their contractors are not employing sweatshop labor. Even former U.S. Labor Secretary Robert Reich got into the act. His department released a national report which showed that almost half of the nation's garment contractors investigated in 1996 were found to be violating federal minimum wage and overtime laws. In response, the secretary invited manufacturers and retailers to help improve compliance with labor laws in the industry by not dealing with contractors known to be labor scofflaws.

THE CHALLENGE OF CHINESE ETHNIC LABOR ORGANIZING
It is important to understand that the Wai Chang workers are no more militant than any others. They acted because they desperately needed the money to live on—as do most people who make only two

or three dollars an hour—and yet their actions caught labor authorities by surprise. But the movement ignited by Wai Chang workers has faded quickly, as all of them have long since returned to their jobs. Besides, they had only drawn fleeting public attention to their most fundamental right: being paid for their labor. They never raised the issue of other basic rights, taken for granted by most working Americans: the minimum wage, the forty-hour workweek, and overtime pay. Their ranks are simply too small to hold back the power of the employers. What's more, their action was purely spontaneous. They would need a bigger and better organization to broaden the scope and maintain the momentum of their cause. Their action could make a real difference only if it were part of a systematic rank-and-file organizing effort.

Chinatown labor has long been dominated by an ethnic economic elite who controls the community's political structure. This structure has the power to define the laws and regulations inside the enclave. It has the power to represent the community externally and has a commanding influence over the local media. The enclave's workers are fighting against great odds. To break up the ethnic elite's hegemonic power, they need intervention by American authorities, if American laws are to be enforced in the Chinese community. However, all too often, American labor officials have been indifferent to the problems of Chinese workers, blaming their inaction on the passivity of the Chinese.

In a town hall meeting held on June 29, 1994, at P.S. 124 in Chinatown, workers were invited to speak about their work environment, attended by administrators from federal and state labor departments and representatives from the offices of members of Congress and New York City Council. Some three hundred Chinatown residents, jammed in the elementary school auditorium, listened to the emotional testimonies of dozens of workers, who listed a litany of abuses at their workplaces. Government representatives learned that a twelve-hour-plus workday was increasingly common, that wages had dropped for many to only $2 an hour, and that owners often employed youth gangs to threaten workers. Still, the most consistent complaint was the nonpayment of wages.

Surprisingly, government representatives saw these problems only in legal terms. One labor official insisted that the failure of owners to pay the minimum wage constituted a violation of law and that such owners should be reported to the authorities. Another state official lectured workers that they must press for "official charges" before her office could take action against owners. The workers gasped with amazement, realizing how out of touch the authorities were with the realities of Chinatown. The Chinese see it as exactly the opposite: it is the labor authorities who do not take Chinese workers' complaints seriously, usually taking years to investigate and act while the workers who filed the complaints risk their lives by continuing to work and live in the community. Chinese workers, in fact, do come forward willingly—if and when they are assured of serious investigation and aggressive prosecution.

THE JING FONG RESTAURANT STANDOFF: A TRUE CLASS STRUGGLE

The struggle at Jing Fong Restaurant is an excellent example. The dispute began in January 1995, when Sheng Gang Deng, a waiter at the restaurant, challenged his bosses for docking his tips and was fired. The CSWA took on Deng's case even though he was the only worker from the restaurant who came forward, because it understood that no one else dared to join the whistle-blower publicly for fear of being fired, particularly knowing that the management would have plenty of others to replace them with. In fact, a number of the new workers at the restaurant were already Fuzhounese undocumented immigrants.

The CSWA helped Deng file a suit against the restaurant charging the management with forcing the workers to work twelve-hour shifts without giving them a day off during the week. In addition, the management was charged with confiscating at least 30 percent of all the waiters' tips to have them shared by the non-working investors in the restaurant—costing the workers at least $35,000 a month in lost tips. In taking on the Jing Fong case, the CSWA has escalated the labor struggle in Chinatown from unionizing workers at one single workplace to a general attack on the Chinatown restaurant industry for minimum wage violations, a challenge to the "slave labor" practices of the entire Chinatown business establishment.

The CSWA organized a picket by bringing together Chinese workers from other trades, union sympathizers, and student activists citywide demanding for Deng to be rehired. A group of one hundred picketers protested every day outside the restaurant, beating drums and displaying a coffin while chanting "slavery must go." During the summer of 1995, five college students went on a hunger strike for the cause. The Jing Fong management immediately understood what CSWA's actions might spawn, and set about organizing all restaurant owners in its defense. It also rallied the Chinatown business community behind it to confront "outsiders" who were intending to "destroy" the Chinatown economy.

Jing Fong is the largest restaurant in Chinatown, capable of accommodating over 1,000 guests. It is the place where all the important public events are held, including annual banquets for community organizations, festive celebrations for associations, and fund-raising dinners for political parties and nonprofit organizations. The owners are well connected with the Chinese business community, the traditional associations, local politicians, and with the New York Consulate General Office of the People's Republic of China. In fact, when Deng Xiaoping's daughter, Yong, came to New York, "community leaders" held an banquet in her honor at the restaurant.

In April 1995, more than 1,000 Chinese businessmen gathered at Jing Fong for a fund-raising dinner hosted by the Chinatown Restaurant Owners Association, an unprecedented show of unity among Chinatown restaurant owners. During the banquet bitter attacks were launched against Wing Lam, the executive director of the CSWA, whose photo appeared on posters in which he was accused of extortion and theft and labeled a "monster," a "blood sucker," and "public enemy number one." Jing Fong hung two bright red, twenty-five-foot banners that read: "Oppose the labor tyrant stirring up trouble," while the crowd chanted "Da dao Wing Lam," meaning "beat down Wing Lam."

Lam and his family received numerous threats after this banquet, and their seriousness should not be underestimated, for the leaders of the Restaurant Owners' Association are also the leaders of China-town's organized crime networks. Yai Chi Chan, president of the Restaurant Owners' Association, is also the Grand National President of the On Leung tong, identified recently by federal authorities as one of the three tongs on the forefront of illegal business in China-town. Wing Yeung Chan, known as "Big Head," is also a leader of the On Leung tong, and is allegedly the *dai lo*—the elder brother—of one of the most violent Chinatown youth gangs, the Ghost Shadow. He had been indicted on a litany of crimes, including murder, rob-bery, extortion, and illegal gambling in a federal case. Chung-ko Cheng, one of the six owners of Jing Fong who accused the Workers Association of trying to destroy the restaurant industry in China-town, is a former president of the Fukien-American Association, an organization suspected by the police for its ties to the Fuching youth gang—the chief "enforcers" controlling Fuzhounese illegals.[16] This coalition of restaurant owners, *tong* leaders, and human smugglers was an unprecedented threat to the civic order inside the Chinese community. With such a show of force, the management was certain of its control over the workers and its ability to force them into signing an anti-union pledge, forming a counterpicket in front of the restaurant, and parading at an anti-CSWA banquet in new uniforms, carrying banners against "outside labor agitators."

The Jing Fong affair was splitting the community wide open, forcing everyone to take sides. Those organizations that had arranged banquets at Jing Fong had to decide whether to change to another restaurant. Either way, they were taking a pro-labor or a pro-management position. Those invited to an event at the restaurant, too, had to decide whether to cross the picket lines. This dilemma affected non-Chinese public officials and politicians as well. Even the local police precinct was not spared, when the CSWA accused the Fifth Precinct Captain Thomas Chan, the first Chinese to hold such a position, of bias against the protestors when he ordered the picket to move fifty feet away from the restaurant on the pretext of the restaurant's construction of a new entranceway. The accusation of bias seemed to stick when the local *Sing Tao Daily* had a photo of Captain Chan accepting an award from members of the Chinese American Restaurant Owners Association, standing alongside Yai Chi Chan—the Grand National President of On Leung tong and the president of the restaurant association.[17] The Jing Fong struggle was historic, insofar as, for the first time, an organization representing Chinese labor interests took on the restaurant association, the Chinese business community, the *tongs,* the human smugglers, the police, and even the local press.

After the summer of 1995 the demonstration cooled off, but the New York State Attorney General's office subpoenaed the Jing Fong workers to testify. Fifteen of them came forward and provided full details of employers' violations, corroborating completely the original charges made by Mr. Sheng Gang Deng. On January 23, 1997, Attorney General Dennis Vacco announced that, after months of investigation, his office had filed a lawsuit against Jing Fong's management for allegedly cheating fifty-eight employees of over $1.5 million in tips and wages and firing the waiter who blew the whistle on the scam. The lawsuit, filed in supreme court in Manhattan, accused the restaurant of paying workers $65 to $100 a week, despite their having worked sixty hours or more. Those employees should have been paid $213.88 per week, factoring in overtime wages. The management was also charged with violations of the Fair Labor Standards Act by making improper tax deductions and providing no documentation on gross wages and deductions.

According to Attorney General Vacco's investigation, waiters were supposed to pool all their tips into one pot and split it among themselves equally—each one got one share. The Jing Fong partners, some of whom had never set foot in the restaurant and were already making millions from the profitable business, took control of the tip distribution and skimmed part of it for themselves. They were so greedy, in fact, that they were not satisfied with taking just an equal share with the waiters; they each appropriated 1.3 shares of the tips. The lowly waiters, who worked a seven-day, seventy-hour week and were dependent on the tips to complement their meager salary of less than $100 a month (another labor law violation), took home only 0.7 share of the tips.[18] On top of all these abuses, Attorney General Vacco's office was told during the investigation that the Jing Fong management had set a rule forbidding workers to congregate. If more than three workers ever assembled, they got punished by having their tips docked.[19] The workers were also asked to sign a blank piece of paper, onto which a text of their defense of the management was later inserted.

Of course, the management denied all these charges and tried to spread disinformation. Even after Attorney General Vacco provided the press with hundreds of pages of written testimony taken from workers at Jing Fong Restaurant against the employers, the Chinese press still carried only management's side of the story, accusing the attorney general of pandering to "racial politics" by attacking the Chinese community in order to gain voter appeal during the election year.[20] Then, a week after Vacco's announcement, the loft space above the CSWA office was set on fire, an incident which the New York Fire Department classified as arson.[21]

The attorney general's full-scale investigation into the labor practices in the Chinese community has jolted the Chinatown establishment. The investigation itself was a belated response to the long-standing demand by the CSWA that labor enforcement be treated as a civil rights issue for the Chinese community. CSWA's effort to pressure official intervention has finally paid off. In recognition of that fact, New York State Senator Basil Paterson passed a resolution in the New York State Senate commending the Chinese Staff and Workers Association for its persistent and courageous efforts on behalf of the New York City Chinese community. The Senate resolution specifically credits the CSWA for its effort in combating sweatshops, its campaign for Chinese construction workers, and its role in exposing the wrongdoings of Jing Fong management in paying "slave wages" and withholding tips from waiters and other workers.[22]

COMMUNITY-BASED WORKERS' ORGANIZATIONS

Significant as they are, the State Attorney General's efforts have barely scratched the surface of the labor problems in the Chinese community. External intervention will not transform the existing conditions without a community-based workers' movement. The Chinese community has always been divided vertically, along the lines of kinship, village ties, trade, and fraternal organizations; no traditional organization cuts across the class lines, with the result that power remains concentrated exclusively in the hands of the wealthy elite. Yet, the overwhelming majority in the community are working people. If they were to form a union across all trades and reorient themselves to speak up and fight for redress of genuine worker concerns, they would be able to challenge the hegemonic power of their Chinese employers within the enclave. The working people need a dynamic and activist community-based workers' organization capable of mobilizing the rank and file for action. Groups like the CSWA could be more effective if they shifted their emphasis from trade unions to community-based workers' organizations. Such organizations would work with workers across all trades and form alliances with other organizations to tackle working-class-related issues, which could include working with parents' associations to improve the community's school board, with local journalists to fight for freedom of the press, with social welfare agencies to broaden their service outreach to non-English-speaking clientele, with law enforcement to get a handle on the Chinese organized crime problem, with American political parties to provide alternatives to stale homeland politics. Most importantly, such organizations should include the undocumented aliens. Their inclusion would prevent the working-class division that has been so deftly exploited by the employers and Chinatown establishment.

Broad working-class organizations of this type could sustain a whole new political and social life in the Chinese community. They would be significantly different from the "workers' centers" currently being promoted by organized labor, which are no more than local extensions of single trade union offices, essentially interested in providing services for their members. For instance, UNITE has established a Garment Workers' Center in Sunset Park, Brooklyn, whose main programs are to teach new immigrants their constitutional rights and American culture, help them adjust, offer them English language classes, and instruct them on filing benefit forms, but impart nothing about labor organizing and activism.

The kind of horizontal political alliance proposed here once existed in New York's Chinatown, but only for a short time. In the 1930s, Chinese working people in New York were locked in the self-employed trades and trapped in the isolated ethnic community dominated by the feudal Chinese informal political structure. They too were silenced, just like the residents of Chinatown today. The majority of the Chinese then were hand-laundrymen. Although they were self-employed small-business operators, they toiled long hours and made a meager income. The traditional Chinese associations levied taxes on them, but would not help when needed.

In 1934, during the Great Depression, white laundry operators in New York, fighting for survival, repeatedly tried to pass city ordinances imposing heavy security bonds on the Chinese when they tried to renew their business licenses, in order to force them out of the trade. Without help from the traditional Chinese associations, Chinese laundrymen finally formed their own organization, the Chinese Hand Laundries Alliance (CHLA). The CHLA was independent from the traditional family, district, and fraternal associations, and it was formed when the laundrymen reached outside Chinatown for assistance. With the help of progressive American lawyers, CHLA challenged the proposed "bond ordinance," arguing that it discriminated specifically against Chinese businesses. Eventually, the city's Board of Aldermen rescinded the fees. This victory taught the Chinese that they could get things done without traditional Chinatown associations, but it came with a price: an assault on the CHLA by the Chinatown establishment.

The CHLA was able to survive the assault because of favorable external conditions. For one thing, there was a civil war in China, where the Nationalist (KMT) Government under the leadership of Chiang Kai-shek pursued an unpopular war against the Chinese Communists instead of rallying the nation to resist Japanese aggression. While the traditional Chinatown establishment supported the policies of the KMT, the CHLA called for a "united front against Japanese aggression"—a position that attracted majority support both in China and in Chinatown. The CHLA became an alternative voice, attracting many "patriotic" Chinese who slowly moved away from the influence of the KMT and the traditional associations. Thus an alternative political center in Chinatown began to emerge.

With its increasing strength, the CHLA was able to support the publication of an independent newspaper, *The China Daily News*. It formed its own youth group and its own women's organization. For the first time, the hegemony of the Chinese political elite was broken. The CHLA was further strengthened by reaching out to the American liberal civil rights groups, immigrants' rights advocates, labor unions, and anti-fascist organizations. Once people could hold different political positions openly, a whole parallel political structure in the Chinese community developed.

Unfortunately, this alternative center collapsed during the McCarthy era and the Korean War, when American politics turned to the right and the conservative KMT government was able to reimpose its control on the Chinese community. Half a century later, the Chinese community still needs a similar alternative—a pro-working-people political center, dedicated to breaking the grip of the traditional establishment.

COMMUNITY UNIONISM

There were plenty of immigrant community-based, multi-trade labor organizations in America's past. Jewish immigrants from Eastern Europe, who came around the turn of the century, lived in ethnic ghettos and worked for Jewish owners under the heavy political and social influence of Jewish religious leaders. In the early 1900s, groups like the Workmen's Circle and the Jewish National Workers Alliance were formed by Jewish trade unionists who were dissatisfied with the quasi-religious ritualism and tone of the existing order in the community.[23] These activists were influenced by socialist ideas, which they had brought over with them from Europe, stressing organizing along class rather than trade lines. They saw no need for separating organizing in the workplace from organizing in the community where they lived. Their groups took over many of the activities that charitable and religious organizations used to perform, such as feeding, lodging, and clothing friendless new immigrants and aiding them in finding employment, but they also started organizing workplaces across all trades. According to Irving Howe, "Where most American unions focused on immediate bread-and-butter issues and were likely to be hostile to heterodox ideas, the Jewish unions reached out towards a wide range of interests, from social insurance plans to co-operative housing, educational programs to Yiddishist cultural activity."[24]

Their class consciousness also led them to extend a helping hand to non-Jewish unions that were on strike. This form of organizing anticipated the "social unionism" later introduced by the Congress of Industrial Organizations (CIO).[25] It was this community-based, grass-roots type of organizing that made the CIO so effective later on in mobilizing unskilled, semi-skilled and immigrant workers.

With the transformation of America's economy into industrial monopolies, American unions too had to adjust by establishing large and centralized national organizations. Small ethnic and community-based unions became obstacles to nationwide organizing and therefore obsolete. The advent of large industrial unions, however, brought along specialization—dealing with a single trade, addressing only the issues affecting the workplace. The task of rank-and-file mobilization was taken over by union bureaucrats and professional organizers. Issues affecting working people after work, like health, housing, unemployment, and others were taken over by separate community and social welfare agencies.

As the division of responsibilities becomes more narrowly defined—with the unions interested only in wage negotiations in their trade affecting only their own membership, and social agencies and community organizations only interested in procuring funding in order to deliver their particular services—the power of labor, formerly embodied in one union, became fragmented. This division was fully institutionalized when trade unions formed district labor councils and connected them politically to the Democratic Party, while community and social welfare groups, such as the neighborhood, civil rights, women rights, welfare rights and 1960s antiwar groups, developed their own political bases through special interest politics or through mass mobilization. Community organizations even developed their own organizing theories. The once popular Saul Alinsky organizing model, for instance, emphasized the building of strong neighborhood-based organizations, which have in recent years been criticized for not addressing the needs of multicultural or multiracial communities.[26]

The split between labor and social organizations became much worse during the 1960s, when the leadership of organized labor turned more conservative and anti-communist, taking pro–Vietnam War and ambiguous women's and civil rights positions. The unions remained on the sidelines during mass mobilizations involving a number of social issues at that time. They certainly gained no adherents among the young antiwar and civil rights activists or among the so-called "New Left." The split has had particularly devastating consequences since the 1980s, when the restructuring of the American economy to one based on flexible and decentralized production made the power of organized labor institutions, originally established to deal with industrial monopolies, no longer viable. And at the same time, with the ascendency of Reaganite Republicans to political power, the "New Left," the intellectuals, and the community-based social welfare liberals were put on the defensive.

Only the less ideological post–Cold War era offers some hope for rapprochement between the left, the liberals, and organized labor, as witnessed by the current AFL-CIO effort to engage in a dialogue with the academic community through a series of teach-ins on college campuses across the nation. However, it is essential that this rapprochement be based on the understanding that a new union movement should be built to confront the current challenges posed by the global economic strategies of restructured capital.

Moreover, the problem with the present shape of organized labor is not simply one of institutional ineptitude or "old age," or the fact that America has turned into a "non-class society." Nor is it simply a question of the restructuring of the American economy. The fact is that the unions have lost the support of the workers. By 1980, for instance, according to a survey, only 13 percent of union members thought that their unions were doing an excellent or good job, 54 percent ranked their union's performance as fair, and 33 percent as poor.[27] The workers believe that union leadership is more interested in the welfare of the unions themselves than the interests of the workers they represent and the communities they are supposed to serve. So it is not surprising when unorganized workers, given the opportunity to decide on union representation, do not necessarily opt for unionization. In 1996, for instance, the AFL-CIO won only 47.6 percent of the total number of representation petitions filed—the worst in its history.[28] One can no longer automatically assume that workers will want to join unions to protect their wages and employment.

In this regard, unions, like political parties, are faced with the challenge of convincing the American public that they deserve to be trusted once again, and they are now serving its interests. They will have to be based on decentralized, grass-roots organizations, capable of addressing both the workplace and daily social needs of the working people—issues like universal health care, low-income housing, community safety, public school and transportation systems. Unions, just like political parties, will have to learn the lesson that "all politics is local."

PROMOTING WORKING-CLASS UNITY

Working people in the Chinese community expect the unions to fight for the enforcement of "American labor standards," challenge the unlawful practices of the traditional Chinese pro-business superstructure, and demolish Chinese employers' efforts to split ethnic Chinese labor into legal and illegal immigrants, in order to better exploit them both.

In view of current economic changes in the United States, what is going on in Chinatown is not at all marginal to the American labor movement. In fact, one could even place the grass-roots, multi-trade, and community-based organizing effort of Chinese workers at the forefront of American labor's fight to prevent the whole of the American working class from sliding down to third world working and living standards. Their ability to succeed should very much be of concern to the entire American labor movement.

By the same token, the Chinese community-based grass-roots movement cannot go very far without the support of a broad-based American labor movement. "There is no possibility that the Chinese can build a viable labor movement alone, within the confines of Chinese community," CSWA's executive director, Wing Lam, explains. "We need to build alliances with other rank-and-file struggles going on elsewhere."

His organization is engaged in the "National Mobilization Against Sweatshops" (NMASS), a campaign focused on the call for "the right to eight-hour workday and a forty-hour workweek." The campaign is focusing on how long people are made to work much more than on how much they are getting paid, as long hours are the most debilitating aspect of sweatshop conditions. Long hours have introduced a score of serious social and health problems, not the least of which is the dramatic shortening of a working person's expected wage-earning life span.

In this country, we define sweatshops as places where workers work long hours at low wages. The general image is that only illegal aliens, particularly the Chinese, are exposed to such conditions, much as we believe that only African Americans are on welfare. Unfortunately, sweatshop conditions are pervasive in the United States today. To be sure, Fuzhounese illegals normally work seventy hours a week, but their deprivation is only relative in comparison to that of all other working people. Millions of Americans are now forced to work longer hours just to make enough to get by. Salespeople, white-collar office workers, nurses, skilled professionals, and even stockbrokers often work much more than forty hours a week as a condition of keeping their jobs. As a result, there are not enough jobs to go around for others, who end up getting hired as temporary workers without job security or benefits. Many individuals, including college instructors with doctoral degrees, health care professionals, computer programmers and janitors, have to find three or four part-time jobs to piece together an income they can live on.

Organized labor has hardly addressed this issue. Confronted with aggressive management assaults, the unions are increasingly willing to make concessions on workers' job security, working hours, and health care benefits, dealing exclusively with the issue of hourly wages. The last major battle won by organized labor, with the help of the Clinton administration, was the raising of the minimum wage.

The forty-hour workweek was an American labor victory won in the 1930s. It is now being re-introduced as a national issue as more American working people realize that their working conditions cannot be taken for granted. They may find this once again as one issue they can unite on across all professional lines. As one speaker at a NMASS teach-in put it: "It's like we're all asleep in a burning building—the people closest to the flame wake up first. Chinatown is waking up first. But we're all in the same house even though many of us don't admit it."[29]

In the end, the American public may realize that the undocumented Fuzhounese immigrant workers are not that different from the rest of American working people—they only happen to be on the breaking edge of the crumbling working-class structure.

A FINAL NOTE

A CONSERVATIVE ESTIMATE OF THE NUMBER OF ILLEGAL IMMIGRANTS currently in the United States is five million, and over 60 percent of them are Mexicans and Central Americans.[1] The number of Fuzhounese illegals is small by comparison, but they are unique. They are victims of a large-scale and sophisticated international human smuggling network. After arrival in the United States, they are forced to work for years under what amounts to indentured servitude to pay off large "transportation" debts, with constant threats of torture, rape, and kidnapping.

In 1862, the U.S. Congress suspected that Chinese laborers were imported to this country under the "coolie system," which was very similar to the system the Fuzhounese are presently submitted to, and passed a law which forbade such trade on American vessels and at American ports. Today, there is still no American law that specifically sanctions "indentured migrant labor trafficking."

Smuggling unfree labor for profit is barbaric and should be outlawed, just as was the slave trade, which was banned in the nineteenth century by European states.[2] In the Immigration Reform Act of 1996 the U.S. Congress imposed tougher penalties on those who smuggle immigrants into the country. But the new act makes no reference to migrant smuggling in conjunction with indentured servitude. Futher, this practice is no longer limited only to the Fuzhounese. Smugglers are now charging $28,000 to bring in Indians and Pakistanis,[3] and $8,000 to bring Poles through Native American reservations on the New York–Canada border. The cost to Southeast Asian women often is years of indentured service as "white slaves" in the prostitution industry. It is high time for the U.S. Congress to pass a law that specifically criminalizes human smuggling and enslavement of individuals and calls for maximum sentencing. Severe additional punishment should be imposed for crimes involving kidnapping and torture.

The United States is by no means the only country afflicted by this curse. Human smuggling and enslavement have reached international proportions. According to the latest information, the smugglers now charge the Chinese $25,000 to enter Japan; to enter Germany, Afghans pay $10,000 for an individual and $33,000 for a family. In Australia, young women from Thailand are forced to work in brothels to pay off "contracted debts" of up to $35,000. The federal police there have recently raised concern about the lack of anti-slavery laws in the country.[4] As the receiving countries tighten their borders and make entry more difficult, the smuggling fees keep rising and the pattern of indentured servitude is likely to be even more prevalent.

International anti-trafficking statutes have existed since the early last century, when the first steps to combat traffic in slaves were taken by European states. Over the course of this century, a number of universal and regional legislations were passed dealing with child labor, forced prostitution, and trafficking in migrants. The International Labor Organization (ILO) Convention 97 (1949) concerning Migration for Employment is one of them, and it calls for punishment of "persons who promote clandestine or illegal immigration." The ILO Convention 143 (1975), which contains punitive measures aimed at employers and traffickers of clandestine migrants, is another. There is also the United Nations Economic and Social Council Resolution 1983/30 on the suppression of the traffic in persons and of the exploitation of the prostitution of others.[5] More recently, there has been a series of international treaties aimed at the protection of children from child labor and other forms of abuses, such as the United Nations Convention on the Rights of the Child, 1989. In a 1994 U.N. General Assembly resolution, the international body reminds member states of their duty to prevent alien smuggling by enforcing human rights and maritime rules.[6]

The problem with these conventions is that they exist piecemeal and do not address migrant trafficking in connection to forced labor in general. Their attention focuses only on child labor and forced prostitution. More importantly, although these declarations and conventions against migrant trafficking have been on the international agenda for a long time, there has been no effort to translate them into uniform criminal legislation in individual countries. In fact, a number of states do not even recognize human smuggling as a crime. In addition, most governments that do deal with the problem of human smuggling concentrate on sanctioning and deporting migrants without effectively attacking the trafficking networks. The overall consequence is reflected in the seriousness of the current migrant trafficking problem in most of the receiving countries.

What is long overdue is an international conference of the United States and other immigrant-receiving states for the purpose of establishing an international convention against forced labor migrant trafficking. It should address migrant smuggling for all forms of indentured labor—not just forced prostitution and child labor—as major targets of law enforcement and severe prosecution. The signatories should establish a comprehensive international criminal code regarding migrant trafficking and forced labor so that the law enforcement authorities in different countries have a clear understanding of their authority and responsibilities. The harmonization of laws is imperative for effectively combating the problem. The code should stipulate that all nations have the responsibility to implement such laws (i.e., to arrest and prosecute trafficking criminals), as well as to cooperate with other states in the pursuit of such crimes. Those that do not would face specific international sanctions.

Insofar as the Chinese human smugglers in the United States are concerned, they can never be effectively dealt with without the cooperation of the governments of Taiwan and mainland China. The Fuzhou local branch of the Chinese Public Security office did cooperate with the Major Case Squad of the New York City Police Department in the arrest of snakeheads involved in the infamous "Peach Blossom" kidnapping and murder case. This kind of cooperation is unfortunately rare and based on local initiatives. The United States should, therefore, present the issue of human smuggling as the top national concern for discussion in all future bilateral negotiations with Taiwan and the People's Republic of China. A special bilateral task force should be formed and put in charge of coordinating efforts for the detection, arrest, and prosecution of suspected human smugglers. The United States should expect full cooperation from the law enforcement authorities of the two countries in providing background files in the investigation of such crimes and in extraditing suspected human smugglers for trial.

The most difficult aspects of dealing with human smuggling are the lack of accurate information on the criminal enterprise and getting people to testify in courts once the criminals are apprehended. The people who know about the smuggling operations are the illegal aliens themselves, and there are no incentives for them to come forward. The only time U.S. law enforcement officials are informed of the activities of the human smugglers is when the illegal aliens come forward under extreme duress, such as when they are being tortured or kidnapped and threatened with death. Even then there is no guarantee that the illegals will cooperate fully. For law enforcement to get the upper hand in the situation, it would have to make it clear to the illegals that they would be protected by U.S. institutions. Undocumented aliens who enter this country through the service of human smuggling networks who are willing to cooperate with law enforcement by providing details of the smuggling process, divulging the names of those who prey upon them (during transit and in safe houses), and by standing in court as witnesses, should be able to expect an adjustment of their immigration status. Moreover, the U.S. government should seek assurance from the PRC government that relatives of individuals who cooperated with U.S. law enforcement will be given full protection against retribution in China.

Amnesty for a few victims would be a small price to pay in order to stop indentured migrant trafficking and the present practice of targeting certain racially distinct immigrant groups as "exploitable" low-wage workers under the subcontracting system. This practice is literally turning them into permanent caste-like subgroups, whose very existence violates the most basic American democratic principles of fairness, justice, and equal opportunity.

Finally, involving law enforcement in curtailing illegal immigration will not be seen as anti-immigrant if the enforcement effort is aimed at putting the criminals out of business. Such action will in fact protect the interests of immigrants, because no immigrant comes to America to help it become just like the third world country left behind. People come to fulfill their dreams of finding well-paying jobs and achieving a high standard of living, while enjoying full political freedom and legal protection. We should not let our immigration policy undermine our ability to preserve America as the land of these fine features, so eagerly sought by immigrants.

ENDNOTES

INTRODUCTION

1. David Reimers, "The Emergence of the Immigration Restriction Lobby Since 1979" (American Political Science Association Annual Convention, San Francisco, 1996), pp. 15–18.

2. *Washington Post*, Aug. 10, 1996, p. A18.

3. *N. Y. Times*, Aug. 8, 1996, A27.

4. *World Journal* (in Chinese), Feb. 28, 1997, p. B1.

5. David Reimers, *Still the Golden Door: The Third World Comes to America* (New York: Columbia University Press, 1985), p. 6.

6. Eric Foner, *Reconstruction: Unfinished Revolution, 1863-1877* (New York: Harper and Row, 1989), p. 16.

7. Herbert Hill, "Black Workers, Organized Labor," in *Race in America: The Struggle for Equality*, Herbert Hill and James Jones, Jr., eds. (Madison, WI: University of Wisconsin Press, 1993), p. 268.

8. Ronald F. Ferguson, "Shifting Challenges: Fifty Years of Economic Change toward Black-White Earning Equality," *Daedalus*, vol. 124 (winter 1995):53.

CHAPTER I.   THE PIG TRADE: THE CONTEMPORARY VERSION

1. Marco Polo, *The Travels of Marco Polo* [The Venetian], Revised from Marsden's Translation and Edited with Introduction by Manuel Komroff (New York: Liveright, 1982), p. 251.

2. Anti-Cobweb Club, *Fukien: A Study of a Province in China* (Shanghai: Presbyterian Mission Press, 1925), p. 8.

3. Lynn Pan, *Sons of the Yellow Emperor: A History of the Chinese Diaspora* (Boston: Little, Brown, 1990), pp. 1–3.

4. Harley MacNair, *The Chinese Abroad* (Shanghai: Commercial Press, 1924), p. 2.

5. Ibid., p. 12.

6. Anti-Cobweb Club, *Fukien: A Study of a Province in China* (Shanghai: Presbyterian Mission Press, 1925), p. 66.

7. Ibid.

8. Michael H. Hunt, *The Making of a Special Relationship: The United States and China to 1914* (New York: Columbia University Press), pp. 7–8.

9. Jim Rohwer, *Asia Rising: Why America Will Prosper as Asia's Economies Boom* (New York: Simon & Schuster, 1995), p. 235.

10. Peter Kwong, *Chinatown, New York: Labor and Politics 1930–1950* (New York: Monthly Review Press, 1979), pp. 124–30.

11. David M. Reimers, *Still the Golden Door* (New York: Columbia University Press, 1985), p. 212.

12. David Devoss, "A New Chinese Export: Labor so Cheap!," *Asia, Inc.*, May 1993, p. 40.

13. Harley MacNair, *The Chinese Abroad* (Shanghai: Commercial Press), 1924, p. 210.

14. Robert L. Irick, *Ch'ing Policy toward the Coolie Trade, 1847–1878* (Taipei: Chinese Material Center, 1982), p. 17.

15. H. M. Lai and P. P. Choy, *Outline History of the Chinese in America* (San Francisco: Chinese American Studies Planning Group: distributed by Everybody's Bookstore, 1972), p. 40.

16. Henry Tsai, *The Chinese Experience in America* (Bloomington, Indiana: Indiana University Press, 1986), p. 5.

17. Lynn Pan, *Sons of the Yellow Emperor: A History of the Chinese Diaspora* (Boston: Little, Brown, 1990), p. 71.

18. Corinne K. Hoexter, *From Canton to California: The Epic of Chinese Immigration* (New York: Four Winds Press, 1976), p. 34.

19. Peter Stalker, *The Work of Strangers: A Survey of International Labor Migration* (Geneva, International Labour Office, 1994), p. 11.

20. James W. Loewen, *The Mississippi Chinese: Between Black and White* (Cambridge, Mass.: Harvard University Press, 1971), pp. 22–23.

21. Mary Coolidge, *Chinese Immigration* (New York: Henry Holt, 1909), p. 77.

CHAPTER 2.   GOING TO AMERICA

1. Carl Riskin, *China's Political Economy: The Quest for Development Since 1949* (New York: Oxford University Press), 1987.

2. Maurice Meisner, *The Deng Xiaoping Era: An Inquiry into the Fate of Chinese Socialism 1978–1994* (New York: Hill and Wang, 1996), p. 239.

3. Su Xiaokang, "Playing Politics with Population in China," *L. A. Times*, Dec. 11, 1995.

4. Smil, Vaclav, *China's Environmental Crisis*, Armonk (N.Y.: M. E. Sharpe, 1993).

5. Su Xiaokang, "The Humanitarian and Technical Dilemmas of Population Control in China," *Journal of International Affairs* 49 (2) 1996: pp. 343–47.

6. Greenhalgh, Susan, Zhu Chuzu, and Li Nan. "Restraining Population Growth in Three Chinese Villages," *Population and Development Review*, 20(2) 1994: pp. 365–95.

7. Zeng Yi et al. "Causes and Implications of the Recent Increase in the Reported Sex Ratio at Birth in China," *Population and Development Review* 19 (2)1993: pp. 283–302.

8. Chen, Cathy. "China Seeks End to Rural-Urban Divide," *Asian Wall Street Journal*, April 25, 1994.

9. Jack A. Goldstone, "A Tsunami on the Horizon?: Potential for International Migration from the People's Republic of China," paper presented at Conference on Asian Migrant Trafficking, sponsored by the Pacific Forum-CSIS, Honolulu, Hawaii, July 26, 1966, p. 19.

10. *Dongfong Daily*, Hong Kong, November 11, 1996, also in *World Journal*, March 4, 1997.

11. *Cheng-min Monthly*, Hong Kong, no. 230 Nov. 1996, p. 11.

12. Sharon Stanton Russell, "Migration Patterns of U.S. Foreign Policy Interest," in Michael S. Teitelbaum and Myron Weiner, eds. *Threatened Peoples, Threatened Borders: World Migration and U.S. Policy* (New York: Norton, 1995), pp. 39–87.

13. Jack A. Goldstone, "A Tsunami on the Horizon?: Potential for International Migration from the People's Republic of China," paper presented at Conference on Asian Migrant Trafficking, sponsored by the Pacific Forum-CSIS, Honolulu, Hawaii, July 26, 1966, abstract.

14. *World Journal*, July 23, 1996, p. B1.

15. All of this conversation was recorded on videotape; an edited version was broadcast on NBC *Dateline* program and on a PBS special in 1995.

16. *Tiger Daily*, Hong Kong, Nov. 10, 1996.

17. *New York Times*, Dec. 12, 1996, p. B1.

18. *World Journal*, January 16, 1997, p. A1.

19. *Ren Yu Shi* (Events and People), Jan. 1, 1997, pp. 24–29.

20. Su Xiao-kang, "The International Consequences of China's Population Pressures," paper present at the Conference on Asian Migrant Trafficking, sponsored by the *Pacific Forum* CSIS, Honolulu, Hawaii, July 1996, p. 11.

21. Maurice Meisner, *The Deng Xiaoping Era*, pp. 312–13.

22. *Apple Daily*, Hong Kong, Mar. 16, 1997.

CHAPTER 3.   SNAKEHEADS

1. Frank D. Bean and Michael Fix, "The Significance of Recent Immigration Policy Reforms in the United States," in *Nations of Immigrants: Australia, the United States, and International Migration*, Gary P. Freeman and James Jupp, eds. (New York: Oxford University Press, 1992), p. 70.

2. Paul Smith, "Smuggling People into Rich Countries Is a Growth Industry," *International Herald Tribune*, June 28, 1996.

3. Sonni Efron, "Chinese Smugglers, Yakuza Flood Japan with Illegal Migrants," *L. A. Times*, Mar. 1, 1997.

4. Paul Kaihla, "Paul the People Smugglers," *Maclean's*, Apr. 29, 1996.

5. *Trafficking in Migrants Quarterly Bulletin*, IOM International Organization for Migration, Geneva, Switzerland, June 1996, p. 3.

6. "Frozen Chinese Migrants Found on Ukraine Border," *Reuters World Service*, June 11, 1996.

7. *Trafficking in Migrants Quarterly Bulletin*, IOM International Organization for Migration, Geneva, Switzerland, Sept. 12, 1996, p. 1.

8. *Trafficking in Migrants Quarterly Bulletin*, International Organization for Migration, Sept. 1996.

9. President of the United States, "Immigration Emergency Resulting from Alien Smuggling by Organized Crime Memorandum for the Attorney General," 60 FR 53677, Oct. 16, 1995.

10. Sonni Efron, "Chinese Smugglers, Yakuza Flood Japan with Illegal Migrants," *L. A. Times*, Mar. 1, 1997.

11. *Chinese Migrants in Central and Eastern Europe: The Cases of the Czech Republic, Hungary and Romania*, published by Migration Information Programme, Budapest, Hungary, September 1995, p. 2, and also in the *New York Times*, June 14, 1995, p. A12.

12. Kaihla, "Paul the People Smugglers," *Maclean's*, April 29, 1996.

13. Marlowe Hood, "The Taiwan Connection," *L. A. Times*, Oct. 9, 1994.

14. Paul J. Smith, "Illegal Chinese Immigrants Everywhere, and No Letup in Sight," *International Herald Tribune*, June 28, 1996.

15. Liu Nin-lung, *Choong Kuo Ren Tsai Taso (Chinese Snakepeople)* (Hong Kong: The Nineties Monthly/Going Fine Ltd., 1996), p. 192.

16. Marlowe Hood, "The Taiwan Connection," *L. A. Times*, Oct. 9, 1994.

17. Liu Nin-lung, *Chinese Snakepeople* (1996), p. 52.

18. Ko-lin Chin, *Chinatown Gangs: Extortion, Enterprise, & Ethnicity* (New York: Oxford University Press, 1996), p. 158.

19. Coast Guard District Fourteen Law Enforcement Branch, "Migrant Smuggling in the 1990s: The Law Enforcement Perspective," Honolulu, Hawaii, 23 July 1996, sponsored by the Pacific Forum CSIS.

20. Gordon Witkin, "One Way, $28,000: Why Smuggling Aliens into America Is a Boom Business," *U.S. News & World Report*, Apr. 14, 1997, p. 41.

21. Ko-lin Chin, "Safe House or Hell House? The Experiences of Newly Arrived Undocumented Chinese," Paper Presented at the Conference on Asian Migrant Trafficking: The New Threat to America's Immigration Tradition, Honolulu, July 25–27, 1996, sponsored by the Pacific Forum CSIS.

22. T. J. English, *Born to Kill: America's Most Notorious Vietnamese Gang and the Changing Face of Organized Crime* (New York: William Morrow, 1995), p. 83.

23. Ying Chan, *The Daily News*, Sept. 10, 1993.

24. Ko-lin Chin, *Chinatown Gangs*, p. 160.

25. William Branigin, "U.S. Official Is Seized for Alien Smuggling: Immigration Aide Tied to Hong Kong Ring," *International Herald Tribune*, July 18, 1996.

26. Paul Smith, "Migrant Trafficking from China—A Temporary Phenomenon or a Sign of Things to Come?" PacNet, Pacific Forum CSIS, Honolulu, Hawaii, August 9, 1996.

27. John Leicester, "Senior U.S. Immigration Official Admits Guilt in Passport Scam," *Associated Press*, July 24, 1996.

28. Brook Larmer and Melinda Lu, "Smuggling People," *Newsweek*, Mar. 17, 1997.

29. Jacquelyn L. William Bridgers, Inspector General of the Department of State. "Statement Before the House Committee on Appropriations Subcommittee on Commerce, Justice, State, the Judiciary, and Related Agencies," Apr. 16, 1996.

30. David E. Kaplan, *Fires of the Dragon: Politics, Murder, and the Kuomintang* (New York: Atheneum, 1995), pp. 227–28.

31. Ibid., pp. 229–30.

32. Ibid., p. 231.

33. Marlowe Hood, "The Taiwan Connection," *L. A. Times*, Oct. 9, 1994.

34. Ibid.

35. From interviews with informants.

36. Marlowe Hood, "The Taiwan Connection," *L. A. Times*, Oct. 9, 1994.

37. Gordon Witkin, "One Way, $28,000: Why Smuggling Aliens into America Is a Boom Business," *U.S. News & World Report*, Apr. 14, 1997, p. 43.

38. Glenn Schloss, "Cadres in Passport Scam," *South China Morning Post*, Aug. 21, 1996.

CHAPTER 4.   THE LIMITS OF KINSHIP NETWORKS

1. Rose Hum Lee, *The Chinese in the United States of America* (Hong Kong: Hong Kong University Press, 1960), p. 304.

2. U.S. Department of Justice, INS file dated Dec. 3, 1972, p. 14.

3. Paul Smith, "The Strategic Implications of Chinese Emigration," *Survival*, vol. 36, no. 2 (summer 1994), pp. 60–77.

4. "The Worsening Fuzhounese Gang Violence," *World Journal*, Mar. 1, 1995, p. B2.

5. Ying Chan, "Horrors of a Kidnap Victim," *Daily News*, Oct. 10, 1993, p. 20.

6. *World Journal*, Mar. 27, 1997, p. B4.

7. Seth Faison, "Brutal End to an Immigrant's Voyage of Hope," *New York Times*, Oct. 3, 1995, p. A1.

8. *World Journal*, Mar. 1, 1995, p. B2.

9. Dan Morrison and Graham Rayman, "Boy Had Ben Kidnaped Before," *Newsday*, Dec. 5, 1996, p. A7.

10. Thomas W. Hainer, "Immigrants Become Smugglers' Prey," *The Seattle Times*, March 8, 1996.

11. *World Journal*, Sept. 26, 1996, p. B4.

12. Lin Baoqing, *World Journal*, Aug. 26, 1996, p. B1.

13. *World Journal*, August 27, 1996, p. B1.

14. Wendy Lau, "Children at a Sewing Machine: Grim Choice for Immigrants," *Chinese Staff and Workers Association News Letters*, vol. 2, issue 1, winter 1990, p. 8.

CHAPTER 5. MANUFACTURING ETHNICITY

1. Sarah J. Mahler, *The Dysfunctions of Transnationalism*, Russell Sage Foundation working paper no. 73.

2. Paul Ong, "Chinatown Unemployment and the Ethnic Labor Market," *Amerasia Journal*, 11:1 (1984), pp. 35–54.

3. Alejandro Portes and Robert Bach, *Latin Journey: Cuban and Mexican Immigrants in the United States* (Berkeley: University of California Press, 1985), p. 351.

4. Min Zhou, *Chinatown: The Socioeconomic Potential of an Urban Enclave* (Philadelphia: Temple University Press, 1992).

5. Jimmy Sanders and Victor Nee, "Limits of Ethnic Solidarity in the Enclave Economy," *American Sociological Review* 52 (1987): 745–73.

6. Paul Ong, "Chinatown Unemployment and the Ethnic Labor Market," *Amerasia Journal*, 11:1(1984), pp. 35–54.

7. Rachel X. Weissman, "Reaping What They Sew," *Brooklyn Bridge*, vol. 2, no. 9, May 1997, pp. 52–53.

8. Gwen Kinkead, *Chinatown: A Portrait of a Closed Society* (New York: HarperCollins, 1992), p. 164.

9. Ibid., p. 163.

10. Ko-lin Chin, *Chinatown Gangs* (New York: Oxford University Press, 1996), p. 160.

11. Peter Kwong and Dusanka Miscevic, "The Year of the Horse," *Village Voice*, July 17, 1990.

12. Gwen Kinkead, *Chinatown: A Portrait of a Closed Society* (New York: Harper-Collins, 1992), p. 166.

13. News release from Attorney General Dennis C. Vacco, Jan. 23, 1997.

14. Jim Dwyer, "Stink of Intimidation in Chinatown," *New York Daily News*, Jan. 31, 1997.

CHAPTER 6. THE EXCLUSION OF CHINESE LABOR

1. Karen Brodkin Sacks, "How Did Jews Become White Folks?" in *Race*, Steven Gregory and Roger Sanjek eds. (New Brunswick, N.J.: Rutgers University Press, 1994), pp. 89–97.

2. Ibid., p. 97.

3. *McGee's Illustrated Weekly*, I (1877), quoted in Stuart Creighton Miller, *The Unwelcome Immigrant: The American Image of the Chinese, 1785-1882* (Berkeley: University of California Press, 1969), p. 199.

4. Ronald Takaki, *A Different Mirror: A History of Multicultural America* (Boston: Little, Brown, 1993), p. 162.

5. Victor G. Nee and Brett de Barry Nee, *Longtime Californ': A Documentary Study of an American Chinatown* (New York: Pantheon, 1972), pp. 40–41.

6. Shih-shan Henry Tsai, *The Chinese Experience in America* (Bloomington, Indiana: Indiana University Press, 1986), p. 17.

7. David Montgomery, *The Fall of the House of Labor* (New York: Cambridge University Press, 1987), p. 67.

8. Ping Chiu, *Chinese Labor in California, 1850–1880: An Economic Study* (State Historical Society of Wisconsin for the Department of History, University of Wisconsin, Madison 1963), p. 47.

9. Chris Friday, *Organizing Asian American Labor: The Pacific Coast Canned-Salmon Industry, 1870–1942* (Philadelphia: Temple University Press), pp. 38–39.

10. Alexander Saxton, *The Indispensable Enemy: Labor and the Anti-Chinese Movement in California* (Berkeley: California University Press, 1971), p. 9.

11. Ibid., p. 10.

12. Ibid., p. 104.

13. Ibid., pp. 214–18.

14. American Social History Project, *Who Built America? Working People and the Nation's Economy, Politics, Culture and Society*, 2 vols. (New York: Pantheon, 1992), p. 118.

15. Stuart Crighton Miller, *The Unwelcome Immigrant: The American Image of the Chinese, 1785–1882* (Berkeley: University of California Press, 1969), p. 196.

16. Philip Foner and Daniel Rosenberg, eds., *Racism, Dissent, and Asian Americans from 1850 to the Present: A Documentary History* (Westport, Conn.: Greenwood Press, 1993), pp. 172–76.

17. David Montgomery, *The Fall of the House of Labor*, p. 85.

18. Herbert Hill, *Reviews in American History*, p. 197.

19. Alexander Saxton, *The Indispensable Enemy*, pp. 214–18.

20. Noel Ignatiev, *How The Irish Became White* (New York: Routledge, 1995).

21. This is the main argument in Alexander Saxton's *The Indispensable Enemy*.

22. Mary Coolidge, *Chinese Immigration* (New York: Henry Holt, 1909), pp. 266–67.

23. Victor G. And Brett deBary Nee, *Longtime Californ': A Documentary Study of an American Chinatown* (New York: Pantheon Books, 1972), p. 53.

24. David Montgomery, "The Irish and the American Labor Movement," in David N. Doyle and Owen D. Edwards, eds., *America and Ireland, 1776–1976* (Westport, Conn.: Greenwood Press, 1980), pp. 211–12.

25. Peter Kwong, *Chinatown, New York: Labor and Politics 1930–1950* (New York: Monthly Review Press, 1979), pp. 88–91.

26. Herbert Hill, "The Problem of Race in American Labor History," *Review of American History*, June 1996.

27. Ibid., p. 198.

28. The New York City Commission on Human Rights, *Building Barriers: A Report on Discrimination Against Women and People of Color in New York City's Construction Trades*, Dec. 1993.

CHAPTER 7.   INEFFECTUAL ENFORCEMENT OF IMMIGRATION
AND LABOR LAW

1. Thomas Muller, *Immigrants and the American City* (New York: New York University Press, 1993), p. 51.

2. Alejandro Portes and Ruben G. Rumbaut, *Immigrant America: A Portrait* (Berkeley: University of California Press, 1990), p. 235.

3. Gary Freeman, "Migration Policy and Politics in the Receiving States," *International Migration Review*, Center for Migration Studies, vol. 26 (winter 1992), p. 1146.

4. *New York Times*, Aug. 4, 1995, pp. A1 and A18.

5. Gordon Witkin, "One Way, $28,000: Why Smuggling Aliens into America Is a Boom Business," *U.S. News & World Report*, Apr. 14, 1997, pp. 39–43.

6. *New York Times*, Sept. 11, 1995, B1 and B6.

7. Ying Chan, *Daily News*, June 2, 1993.

8. Kenneth Yates, "Canada's Growing Role as a Migrant Trafficking Corridor into the United States," paper presented at Conference on Asian Migrant Trafficking, sponsored by the Pacific Forum, CSIS, Honolulu, Hawaii, July 1996.

9. *Mercury Newscenter*, Text, Presidential News Conference, June 18, 1993.

10. "Migrant Smuggling in the 1990s: The Law Enforcement Perspective," by Coast Guard District Fourteen Law Enforcement Branch, presented at Conference on Asian Migrant Trafficking, sponsored by the Pacific Forum CSIS, Honolulu, Hawaii, July 23, 1996, p. 1.

11. Willard H. Myers III, "Of Qinqing, Qinshu, Guanxi, and Heiyu: The Dynamic Elements of Chinese Irregular Population Movement," presented at the Conference on Asian Migrant Trafficking, sponsored by the Pacific Forum CSIS, Honolulu, Hawaii, July 26, 1996.

12. Sam Dillon, "U.S. Cracks Ring That Smuggled Asians via Mexico," *International Herald Tribune*, May 31, 1996.

13. "Migrant Smuggling in the 1990s: The Law Enforcement Perspective," by Coast Guard District Fourteen Law Enforcement Branch, presented at the Conference on Asian Migrant Trafficking, sponsored by the Pacific Forum CSIS, Honolulu, Hawaii, July 23, 1996.

14. Gwen Kinkead, *Chinatown: A Portrait of a Closed Society* (New York: Harper-Collins), p. 163.

15. Ying Chan, "Smuggler 'Queen' Is Out of Biz," *Daily News*, Jan. 19, 1995, p. 14.

16. Willard H. Myers III, "The Dynamic Elements of Chinese Irregular Population Movement," presented at Conference on Asian Migrant Trafficking, sponsored by the Pacific Forum CSIS, Honolulu, Hawaii, July 26, 1996, p. 22.

17. Paul Smith, "The Rising Tide of Human Smuggling," *Christian Science Monitor*, Nov. 30, 1994, p. 19.

18. Wade Graham, "Masters of the Game: How the U.S. Protects the Traffic in Cheap Mexican Labor," *Harper's*, July 1996, pp. 35–50.

19. Ibid. P · \]o

20. Quoted in Thomas Muller, *Immigrants and the American City* (New York: New York University Press, 1993), p. 54. P- \]\

21. Quote from Lawrence H. Fuchs, "The Search for a Sound Immigration Policy: A Personal View," in Nathan Glazer, ed., *Clamor at the Gates* (San Francisco: Institute for Contemporary Studies, 1985), p. 33.

22. Frank D. Bean and Michael Fix, "The Significance of Recent Immigration Policy Reforms in the United States," in *Nations of Immigrants: Australia, the United States, and International Migration*, Gary Freeman and James Jupp, eds. (New York: Oxford University Press, 1992), p. 62. P .\]\

23. "Service Provider / Advocate Manual" issued by Coalition for Immigrant & Refugee Rights and Services, pp. 2–3.

24. Goran Rystad, "Immigration History and the Future of International Migration," *International Migration Review*, vol. 26, winter 1992, Center for Migration Studies, p. 1187.

25. Coalition for Humane Immigration Rights of Los Angeles, Center for Immigration Rights, Inc., "Employer Sanctions—A Costly Experiment," in pamphlet *A National Report About the Harmful, Discriminatory Effects of Employ Sanctions on the Community*, Mar. 1990.

26. Eric Schmitt, "Illegal Immigrants Rose to 5 Million in '96s," *New York Times*, Feb. 8, 1997, p. 9.

27. United States General Accounting Office, "Sweatshops in New York City, A Local Example of a Nationwide Problem," June 1989, p. 3.

28. Aurelio Rojas, "Growers Hire Illegals with Impunity," *San Francisco Chronicle*, Mar. 19, 1996, p. A6.

29. *Chinese Staff and Workers Association Newsletter*, May 1988, p. 6.

30. Aurelio Rojas, "Border Guarded, Workplace Ignored," *San Francisco Chronicle*, Mar. 18, 1996, p. A6.

31. Peter B. Doeringer and Michael J. Piore, *Internal Labor Markets and Manpower Analysis* (Lexington, Mass: D.C. Heath, 1971).

32. Daniel Luria, "Why Markets Tolerate Mediocre Manufacturing," *Challenge*, July–Aug. 1996, pp. 11–16.

33. Kenneth C. Crowe, "Chinese Immigrants Question Wages in City Work Program," *Newsday*, January 9, 1989, also see brief prepared by NLRB–*NLRB vs. Chinatown Planning Council*, United States Court of Appeals for the Second Circuit, No. 88–4152.

34. Steve Greenhouse, "Big Chinatown Restaurant Sued on Wages and Tips," *New York Times*, Jan. 24, 1997, p. A5.

35. "Made in the U.S.A.: The Clothing Is Brand Name, and Millions of Americans Wear it Every Day. Who Knew it Was Made in Sweatshops?" *U.S. News & World Report*, Nov. 22, 1993, p. 55.

36. Interview and information from New York State Senator Franz Leichter's office.

37. Memorandum of Understanding Between the Immigration and Naturalization Service, Department of Justice and the Employment Standards Administration, Department of Labor.

38. Elizabeth Ruddick, "Silencing Undocumented Workers: U.S. Agency Policies Undermined Labor Rights and Standards," *Immigration Newsletter*, National Lawyers Guild, June 1996, vol. 23, no. 3, p. 1.

39. *Interpreter Releases*, "INS Targets Worksites, Apprehends Over 3,600 Undocumented Workers," vol. 73, no. 34, Sept. 9, 1996, p. 1191.

40. U. S. Congress, Senate Committee on the Judiciary, Subcommittee on Immigration and Refugee Affairs, "How Employer Sanctions Undermine the Enforcement of Federal Laws: A Study," Heading, 102d Cong., 2d Sess., April 3 and 10, 1992 (Washington, U. S. Government Printing Office, 1993), p. 411.

41. David Reimers, *Still the Golden Door: The Third World Comes to America* (New York: Columbia University Press, 1985), pp. 232–33.

42. Public statement addressed to the president of the United States by seven AFL-CIO presidents.

CHAPTER 8.   WAITING FOR ORGANIZED LABOR

1. Robert Kuttner, *Everything for Sale: The Virtues and Limits of Markets* (New York: Knopf, 1997), p. 100.

2. Lawrence Mishel, "Rising Tides, Sinking Wages," *Ticking Time Bombs*, Robert Kuttner, ed. (New York: The New Press, 1996), pp. 81–84.

3. Robert Kuttner, *Everything for Sale*, p. 103.

4. David R. Howell, "The Skills Myth," in *Ticking Time Bombs*, Robert Kuttner, ed. (New York: The New Press, 1996), pp. 89–93.

5. PBS, *The News Hour With Jim Lehrer*, Monday, June 23 1997.

6. David R. Howell, "The Skills Myth," in *Ticking Time Bombs*, pp. 100–102.

7. Editorial, "Towards a New Unionism," in *Social Policy*, vol. 25, no. 2 (winter 1994), p. 2.

8. From *The Chinese Staff and Workers' Association Newsletter*, 1988 issue.

9. Peter Kwong and JoAnn Lum, "How the Other Half Lives Now," *The Nation*, June 18, 1988, p. 899.

10. Pamphlet issued by UNITE's research department.

11. Samuel Gompers, "Struggles in the Garment Trades," in *Out of the Sweatshop: The Struggle for Industrial Democracy*, Leon Stein, ed. (New York: Times Books, 1977), pp. 140–48.

12. Susan A. Glenn, *Daughters of the Shtetl: Life and Labor in the Immigrant Generation* (Ithaca, N.Y.: Cornell University Press 1990), p. 169.

13. Altagacia Ortiz, "Puerto Rican Workers in the Garment Industry of New York City, 1920–1960," in *Labor Divided: Race and Ethnicity in United States Labor Struggles, 1835-1960*, Robert Asher and Charles Stephenson, eds. (Albany, N.Y.: State University of New York Press, 1990), p. 112.

14. Ibid., p. 117.

15. Clara E. Rodriguez, "Economic Factors Affecting Puerto Ricans," in *Labor Migration Under Capitalism: The Puerto Rican Experience*, ed. Contro de Estudios Puertorriquenos, History Task Force (New York: Monthly Review Press, 1979), pp. 214–15.

16. *Chinese Garment Industry Study*, by Abeles, Schwartz, Hackel, and Silverblatt, Inc., study commissioned by Local 23–25 International Ladies Garment Workers Union and the New York Skirt and Sportswear Association, 1983.

17. Peter Kwong, *The New Chinatown* (New York: Hill & Wong, 1979), p. 152.

18. Steve Greenhouse, "Apparel Industry Group Moves to End Sweatshops," *New York Times*, Apr. 9, 1997, p. A14.

19. *China Daily News*, April 1, 1997.

20. "Teamsters Plan an Organizing Drive in Chinatown," *New York Times*, May 13, 1979, p. 36.

21. Peter Kwong, *The New Chinatown*, 2nd ed. (New York: Hill and Wang, 1996), p. 145.

22. Hector Figueroa, "The Growing Force of Latino Labor," in *NACLA Report on the Americas*, vol. xxx, no. 3, Nov.–Dec. 1996, p. 21.

23. Michael Tomasky, "Waltzing with Sweeney: Is the Academic Left Ready to Join the AFL-CIO," *Lingua Franca*, vol. 7, no. 2, February 1997, p. 42.

24. Selwyn Raab, "At Union's Headquarters, Cleaners Have No Union," *New York Times*, June 9, 1997, p. 43.

25. Michael Tomasky, *Lingua Franca*, p. 42.

26. Ibid., p. 45.

27. Bob Fitch, "Labor Pain," *The Nation*, Nov. 25, 1996, p. 27.

28. Ibid.

CHAPTER 9.   THE UNDOCUMENTED IMMIGRANT AS PART
OF AMERICAN LABOR

1. Robert Pear, "Academy's Report Says Immigration Benefits the U.S.," *New York Times*, May 18, 1997, p. 1.

2. Ronald F. Ferguson, "Shifting Challenges: Fifty Years of Economic Change Toward Black-White Earning Equality," *Daedalus*, vol. 124 (winter 1995):53.

3. Testimony of Richard M. Estrada before the U.S. House of Representatives Committee on the Judiciary Subcommittee on Immigration and Claims, Dec. 7, 1995.

4. Ibid.

 5. Marc Cooper, "The Heartland's Raw Deal," *The Nation*, Feb. 3, 1997, p. 12.

6. Hector L. Delgado, *New Immigrants, Old Unions: Organizing Undocumented Workers in Los Angeles* (Philadelphia: Temple University Press, 1993), p. 10.

7. Manuel Castels, "Immigrant Workers and Class Struggles in Advanced Capitalism: The Western European Experience," *Politics and Society*, 5 (1985), pp. 33–66.

8. Carey Goldberg, "Hispanic Households Struggle Amid Broad Decline in Income," *New York Times*, January 30, 1997, p. 1.

9. Rodolfo F. Acuna, *Anything but Mexican: Chicanos in Contemporary Los Angeles* (New York: Verso), 1996.

10. Hector Figueroa, "The Growing Force of Latino Labor," in *NACLA Report on the Americas*, vol. xxx, no. 3, Nov.–Dec. 1996, p. 19.

11. Ibid., pp. 19–20.

12. Fuyuki Kurasawa, *Third Force*, Jan.–Feb. 1996, pp. 20–24.

13. Suzanne Tay-Kelley, "Janitors Protest Swells to Include a New Coalition," *Cupertino Courier*, May 8, 1991, vol. 44, no. 20.

14. Fuyuki Kurasawa, "Topple the Pyramid: Organizing Against Subcontracting," *Third Force*, Jan.–Feb. 1996, p. 28.

15. Serge F. Kovaleski, "A Fear Day's Pay?" *New York Daily News*, May 15, 1991.

16. Vivian Huang and Tom Robbins, "Chinatown Wages War," *New York Daily News*, Apr. 20, 1995.

17. *Sing Tao Daily News*, Feb. 28, 1995.

18. From exhibits to petition, *People of the State of New York Against Jing Fong Restaurant, Inc.*, Supreme Court of the State of New York County of New York.

19. Angela C. Allen, "Slave Wages, Vacco Says," *New York Post*, Jan. 24, 1997, p. 1.

20. Jim Dwyer, "Stink of Intimidation in Chinatown," *New York Daily News*, Jan. 31, 1997.

21. Ibid.

22. New York State Senate Legislative Resolution No. 870, adopted in Senate on Apr. 2, 1997.

23. Moses Rischin, *The Promised City: New York's Jews, 1870–1914* (Cambridge, Mass.: Harvard University Press, 1977), p. 105.

24. Irving Howe, *World of Our Fathers: The Journey of the East European Jews to America and the Life They Found and Made* (New York: Schocken Books, 1989), p. 308.

25. Ibid.

26. Francis Calpotura and Kim Fellner, "Square Pegs Find Their Groove: Reshaping the Organizing Circle," published by Center for Third World Organizing in Oakland, CA, 1996.

27. Seymour Martin Lipset and William Schneider, *The Confidence Gap* (New York: Free Press, 1983), p. 205.

28. Bob Fitch, "Labor Pain," *The Nation*, Nov. 25, 1996, p. 25.

29. *CSWA News: The Voice of the Chinese American Worker*, vol. 5, no. 1, spring 1977, p. 2.

A FINAL NOTE

1. Eric Schmitt, "Illegal Immigrants Rose to 5 Million in '96," *New York Times*, Feb. 8, 1997, p. 9.

2. Walton Look Lai, *Indentured Labor, Caribbean Sugar: Chinese and Indian Migrants to the British West Indies, 1838-1918* (Baltimore, Md.: The Johns Hopkins University Press, 1993), pp. 1–3, and also "Combating Migrant Trafficking Through Legislation," in *Trafficking in Migrants Quarterly Bulletin*, Sept. 1996, p. 1.

3. Sam Dillon, "U.S. Cracks Ring That Smuggled Asians via Mexico," *International Herald Tribune*, May 31, 1996.

4. *Trafficking in Migrants*, Quarterly Bulletin, International Organization for Migration, no. 13, December 1996.

5. "Recent International Legal Instruments and Measures Relating to Illicit Trafficking in Migrants: Trends and Efficiency," Paper no. 4, submitted by Federal Ministry of the Interior Vienna, Austria at the Eleven IOM Seminar on Migration, Oct. 26–28, 1994, Geneva.

6. U.N. General Assembly, *Prevention of the Smuggling of Aliens*, resolution adopted by the General Assembly, March 8, 1994.

BIBLIOGRAPHY

Acuna, Rodolfo F. *Anything But Mexican: Chicanos in Contemporary Los Angeles.* New York: Verso, 1996.

Allen, Angela C. "Slave Wages, Vacco Says," *New York Post*, January 24, 1997, p. 1.

American Social History Project. *Who Built America? Working People and the Nation's Economy, Politics, Culture and Society.* 2 vols. New York: Pantheon Books, 1992.

Anti-Cobweb Club. *Fukien: A Study of a Province in China.* Shanghai: Presbyterian Mission Press, 1925.

Bean, Frank D. and Michael Fix. "The Significance of Recent Immigration Policy Reforms in the United States," in *Nations of Immigrants: Australia, the United States, and International Migration.* Gary P. Freeman and James Jupp, eds. New York: Oxford University Press, 1992.

Branigin, William. "U.S. Official Is Seized for Alien Smuggling: Immigration Aide Tied to Hong Kong Ring." *International Herald Tribune*, July 18, 1996.

Castels, Manuel. "Immigrant Workers and Class Struggles in Advanced Capitalism: The Western European Experience." *Politics and Society* 5 (1985), 33–66.

Chaio-pao [China Daily News] New York City, 1990–97.

Chan, Ying."Horrors of a Kidnap Victim." *New York Daily News*, October 10, 1993, p. 20.

Chen, Cathy. "China Seeks End to Rural-Urban Divide." *Asian Wall Street Journal.* April 25, 1994.

Cheng-min [Cheng-min Monthly] Hong Kong, 1989–97.

Chin, Ko-lin. *Chinatown Gangs: Extortion, Enterprise, and Ethnicity.* New York: Oxford University Press, 1996.

Chinese Garment Industry Study. Abeles, Schwartz, Hackel, and Silverblatt, Inc., commissioned by Local 23–25 International Ladies Garment Workers Union and the New York Skirt and Sportswear Association, 1983.

Chinese Migrants in Central and Eastern Europe: The Cases of the Czech Republic, Hungary, and Romania, published by Migration Information Programme, Budapest, Hungary, Sept. 1995.

Chiu, Ping. *Chinese Labor in California, 1850–1880: An Economic Study*. State Historical Society of Wisconsin for the Department of History, University of Wisconsin, Madison, 1963.

Coalition for Humane Immigrant Rights of Los Angeles, Center for Immigration Rights, Inc.

Coolidge, Mary. *Chinese Immigration*. New York: Henry, 1909.

Cooper, Marc. "The Heartland's Raw Deal." *The Nation*, Feb. 3, 1997, p. 12.

Crowe, Kenneth C. "Chinese Immigrants Question Wages in City Work Program." *Newsday*, Jan. 9, 1989.

CSWA News: The Voice of the Chinese American Worker. vol. 5, issue 1 (spring 1977).

Delgado, Hector L. *New Immigrants, Old Unions: Organizing Undocumented Workers in Los Angeles*. Philadelphia: Temple University Press, 1993.

Devoss, David. "A New Chinese Export: Labor so Cheap!" *Asia, Inc.*, May 1993.

Dillon, Sam. "U.S. Cracks Ring That Smuggled Asians via Mexico." *International Herald Tribune*, May 31, 1996.

Doeringer, Peter B. and Michael J. Piore. *Internal Labor Markets and Manpower Analysis*. Lexington, Mass: D.C. Heath 1971.

Dong-fong Jih-pao [Eastern Daily] Hong Kong, 1990–97.

Dwyer, Jim. "Stink of Intimidation in Chinatown." *New York Daily News*, Jan. 31, 1997.

Efron, Sonni. "Chinese Smugglers, Yakuza Flood Japan With Illegal Migrants." *L. A. Times*, March 1, 1997.

"Employer Sanctions—A Costly Experiment," A National Report About the Harmful, Discriminatory Effects of Employer Sanctions on the Community, March 1990.

English, T. J. *Born to Kill: America's Most Notorious Vietnamese Gang and the Changing Face of Organized Crime*. New York: William Morrow, 1995.

Faison, Seth. "Brutal End to an Immigrant's Voyage of Hope." *New York Times*, Oct. 3, 1995, p. A1.

Ferguson, Hayes. "Border Crackdown Moves Illegal Tide," *The Times-Picayune*, Aug. 18, 1996, p. A1.

Ferguson, Ronald F. "Shifting Challenges: Fifty Years of Economic Change Toward Black-White Earning Equality." *Daedalus*, vol. 124 (winter 1995).

Figueroa, Hector. "The Growing Force of Latino Labor." *NACLA Report on the Americas*, vol. xxx, no. 3 (Nov.–Dec. 1996).

Fitch, Bob. "Labor Pain." *The Nation*, Nov. 25, 1966, p. 27.

Foner, Eric. *Reconstruction: Unfinished Revolution, 1863–1877*. New York: Harper and Row, 1989.

Foner, Philip and Daniel Rosenberg, eds. *Racism, Dissent, and Asian Americans from 1850 to the Present: A Documentary History*. Westport, Connecticut: Greenwood Press, 1993.

Freeman, Gary. "Migration Policy and Politics in the Receiving States." *International Migration Review*, Center for Migration Studies, vol. 26 (winter 1992), p. 1146.

Friday, Chris. *Organizing Asian American Labor: The Pacific Coast Canned-Salmon Industry, 1870–1942*. Philadelphia: Temple University Press, 1994.

Glazer, Nathan, ed. *Clamor at the Gates*. San Francisco: Institute for Contemporary Studies, 1985.

Glenn, Susan A. *Daughters of the Shtetl: Life and Labor in the Immigrant Generation*. Ithaca, N.Y.: Cornell University Press, 1990.

Greenhouse, Steve. "Big Chinatown Restaurant Sued on Wages and Tips." *New York Times*, Jan. 24, 1997, p. A5.

Goldberg, Carey. "Hispanic Households Struggle Amid Broad Decline in Income," *New York Times*, Jan. 30, 1997, p. 1.

Goldstone, Jack A. "A Tsunami on the Horizon?: Potential for International Migration from the People's Republic of China."

Paper presented at Conference on Asian Migrant Trafficking, sponsored by the Pacific Forum-CSIS, Honolulu, Hawaii, July 26, 1966.

Graham, Wade. "Masters of the Game: How the U.S. Protects the Traffic in Cheap Mexican Labor." *Harper's,* July 1996, pp. 35–50.

Greenhalgh, Susan, Zhu Chuzu, and Li Nan. "Restraining Population Growth in Three Chinese Villages." *Population and Development Review,* 20(2) 1994, pp. 365–95.

Greenhouse, Steve. "Apparel Industry Group Moves to End Sweatshops." *New York Times,* Apr. 9, 1997.

Hill, Herbert. "Black Workers, Organized Labor." *Race in America: The Struggle for Equality,* Herbert Hill and James Jones, Jr., eds. Madison, WI: University of Wisconsin Press, 1993.

————. "The Problem of Race in American Labor History." *Review of American History,* June 1996.

Hainer, Thomas W. "Immigrants Become Smuggler's Prey," *The Seattle Times,* March 8, 1996.

Hoexter, Corinne K. *From Canton to California: The Epic of Chinese Immigration.* New York: Four Winds Press, 1976.

Hood, Marlowe. "The Taiwan Connection." *L. A. Times,* Oct. 9, 1994.

Howe, Irving. *World of Our Fathers: The Journey of the East European Jews to America and the Life They Found and Made.* New York: Schocken Books, 1989.

Howell, David R. "The Skills Myth." *Ticking Time Bombs,* Robert Kuttner, ed. New York: The New Press, 1996.

Huang, Vivian and Tom Robbins. "Chinatown Wage War." *New York Daily News,* Apr. 20, 1995.

Hua-chiao Chih-kung tung-hsin [Chinese Staff and Workers Association Newsletter] 1980 on

Hu Pao [Tiger Daily] Hong Kong, 1990–97.

Hunt, Michael H. *The Making of a Special Relationship: The United States and China to 1914.* New York: Columbia University Press, 1983.

Ignatiev, Noel. *How The Irish Became White*. New York: Routledge, 1995.

Irick, Robert L. *Ch'ing Policy Toward the Coolie Trade, 1847–1878*. Taipei: Chinese Material Center, 1982.

Jen Yu Shih [People and Issues] (New York: Chinatown Report Inc.) 1983–97.

Jiushi Niadai [Nineties Monthly] (Hong Kong: Chinese Periodicals Distribution Inc.) 1990–97.

Kaihla, Paul. "The People Smugglers." *Maclean's*, Apr. 29, 1996.

Kaplan, David E. *Fires of the Dragon: Politics, Murder, and the Kuomintang*. New York: Atheneum, 1995.

Kinkead, Gwen. *Chinatown: A Portrait of a Closed Society*. New York: HarperCollins 1992.

Kurasawa, Fuyuki. "Toppling the Pyramid: Organizing Against Subcontracting," *Third Force*. Jan.–Feb. 1996, pp. 20–24.

Kuttner, Robert. *Everything for Sale: The Virtues and Limits of Markets*. New York: Knopf, 1997.

Kwong, Peter. *Chinatown, New York: Labor and Politics, 1930–1950*. New York: Monthly Review Press, 1979.

———. *The New Chinatown*. 2nd ed. New York: Hill and Wang, 1996.

Kwong, Peter and Dusanka Miscevic. "The Year of the Horse." *Village Voice*, July 17, 1990.

Kwong, Peter and JoAnn Lum. "How the Other Half Lives Now." *The Nation*, June 18, 1988, p. 899.

Lai, H.M. and P. P. Chbyy. *Outline History of the Chinese in America*. San Francisco: Chinese-American Studies Planning Group: distributed by Everybody's Bookstore, 1972.

Lai, Walton Look. *Indentured Labor, Caribbean Sugar: Chinese and Indian Migrants to the British West Indies, 1838–1918*. Baltimore, Md.: Johns Hopkins University Press, 1993.

Larmer, Brook and Melinda Lu. "Smuggling People." *Newsweek*, Mar. 17, 1997.

Lau, Wendy. "Children at a Sewing Machine." *Chinese Staff and Workers Association News Letter*, vol. 2, no. 1 (winter 1990), p. 8.

Lee, Rose Hum. *The Chinese in the United States of America*. Hong Kong: Hong Kong University Press, 1960.

Leicester, John. "Senior U.S. Immigration Official Admits Guilt in Passport Scam." *Associated Press*, July 24, 1996.

Lipset, Seymour Martin and William Schneider. *The Confidence Gap*. New York: Free Press, 1983.

Liu Nin-lung. *Chinese Snakepeople [Choong Kuo Ren Tsai Taso]*. Hong Kong: *The Nineties Monthly*/Going Fine Ltd., 1996.

Loewen, James W. *The Mississippi Chinese: Between Black and White*. Cambridge, Mass.: Harvard University Press, 1971.

Luria, Daniel. "Why Markets Tolerate Mediocre Manufacturing." *Challenge*, July–Aug. 1996, pp. 11–16.

MacNair, Harley. *The Chinese Abroad*. Shanghai: Commercial Press, 1924.

Mahler, Sarah J. *The Dysfunctions of Transnationalism*. Russell Sage Foundation working paper no. 73.

Meisner, Maurice. *The Deng Xiaoping Era: An Inquiry into the Fate of Chinese Socialism 1978–1994*. New York: Hill and Wang, 1996.

Miller, Stuart Crighton. *The Unwelcome Immigrant: The American Image of the Chinese, 1785–1882*. Berkeley: University of California Press, 1969.

Ming Pao [Ming Pao Daily News] (Ming Pao Inc. [New York]), 1997.

Min Pao Yuo-kan [Min Pao Monthly] (Hong Kong: Ming Pao Magazine Limited), 1989–97.

Mishel, Lawrence. "Rising Tides, Sinking Wages." *Ticking Time Bombs*, Robert Kuttner, ed. New York: The New Press, 1996.

Montgomery, David. *The Fall of the House of Labor*. New York: Cambridge University Press, 1987.

———. "The Irish and the American Labor Movement." *American and Ireland, 1776–1976*, David N. Doyle and Owen D. Edwards, eds., Westport, Conn.: Greenwood Press, 1980.

Morrison, Dan and Graham Rayman. "Boy Had Been Kidnapped Before." *Newsday*, Dec. 5, 1996, p. A7.

Muller, Thomas. *Immigrants and the American City*. New York: New York University Press, 1993.

Myers, Willard H. III. "The Dynamic Elements of Chinese Irregular Population Movement." Paper presented at Conference on Asian Migrant Trafficking, sponsored by the Pacific Forum CSIS, Honolulu, Hawaii, July 26, 1996, p. 22.

Nee, Victor G. and Brett deBary Nee. *Longtime Californ': A Documentary Study of an American Chinatown*. New York: Pantheon 1972.

New York City Commission on Human Rights. *Building Barriers: A Report on Discrimination Against Women and People of Color in New York City's Construction Trades*. Dec. 1993.

New York State Attorney General. News release from New York State Attorney General Dennis C. Vacco, Jan. 23, 1997.

NLRB vs. Chinatown Planning Council, United States Court of Appeals for the Second Circuit, no. 88–4152.

Ong, Paul. "Chinatown Unemployment and the Ethnic Labor Market." *Amerasia Journal*, 11:1(1984), pp. 35–54.

Ortiz, Altagacia. "Puerto Rican Workers in the Garment Industry of New York City, 1920–1960." *Labor Divided: Race and Ethnicity in United States Labor Struggles, 1835–1960*, Robert Asher and Charles Stephenson, eds. Albany, N.Y.: State University of New York Press, 1990.

Pan, Lynn. *Sons of the Yellow Emperor: A History of the Chinese Diaspora*. Boston: Little, Brown, 1990.

Pear, Robert. "Academy's Report Says Immigration Benefits the U.S." *New York Times*, May 18, 1997, p. 1.

Polo, Marco. *The Travels of Marco Polo* [The Venetian]. Revised from Marsden's translation and edited with introduction by Manuel Komroff. New York: Liveright, 1982.

Portes, Alejandro and Robert Bach. *Latin Journey: Cuban and Mexican Immigrants in the United States*. Berkeley: University of California Press, 1985.

Recent International Legal Instruments and Measures Relating to Illicit Trafficking in Migrants: Trends and Efficiency. Paper no. 4 submitted by Federal Ministry of the Interior, Vienna, Austria, at the *Eleven IOM Seminar on Migration,* 26–28 Oct. 1994, Geneva.

Reimers, David. *Still the Golden Door: The Third World Comes to America.* New York: Columbia University Press, 1985.

———. "The Emergence of the Immigration Restriction Lobby Since 1979." American Political Science Association Annual Convention, San Francisco, 1996.

Rischin, Moses. *The Promised City: New York's Jews, 1870–1914.* Cambridge: Harvard University Press, 1977.

Riskin, Carl. *China's Political Economy: The Quest for Development Since 1949.* New York: Oxford University Press, 1987.

Rodriguez, Clara E. "Economic Factors Affecting Puerto Ricans in New York." *Labor Migration Under Capitalism: The Puerto Rican Experience,* ed. Contro de Estudios Puertorriquenos, History Task Force. New York: Monthly Review Press, 1979, pp. 214–15.

Rohwer, Jim. *Asia Rising: Why America Will Prosper as Asia's Economies Boom.* New York: Simon & Schuster, 1995.

Rojas, Aurelio. "Border Guarded, Workplace Ignored." *San Francisco Chronicle,* March 18, 1996, p. A6.

Ruddick, Elizabeth. "Silencing Undocumented Workers: U.S. Agency Policies Undermined Labor Rights and Standards." *Immigration Newsletter,* National Lawyers Guild, June 1996, vol. 23, no. 3.

Rystad, Goran. "Immigration History and the Future of International Migration." *International Migration Review,* Center for Migration Studies, vol. 26, winter 1992.

Sacks, Karen Brodkin. "How Did Jews Become White Folks?" *Race,* Steven Gregory and Roger Sanjek, eds. New Brunswick, N.J.: Rutgers University Press, 1994, pp. 89–97.

Sanders, Jimmy and Victor Nee. "Limits of Ethnic Solidarity in the Enclave Economy." *American Sociological Review* 52 (1987): 745–73.

Saxton, Alexander. *The Indispensable Enemy: Labor and the Anti-Chinese Movement in California.* Berkeley: California University Press, 1971.

Schloss, Glenn. "Cadres in Passport Scam." *South China Morning Post*, Aug. 21, 1996.

Schmitt, Eric "Illegal Immigrants Rose to 5 Million in '96," *New York Times*, Feb. 8, 1997, p. 9.

Service Provider/Advocate Manual. Coalition for Immigrant and Refugee Rights and Services. San Francisco, 1992.

Sing-tao jih-pao [Singtao Daily News] New York City, 1990–97.

Smil, Vaclav. *China's Environmental Crisis.* Armonk, N.Y.: M. E. Sharpe, 1993.

Smith, Paul. "Smuggling People Into Rich Countries Is a Growth Industry." *International Herald Tribune*, June 28, 1996.

———. "Illegal Chinese Immigrants Everywhere, and No Letup in Sight." *International Herald Tribune*, June 28, 1996.

———. "The Strategic Implications of Chinese Emigration." *Survival*, vol. 36, no. 2, 1994, pp. 60–77.

———. "The Rising Tide of Human Smuggling." *Christian Science Monitor*, Nov. 30, 1994, p. 19.

Stalker, Peter. *The Work of Strangers: A Survey of International Labor Migration.* Geneva: International Labour Office, 1994.

Stein, Leon, ed. *Out of the Sweatshop: The Struggle for Industrial Democracy.* New York: Times Books, 1977.

Su Xiaokang. "Playing Politics with Population in China." *L. A. Times*, Dec. 11, 1995.

———. "The Humanitarian and Technical Dilemmas of Population Control in China." *Journal of International Affairs* 49 (2) 1996, pp. 343–47.

———. "The International Consequences of China's Population Pressures. Paper presented at the Conference on Asian Migrant

Trafficking, sponsored by the Pacific Forum CSIS, Honolulu, Hawaii, July 1996.

Supreme Court of the State of New York, County of New York. "Exhibits to Petition." *People of the State of New York against Jing Fong Restaurant, Inc.*, 1997.

Szu-chieh jih-apo [The World Journal] (New York: T. W. Wang, Inc.) 1990–97.

Takaki, Ronald. *A Different Mirror: A History of Multicultural America*. Boston: Little, Brown, 1993.

Tay-Kelley, Suzanne. "Janitors Protest Swells to Include a New Coalition," *Cupertino Courier*, May 8, 1991, vol. 44, no. 20.

Teitelbaum, Michael S. and Myron Weiner, eds. *Threatened Peoples, Threatened Borders: World Migration and U.S. Policy*. New York: Norton, 1995.

Tomasky, Michael. "Waltzing with Sweeney: Is the Academic Left Ready to Join the AFL-CIO?" *Lingua Franca*, vol. 7, no. 2, Feb. 1997.

Trafficking in Migrants Quarterly Bulletin. Geneva, Switzerland: IOM International Organization for Migration.

Tsai, Shih-shan Henry. *The Chinese Experience in America*. Bloomington, Indiana: Indiana University Press, 1986.

U.N. General Assembly. *Prevention of the Smuggling of Aliens*. Resolution adopted by the General Assembly, Mar. 8, 1994.

U. S. Congress, Senate Committee on the judiciary, subcommittee on Immigration and Refugee Affairs, "How Employer Sanctions Undermine the Enforcement of Federal Laws: A Study." Hearing, 102d cong., 2d sess., Apr. 3 and 10, 1992. Washington: U.S. Government Printing Office 1993), p. 411.

United States Coast Guard. "Migrant Smuggling in the 1990s: The Law Enforcement Perspective," by Coast Guard District Fourteen Law Enforcement Branch, presented at Conference on Asian Migrant Trafficking, sponsored by the Pacific Forum CSIS, Honolulu, Hawaii, 23 July, 1996.

United States Department of Justice. "Memorandum of Understanding" between the Immigration and Naturalization Service, Department of Justice and the Employment Standards Administration, Department of Labor, June 2, 1992, in "Worksite Enforcement Portion of the U.S. Commission on Immigration Reform's Report to Congress." *Daily Labor Report*, Oct. 3, 1994.

U.S. Department of State (Jacquelyn L. William Bridgers, Inspector General of the Department of State). "Statement Before the House Committee on Appropriations Subcommittee on Commerce, Justice, State, the Judiciary, and Related Agencies," Apr. 16, 1996.

United States General Accounting Office. "Sweatshops in New York City: A Local Example of a Nationwide Problem." June 1989.

U.S. House of Representatives Committee on the Judiciary Subcommittee on Immigration and Claims, testimony of Richard M. Estrada, Dec. 7, 1995.

Weissman, Rachel X. "Reaping What They Sew," *Brooklyn Bridge*, vol. 2, no. 9 (May 1997), pp. 50–55.

Witkin, Gordon. "One Way, $28,000: Why Smuggling Aliens into America Is a Boom Business," *U.S. News & World Report*, Apr. 14, 1997.

Yates, Kenneth. "Canada's Growing Role as a Migrant Trafficking Corridor into the United States." Paper presented at Conference on Asian Migrant Trafficking, sponsored by the Pacific Forum, CSIS, Honolulu, Hawaii, July 1996.

Yi, Zeng et al. "Causes and Implications of the Recent Increase in the Reported Sex Ratio at Birth in China." *Population and Development Review* 19 (2)1993, pp. 283–302.

Zhou, Min. *Chinatown: The Socioeconomic Potential of an Urban Enclave*. Philadelphia: Temple University Press, 1992.

INDEX

AFL-CIO, 152, 204–5, 209, 230
African Americans, 13, 14–15, 16, 140,
  141, 142, 149, 161, 192, 207, 208
  enslavement of, 14, 42, 43, 44, 45,
  140, 141, 142
  ghettos of, 115, 131, 135
  in unions, 151, 152
agriculture, 173
Ah Kay, 87–88, 166, 167
American Federation of Labor (AFL),
  147, 150, 151
amnesty, 29–30, 95, 162, 164, 165, 238
Anti-Terrorism and Effective Death
  Penalty Act (1996), 5, 6, 72
associations, 124–32
asylum, 32, 49, 54, 62, 63, 164, 165

Bevona, Gus, 204
boat people, 65, 75, 165
border controls, 161, 164, 169–70
Burlingame Treaty (1868), 46
Bush, George, 32, 54, 95, 164–65

California, 44–45, 142, 145, 148, 149,
  150, 171, 172, 173, 182, 211
  Proposition 187 in, 5, 147, 207–8
Canales, Gloria, 83, 84
Cantonese, 9, 19, 92, 93, 95, 108–9
  Fuzhounese as viewed by, 19, 20, 56
Carter, Jimmy, 59–60
Cheng Chung-ko, 135, 176, 222
Chiang Kai-shek, 85, 157, 227
children, 108–10
China, 26–27, 67, 227, 237–38
  Burlingame Treaty with, 46
  Chinese emigration as viewed by,
  60, 64–65

economy of, 48, 51, 54, 55, 56–59,
  60, 88
floating population in, 54–56, 59, 95
Fuzhou in, see Fuzhou
Fuzhounese associations and, 131–32
governmental corruption in, 63–64,
  65–66
one-child policy in, 32, 49, 54, 57,
  164, 165
organized crime in, 88–89
population of, 56–57, 60
revolts in, 59
rural industries in, 51
Tienanmen Massacre in, 31–32, 64,
  65, 67, 164
U.S. investments and, 66
Vietnamese in, 75
Wenzhou in, 48, 55, 168
in World War II, 157
Chinatown Planning Council (CPC),
  201–3, 215
Chinatowns, 113–17, 158–59
  in New York, 19–21, 27, 56, 114, 115,
  121, 131–32, 158, 188, 219–20, 226
Chinese Consolidated Benevolent
  Association (CCBA), 126
Chinese Construction Workers
  Association (CCWA), 203
Chinese Hand Laundries Alliance
  (CHLA), 226–27
Chinese immigrants, Chinese labor,
  139–59, 188–203
  Cantonese, see Cantonese
  coolie, 41–46, 75, 235
  exclusion of, 139–59
  female, 201
  Fuzhounese, see Fuzhounese

and immigration and labor law
enforcement, 162–74
labor and, 145–59, 188–91, 213–17,
231
in 19th century, 142–45
numbers of, 37, 59
postwar, 157–59
strikes by, 143–44, 145
see also specific industries
Chinese Labor Exclusion Act (1882), 13,
77, 93, 113, 142, 149, 156, 157, 158
Chinese Staff and Workers Association
(CSWA), 196, 197, 198, 199–201,
215, 217, 220–25, 231
Civil Rights Act (1964), 13, 14, 16,
114, 152
Clinton, Bill, 4, 6, 7, 49, 54, 72, 166, 186
Confucianism, 135–36
Congress of Industrial Organizations
(CIO), 151, 228
construction industry, 201–3
coolie labor, 41–46, 75, 235
Cubans, 115
Cuomo, Mario, 176

delegation schemes, 61–62
Deng, Sheng Gang, 220, 221, 223
Deng Xiaoping, 29, 51, 57, 58, 59–60,
64–65, 221
drug trade, 7, 70, 77, 83, 86–87, 164

economy, U.S., 3, 7, 15, 162, 174–75,
186–87, 207–9, 228, 230, 231
employers, 117–27, 208
exploitation by, 6, 10, 102–5, 163,
173–74, 185, 231
kick-backs to, 119–20
kinship networks and, 117
payment by, 104–5, 118–19, 174, 178,
182, 213–21, 223–24
penalties imposed on, 162, 170–74,
178–80, 181, 185

public assistance and, 119
social organizations and, 124–32
wage withholding by, 104–5, 178, 182,
213–21, 223–24
employment agencies, 33–36
English language, 108–9, 116, 120
ethnic enclaves, 11–12, 16, 113–17, 135,
202, 219
see also Chinatowns
ethnicity, 113–37
European immigrants, 11–12, 14, 113,
139, 140, 148, 149, 161

families, 27, 91–111
farm workers, 173
fongs, 125
food processing industry, 208
Fujian Province, 3, 22, 23, 92
Fukien-American Association, 20, 27,
41, 83, 127, 128, 222
Fuzhou, 22, 23, 24, 25, 30–31, 42, 48,
53–54, 55, 56, 60, 61, 64, 65–66,
75, 91
Fuzhounese, 9, 11, 16, 17, 19–41,
45–46, 48, 50, 53–54, 61, 63–64, 65,
83, 92, 113, 117, 162, 165, 168, 220
children of, 108–10
elite in, 127–33
employment agencies and, 33–36
family dysfunction in, 107–11
history of, 23–26
illegal, population of, 37
illness in, 105–7
IRCA and, 29–30, 32
jobs of, 34–36, 38, 101, 102
kinship networks of, 27, 91–111
labor activism of, 213–17
as smugglers, 87–88
smuggling of, 28–33, 235; *see also*
smugglers, smuggling

gangs, 40, 81, 82, 83, 87, 99, 100, 110, 222

garment workers, 16, 47, 101–6, 110, 114, 118, 122, 176–78, 180, 191–96, 201–3, 213–17, 218

Gentlemen's Agreement (1907), 13, 147

Golden Triangle, 85–86, 87

Golden Venture, 1–3, 4, 6–7, 9, 32, 46, 47, 49, 50, 52, 53, 60, 67, 77, 79, 88, 165–66

Guangdong Province, 19, 22, 92

Guo Leong Chi (Ah Kay), 87–88, 166, 167

Hispanic workers, 204, 209–10

Hong Kong, 28–29, 42, 55, 63, 64–65, 83, 88, 104, 132, 190

housing scams, 103–4

Illegal Immigration Reform and Immigration Responsibility Act (1996), 72

immigrants, immigration, 3–4, 69, 71, 72
cultural values and, 12–13
enforcement of laws on, 161–83, 185
ethics myth and, 135–37
in ethnic enclaves, 11–12, 16, 113–17, 135
hostility toward, 5–6, 15–16, 71, 139
illegal, numbers of, 172, 235
incorporation into American life, 11–12
labor organization of, 207–33
laws on, 5, 6, 7, 13, 29–30, 32, 56, 60, 71, 72, 77, 93, 113, 114, 142, 149, 158, 161–83, 185, 235–39
and need for labor, 10–11, 161
smuggling of, *see* smugglers, smuggling
see also specific groups

Immigration Act (1965), 13, 15, 56, 114, 158, 161

Immigration and Naturalization Service (INS), 7, 28, 36, 61, 78, 83, 84, 100, 119, 164, 166, 167, 169, 171, 172–73, 178, 215
Confession Program of, 94
Labor Department and, 178–80, 181
unions and, 212

Immigration Reform and Control Accountability Act (IRCA) (1986), 29–30, 32, 161–62, 170–74, 182

Immigration Reform and Immigration Responsibility Act (1996), 165, 185, 235

International Ladies Garment Workers Union (ILGWU), 122, 177, 178, 188–93, 194, 217

Irish immigrants, 140–42, 149, 150, 164

janitors, 210–12

Japan, 13, 31, 61, 75, 147, 227

Jewish immigrants, 228

Jing Fong Restaurant, 134–35, 176–77, 220–25

Judy's Place Fashion, 217

Jung Sheng No. 8, 80–81, 167

kinship networks, 27, 91–111, 117

KMT (Kuomintang; Nationalist Party), 63, 85, 86, 227

Korean immigrants, 131

labor, organized, 10–11, 16–17, 105, 139, 145, 157–59, 185–205, 212, 228–31
Chinese immigrants and, 145–59, 188–91, 213–27, 231
community-based, 225–27, 231, 228–29
craft unions, 145, 148, 149, 151
decline of, 185–88
employers' depictions of, 122–23
in Fuzhounese community, 213–17
in Hispanic community, 210–11
industrial unions, 151–53, 228–29

social organizations vs., 229–30
support lacking for, 230–31
undocumented immigrants and, 207–33
Labor Department, 178–80, 181–82, 217, 218
labor export schemes, 62–63
labor laws, enforcement of, 161–83, 185
Latino immigrants, 13, 15, 16
Lau, Alan, 128
laundry operators, 226–27
Lee Ginsing, 1, 6–7
Lin, Mr. and Mrs., 41, 45–46
Lin, Xiao, and family, 53–54, 56, 67, 77

McNeill, George, 146–47
Ma organization, 86
Mao Zedong, 57–58
Meissner, Doris, 167
Mexican immigrants, 3, 59, 76, 161, 162, 204, 235
Mexico, 69, 74, 77, 83, 147, 169–70
Myers, Willard, 86–87

NAFTA, 69
Nationalist Party (Kuomintang; KMT), 63, 85, 86, 227
Nationality Act (1790), 142
National Maritime Union (NMU), 153–57, 158
National Mobilization Against Sweatshops (NMASS), 231, 232
National Origins Act (1924), 161
newspapers, 133–34, 227
New York, N.Y., 83, 114, 172–73, 176
Chinatown in, 19–21, 27, 56, 114, 115, 121, 131–32, 158, 188, 219–20, 226
Fuzhounese in, *see* Fuzhounese
Golden Venture and, *see* Golden Venture

Oriental Exclusion Act (1924), 13

paper son scheme, 93–95
passports, 31, 33, 63–64, 83–84, 88
Pataki, George, 135, 176, 218
piglets (coolies), 41–45, 75, 235
Ping, Cheng Chui (Big Sister Ping), 127–28, 134, 168
political asylum, 32, 49, 54, 62, 63, 164, 165
Puerto Ricans, 192, 204

railroads, 142–43, 145
refugees, 65, 75
restaurant industry, 102, 105, 110, 114, 134–35, 176–77, 196–99, 202, 217–18, 220–25
Restaurant Owners' Association, 221–22, 223
Roosevelt, Franklin D., 157

safe houses, 81, 82, 84, 98
Saxton, Alexander, 144, 148
Scharrenberg, Paul, 150
schools, 108–9
seamen, 153–57
Service Employers International Union (SEIU), 210–12
Silver Palace Restaurant, 105, 176, 198–99
slavery, 40, 42, 163, 235–36
African-American, 14, 42, 43, 44, 45, 140, 141, 142
slot system, 93–95
Smith, Paul, 37, 97
smugglers (snakeheads; snaketails), smuggling, 2, 6–7, 30, 38, 47–54, 60–67, 69–89, 134, 163, 235–39
air travel in, 77–79
Chinese government and, 60, 63
clients' relationship with, 81
conventions and treaties on, 236–37
in delegation schemes, 61–62
and enforcement of immigration and

labor laws, 161–83

fees paid to, 2, 3, 16, 29, 33, 37–40, 45, 47–50, 52, 60–63, 67, 73–75, 81–83, 87, 91, 94, 96–102, 107, 111, 127, 163, 165, 167, 168, 235, 236

of Fuzhounese, 28–33, 235; *see also* Fuzhounese

Fuzhounese as, 87–88

Fuzhounese elite and, 127, 128–29, 132–33

global operations of, 73–74, 75–77

on *Golden Venture,* 1–3, 4, 6–7, 9, 32, 46, 47, 49, 50, 52, 53, 60, 67, 77, 79, 88, 165–66

government cooperation against, 237–38

informants on, 238

on *Jung Sheng No. 8,* 80–81, 167

kidnapping by, 39, 96, 98–99, 100, 164, 235

kinship networks and, 91–111

in labor export schemes, 62–63

networks of, 28–33, 82–87, 88–89, 91, 95–96, 163–64, 167–68

passports and, 31, 33, 63–64, 83–84, 88

in scholarly exchange schemes, 62

sea travel in, 79–81, 166, 167

torture by, 39, 80, 82, 96, 98–99, 164, 235

visas and, 61, 62, 77–79, 83, 84

Stuchiner, Jerry, 83–84

students, 62, 67

subcontracting, 211

sweatshops, 101–2, 104, 123–24, 176, 180, 190, 218, 231–32

Sweeney, John, 204–5

Taiwan, 29, 55, 56, 76, 79–80, 84–85, 86, 87, 88, 132, 237–38

Thailand, 77, 85

Tienanmen Massacre, 31–32, 64, 65, 67, 164

tongs, 63, 126, 133, 198, 222, 223

training programs, 201–2

triads, 63, 85, 88, 128

unions, *see* labor, organized

UNITE, 122, 177, 195, 218, 226

universities, 67

Vacco, Dennis, 133–34, 223, 224

Vietnam, 75

visas, 61, 62, 77–79, 83, 84

wages, 186–87, 207–8, 209, 232

withholding of, 104–5, 178, 182, 213–21, 223–24

Wai Chang factory, 213–17, 218–19

Wang, Charles, 176

Wang, Mr. and Mrs., 47–48, 49–50, 52–53, 67

Welfare Reform Bill (1996), 5–6

Wenzhou, 48, 55, 168

Wenzhounese, 47–53, 168–69

Wing Lam, 174, 196, 221–22, 231

workweek, 232

World War II, 155–56, 157–58

Ying Chan, 48, 60, 134